# New Hollywood Cinema

# New Hollywood Cinema

## An Introduction

Geoff King

Columbia University Press

NEW YORK

Columbia University Press
Publishers Since 1893
New York
Copyright © Geoff King, 2002
All rights reserved

First published in the United Kingdom in 2002 by I.B.Tauris & Co Ltd

A full CIP record for this book is available from the Library of Congress

Library of Congress catalog card: available

ISBN 0-231-12758-8 (cloth: alk. paper)
ISBN 0-231-12759-6 (pbk.: alk. paper)

∞ Casebound editions of Columbia University Press books are printed on
permanent and durable acid-free paper.

Printed in Great Britain by MPG Books Ltd

c 10 9 8 7 6 5 4 3 2 1
p 10 9 8 7 6 5 4 3 2 1

# Contents

# Illustrations

# Acknowledgements

Thanks to Thomas Austin and Alan Miller for reading the manuscript, making a number of useful suggestions and sparing me from some errors and omissions. I am also grateful to Barry Salt for sharing as-yet unpublished statistical data on shot lengths to back up part of my argument in chapter 7. Ian Daniels and Tanya Krzywinska helped in the design and preparation of the graphics used in chapter 6. Much of the material in this book has been tried out in the form of lecture material in my New Hollywood module at Brunel University and has benefited from the input and reaction of both students and colleagues at Brunel. Finally, thanks to Alison, Jordan and Maya, for putting up with my sometimes excessive hours on this project at home.

# Introduction

## Dimensions and Definitions of New Hollywood

> Hollywood, as a total institution, is a multi-faceted creature: which of its facets are of most significance in understanding its evolution?
>
> Murray Smith[1]

A complex American 'art' cinema of innovation and experimentation, or the simplistic world of the comic-book blockbuster? The introverted obsessions of Travis Bickle and Harry Caul, or the action heroics of Luke Skywalker, Indiana Jones or Buzz Lightyear? Street-level independent production, or giant multimedia conglomerates? Radical visions or conservative backlash? Unsettling departures from 'classical' Hollywood style, or superficial glitz and over-insistent rhetoric drawn from advertising and MTV? Filmmakers as visionary artists, or as emptily stylish raiders of the cinematic past? 'Modernism' or 'postmodernism'? Wholesale change, or important continuities with the past?

The label 'New Hollywood' has been attached to what sometimes seems a bewildering and contradictory range of features of Hollywood cinema in recent decades, including all of the above and more. What exactly does it mean? Can any single definition be established? The simple answer is: no. There is no agreement on an unambiguous definition of 'New Hollywood', or even that it exists in a clear-cut manner. The reason for this confusion is quite simple. The term has been used on various occasions to describe different aspects of Hollywood cinema in the post-war period. Its meaning has depended on the particular object of attention at any one time. Two main sets of claims can be identified. First, that New Hollywood represents a *style of filmmaking* different from that which went before. Second, that it signifies a changed *industrial context*. Each of these might also be related, in varying degrees, to changes in a broader *social, cultural or historical context*.

Hollywood is, as Murray Smith suggests, 'a multi-faceted creature' and cannot be reduced to a single essence, 'Old' or 'New'. Changes at one level are related to changes at another, but there is no guarantee that they match up tidily. Much has changed in Hollywood since the 'classical' or 'studio' era, a period that is itself subject to conflicts of definition. But a good deal has remained the same. In some cases different strategies have been used to secure more familiar ends. Sweeping definitions of 'New' Hollywood as something entirely different overlook important continuities and are often based on simplified generalizations about the earlier period. How do we find a way around these confusions?

We need to establish precisely what is and is not new about 'New' Hollywood, to identify its distinctive characteristics – sometimes contradictory – and its points of similarity with the Hollywood of the past. *New Hollywood Cinema: An Introduction* will seek to do this by focusing on the three levels of analysis listed above: an examination of film style, industrial context and social-historical context. Each of these levels can be explored more or less separately. One of the aims of this book, however, is to make connections between the different approaches. As a 'multi-faceted creature', Hollywood is shaped by a combination of forces ranging from the most local and industry-specific detail to the scale of national or global social and economic movements.

The stylistic and industrial levels of New Hollywood cinema obey their own distinctive logics, but they are far from autonomous. The industrial level sets particularly important horizons of possibility, as should be expected in a form of cultural production so strongly governed by commercial imperatives. Hollywood remains, above all, a business. Hollywood cinema, 'Old' or 'New', is regularly subjected to critical interrogation for what it tells us about the society in which it is produced and consumed. It is often taken to 'reflect' or 'express' something about its time and place. This kind of reading can be based both on the subject matter of Hollywood films and the stylistic devices employed. But analysis of this kind that ignores the industrial dimension can be misleading or, at least, incomplete. Do the features of a popular blockbuster reflect and/or tackle issues of social concern? Or are they merely the components of a particular strategy designed to attract audiences? The answer is probably: both, but in a manner that requires a distinct awareness of the part played by each element in the process.

If New Hollywood is to be understood in terms of stylistic, industrial and socio-historical contexts – and the interrelations between them – there is still no single definition available from any one of these perspectives. The different aspects of New Hollywood listed at the start of this introduction fall, broadly, into two main 'versions' that will be explored in the first two chapters. The term gained widespread use initially to describe a wave of films and filmmakers that came to critical attention from the mid-to-late 1960s to the mid-to-late 1970s, a phenomenon also labelled as the Hollywood 'Renaissance'. Some insist that the term 'New Hollywood' should still be reserved for this period, little more than a decade. Subsequently, the term has been applied in two additional ways. 'New Hollywood' has been used since the 1980s to define a brand of filmmaking almost entirely opposite to that of the Hollywood Renaissance: the Hollywood of giant media conglomerates and expensive blockbuster attractions. Alternatively, as in this book, the term can be used to encompass both, and a broader context dating back to the 1950s, the Hollywood Renaissance being viewed as one specific phase.

## Film style: 'post-classical'?

Does New Hollywood cinema represent a significant shift in film style? New Hollywood style has been defined in a number of different ways, as might be expected given the existence of contradictory versions of 'New Hollywood.' One proposition is that New Hollywood has seen a move away from what is defined as the 'classical' Hollywood style. Some have argued for the establishment of a distinctly 'post-classical' style. In style-oriented accounts, the term 'post-classical Hollywood' is often used instead of New Hollywood. The classical style forms the main point of departure for stylistically-inclined definitions of New Hollywood. What, then, is 'classical' Hollywood style?

A brief definition will be sufficient for now, focusing on two principal aspects of the classical style. One concerns shot arrangement and editing style. The other focuses on the centrality of a particular form of narrative (or story) organization. The films of classical Hollywood are in general shot and put together according to the conventions of continuity editing. A range of different camera positions and movements are used to present the viewer with a selection of different viewpoints on the action, an approach often described as offering something close to an 'ideal' perspective on the key events of a scene or sequence. The conventions of continuity editing are designed to ensure a smooth and continuous flow across and between these various perspectives.

Close-up shots of detail, for example, are preceded by longer 'establishing shots' designed to provide general orientation. The 180 degree 'rule', according to which the camera should stay on the same side of an imaginary line drawn through the action in any one set–up, serves to ensure a consistency of space and direction. Techniques such as the eyeline match (cutting from the look of a character to the object of the gaze) and match–on–action (cutting in such a way as to continue a particular action across the cut) are used to link one image to that which follows. The aim is to render the editing itself largely 'invisible', to lead the viewer seamlessly into the space of the action. Emphasis is put not on the construction of the sound and images but on the narrative events. The narratives of classical Hollywood are usually characterized as quite tightly organized sequences governed by rules of cause-and-effect. Each development in the story is meant to be given careful motivation and explanation.

A post-classical style in New Hollywood has been described in terms of departures at both levels. Some films of the Hollywood Renaissance are characterized partly by breaches of the continuity editing regime of classical Hollywood, inspired largely by the films of the French New Wave (*Nouvelle Vague*) of the late 1950s and early 1960s. Some also undermine aspects of classical narrative such as the clear motivation of the actions of the hero. A different set of departures from classical style has been identified more recently as a result of developments such as the contemporary corporate blockbuster format and the growing importance of video and broadcast media to the Hollywood economic equation. Traditional editing regimes are said by some to have been undermined by the importation into feature films of the rapid cutting and 'shallow' imagery of advertising or MTV. The concern of the contemporary blockbuster to offer a spectacular big-screen experience and to generate profitable spin-offs in other media, ranging from computer games to theme parks, has led others to herald the demise of the narrative coherence said to characterize classical Hollywood.

Each of these potential departures from classical Hollywood style is examined in this book. The impact of the Hollywood Renaissance is considered in the first chapter. The stylistic implications of the blockbuster and of the impact of media designed to fit the confines of the television screen are the subject of chapters 6 and 7. In each case, any proclamation of the arrival of a post-classical style are subject to question. The different versions of New Hollywood have seen changes and innovations, as a consequence of a range of specific influences. But the classical style has not been abandoned. Far from it. The conventions of continuity editing and cause–effect narrative structure remain largely in place. Apparent departures can be explained in some cases as much by a qualification of our understanding of what happened in the supposedly 'classical' era as by any major shifts in more recent decades. The term 'classical' itself, in its current usage in this context, was largely elaborated post-hoc, an object defined in terms of its apparent disappearance or modification.

## Industrial context: post-studio or post-Fordism?

If New Hollywood has sometimes been defined in terms of stylistic change, rival or complementary cases have been made for a definition based on the existence of a changed industrial context. That which is described as the 'classical' period in terms of style is generally known as the era of the 'studio system' at the industrial level. The term is generally used to describe the way Hollywood operated economically from the 1920s to some point during the 1950s. The term conjures up images of the giant studio system of production: enormous 'dream factories' in which hordes of contracted employees laboured to create the movies of a period often celebrated as the 'golden age' of Hollywood. This image is misleading, as is the term itself. 'Studio' system puts the emphasis on production, the activity of actually making films. The term draws attention away from one of the essential characteristics of the industry in this period.

The big studios gained their overwhelming power through the control of not just production but also the distribution and exhibition of films, a form of organization known as vertical integration, to which we will return in the first two chapters. This system was undermined in the post-war years, especially the 1950s. The vertically integrated companies were obliged to sell their cinema chains as a result of government action against uncompetitive practices. This, combined with a large fall in cinema-going, led to the end of the factory-like system of production. Films had been produced in whole slates reeled off by the major studios. Instead, they came to be made and sold on something closer to a one-off basis. Individual packages were put together, a system that increased the power of major stars, directors and agents, the latter coming to replace the studio heads of old to a significant extent as the initiators of film projects.

The implications of this change will be seen in numerous chapters of this book. Space for the departures of the Hollywood Renaissance was to some extent created by the advent of a more fragmented production system. This environment also helped to shape the contemporary blockbuster syndrome. As with stylistically-defined versions of New Hollywood, however, it is easy to overstate or misunderstand the nature of what happened at the industrial level. The old form of the vertically integrated studio system was undermined. Some have used this as an example of an economic form known as post-Fordism.[2] The old studios system is, according to this account, defined as a 'Fordist' business, akin to the production-line system of motor manufacturing pioneered by Henry Ford. Large quantities of relatively standardized products are churned out by a large-scale factory system of production. Post-Fordist manufacturing is more fragmented. Smaller quantities of products are manufactured by a range of more specialized producers.

The system of production in Hollywood fits into this framework to some extent, even if the movies of the studio era were never as standardized a mass product as the term Fordism implies. But the big studios never really relinquished their power. They kept control of distribution, which did not fragment and proved to be the key to overall control of the industry. They have also become part of new and very powerful forms of corporate integration, between film and other media such as video, television and the internet, as will be seen in chapter 2. Defined in terms of its industrial structure, New Hollywood is in some respects very different from the Hollywood of the studio era. But important continuities can also be traced.

## Social context

It is less easy to define New Hollywood strictly or directly in terms of social or historical context. There are overlaps between the industrial and social contexts. Major social and demographic trends in the United States in the post-war era played a significant part in shaping the strategies of Hollywood, not least by reducing and altering the audience for its products. These are considered in the first two chapters. Some New Hollywood films, or trends, seem more directly to be products of a changed social context, an era less hidebound and constrained than the studio period. Films like *Bonnie and Clyde* (1967) or *Taxi Driver* (1976), considered in detail in chapter 1, come from a very different world.

But readings of films simply as reflectors of their times are fraught with difficulties and scope for misunderstanding. It is as easy to oversimplify change at this level as at the formal or industrial. The past often appears to be a more simple and 'innocent' time than recent decades. Films made since the late 1950s or early 1960s are able to express more 'adult' or explicit material than most of those of the studio era, for reasons explored in chapter 1. They might be viewed as a reflection of a more 'permissive' social and historical context. There is some truth in this, but it is not simple. There is not a straightforward historical progression in terms of the material permitted within the bounds of Hollywood expression. Some films of the 1920s and early 1930s, for example, are far more adventurous in their representation of issues such as sexuality than those from the mid 1930s to the 1950s.[3]

The constraints imposed on Hollywood in the later of these periods were less a reflection of social attitudes than of the self-regulation provided by the industry's Production Code. This was itself a response to pressures from the society of the time, but only from particular sectors, notably the Catholic church. The aim of the Production Code was to use self-censorship to forestall the possibility of stricter control by others. The limitations on what could be depicted in this period were related to the social-historical context, in other words, but in a complex and mediated fashion. The same goes for the liberalization that occurred in the 1950s and especially the 1960s. Much more explicit depiction of sex and violence and controversial social issues became possible. This was part of broader social and cultural changes in the post-war decades. But it was also closely linked to changes in the industrial situation of Hollywood, especially in terms of its strategies of audience targeting, as will be seen in chapter 1.

The Hollywood Renaissance is often understood as a response to, or part of, a range of social upheavals in the United States in the late 1960s and early 1970s. It is hard to imagine some of its key films existing without that specific social context. There is no guarantee, however, that social upheaval is automatically translated into commercial products such as Hollywood films. Industrial factors again play an important part. The films of the Hollywood Renaissance have been celebrated for offering some degree of radical political potential, in both content and departures from classical style. This is seen as a reflection of some of the radical currents in American culture in the period. The version of New Hollywood associated with the corporate blockbuster is usually seen as more conservative in its ideological implications. The dominance of the contemporary blockbuster format is often linked historically with a reactionary backlash in American culture, especially in the years leading up to and during the Reagan administrations.[4] These films do seem in many respects to reflect a changing social-political context. But, again, the picture is more complex. The generally conservative nature of the contemporary blockbuster can also be explained by industrial factors, principally the need to appeal to a wide cross-section of audiences. Politically explicit or controversial material is generally avoided to minimize the risk of alienating potential audience groups.

At each of these levels – the stylistic, the industrial and the social-historical – the newness of 'New' Hollywood, and its precise delineation, remains open to debate. Even as brief a sketch as that given so far makes it clear that New Hollywood is a complex phenomenon that can only be understood through a combination of levels of analysis. This is demonstrated in more detail in the first chapter. The Hollywood Renaissance is considered through the framework of the three levels of analysis outlined above. Other chapters combine these different perspectives in varying proportions.

The second chapter examines the blockbuster format of contemporary Hollywood through an emphasis primarily at the level of industrial context. Chapters 3, 4 and 5 move between the three perspectives in an examination of three major frameworks within which New Hollywood films have been produced and consumed: authorship, genre and stardom. These frameworks are examined both in general and in their specific articulation in different aspects of New Hollywood. The last two chapters focus primarily on the interface between the industrial and stylistic dimensions in their analysis of the relationship between spectacle and narrative in the contemporary blockbuster format (chapter 6) and the impact of the growing importance of small screen media to the overall economy of Hollywood (chapter 7).

# New Hollywood, Version I
## The Hollywood Renaissance

The thirteen years between *Bonnie and Clyde* in 1967 and *Heaven's Gate* in 1980 marked the last time it was really exciting to make movies in Hollywood, the last time people could be consistently proud of the pictures they made, the last time the community as a whole encouraged good work, the last time there was an audience that could sustain it.

Peter Biskind[1]

Not since the mid 1970s has American cinema promised so much. Taut screenplays, subtle performances and moral ambiguities.

*Observer*, January 2000[2]

A giant pair of red lips fills the screen. The face turns away and we see the reflection in a mirror. The distinctive arched features of Faye Dunaway. Half a smile as she peers into the glass before turning away. Cut to a mid-shot in which Dunaway continues to turn and rises. But the match between shots is not quite right. An instant of transition is missing. The cut is abrupt, disarming. Dunaway pouts, naked to the waist but framed above the line of the breasts. She looks around her, moves to lie down on a bed. Cut to the final movement from a lower angle and a different position. Again the shift is not quite what we expect. Jumpy. As if a number of frames have been omitted. Dunaway's character grabs at a passing insect. Thumps the bedstead in frustration.

She pulls herself up, head framed through the horizontal bars. A sultry pose. The camera lurches awkwardly into a big close-up on her eyes and nose. Focus is lost momentarily in the process.

Thus begins *Bonnie and Clyde* (1967) and with it, arguably, the version of New Hollywood that became known and widely celebrated as the Hollywood 'Renaissance'. The jump cuts and other disorienting effects are direct borrowings from the films of the French New Wave, but used here to potent and specific effect. The impression created is one of restlessness, edginess and a palpable sense of sexual hunger or longing. These are expressions of the state of the fictionalized character played by Dunaway, the Depression-era bank-robber-to-be Bonnie Parker, but also perhaps of the moment in which the film appeared. Parker is presented, in a few bold stylistic strokes, as a figure as barely contained by her humdrum surroundings as the opening of the film is constrained by the 'rules' of classical Hollywood style. She is bursting with desire to escape. So, it seems, were some of the filmmakers coming to the fore in the late 1960s, along with a whole stratum of American culture and society.

The same year saw the release of *The Graduate*. Dustin Hoffman is Benjamin Braddock, a brilliant student and track star, newly home from college and also imprisoned, if in a more wealthy suburban milieu. His parents buy him a diving suit to celebrate, in which he lurks at the bottom of their swimming pool. Another expressive image of youthful alienation and incipient rebellion. Both films were box office hits, although *Bonnie and Clyde* was not initially given a very wide release. Two years later, in 1969, two unkempt figures high on drugs and laid back on motorcycles dispelled any doubts about whether these films were part of what was becoming a significant shift within the Hollywood landscape. *Easy Rider*, made on a budget of $500,000 by a first-time director, was another box-office success, sparking a rush among the studios to cash in as the 1960s youth culture phenomenon finally gained a hold in the Hollywood mainstream. A key development was the fact that *Easy Rider* was released by Columbia Pictures, one of the major studios, rather than, as originally planned, American International Pictures (AIP). AIP was a low-budget operation that had specialized since the mid-1950s in cheap 'exploitation' material such as biker films, horror movies, beach movies and others aimed at the growing teenage audience. *Easy Rider* marked a point at which this kind of filmmaking crossed over into the Hollywood mainstream. Money flowed more freely, if not in huge amounts, to a new generation of filmmakers who, if they did not exactly 'take over' (as the title of one classic account suggests[3]), made considerable inroads into the culture and business of Hollywood.

The period from the late 1960s until the mid or late 1970s has gained almost mythical status in the annals of Hollywood, its advent marked usually by the appearance and success of *Bonnie and Clyde*, *The Graduate* and *Easy Rider*, although there were earlier foreshadowings. It is remembered as an era in which Hollywood produced a relatively high number of innovative films that seemed to go beyond the confines of conventional studio fare in terms of their content and style and their existence as products of a purely commercial or corporate system. For some, this period represented the birth (or rebirth) of the Hollywood 'art' film, or something very like it. For others, it was a time when Hollywood made a gesture towards the more liberal or radical forces in American society. The period is often taken as a benchmark for measuring the state of Hollywood in subsequent decades. The products of the 1980s, 1990s and early 2000s are generally found wanting by comparison. Occasional signs of intelligent life in Hollywood today are often referred back to this earlier period, as suggested by the newspaper comment cited at the start of this chapter.

But what exactly happened in the Hollywood of the late 1960s and the 1970s, and why has it gained such resonance? A distinctive group of films did appear in this period, although exactly how far they stray from more familiar Hollywood themes and forms remains subject to debate. This chapter will explore some of the characteristics of these films and the debates surrounding them, and seek to explain why they appeared when they did. In doing so, it will follow closely the pattern suggested in the introduction, examining the Hollywood Renaissance from social, industrial and formal perspectives. The Hollywood Renaissance provides a good illustration of the need to combine such approaches.

It was, quite clearly, to some extent a product of a particular social and historical context: from the fervid brew of 1960s radicalism and counterculture to the icy paranoia of the post–Watergate period. Yet, as will be seen, the ability of this context to become translated into the cinema was conditioned to a large extent by developments in the industrial structure and strategies of Hollywood from the 1950s onwards. The distinctive nature of the Hollywood Renaissance also needs to be considered at the level of film style. This is related in part to the social dimension. To question dominant myths and ideologies entails at least some departure from the formal conventions that play a significant part in their maintenance. The stylistic innovations of the Renaissance also have their own dynamic, however, traceable to sources such as the European 'art' film.

## From counterculture to Watergate: the social context of the Hollywood Renaissance

The civil rights movement, race riots: 'black power'. The counterculture, hippies, drug-taking: 'flower power'. Youth, popular music and fashion. Protests against the war in Vietnam. Student radicalization and the 'New Left'. A new wave of feminism and demands for gay rights. Political hopes, dreams and nightmares. Kennedy, the Kennedy assassination. Another Kennedy: another assassination. Martin Luther King: assassination. My Lai, Cambodia and the shooting of students at Kent State. Battles on the streets of Chicago. Nixon. Watergate. Humiliating withdrawal from Vietnam. The oil crisis and a reduced scale of global American economic power. Making connections between Hollywood movies and the times in which they appear is not as straightforward a business as it might often appear. Sometimes, however, the case seems more clear-cut; the times are such that they appear to impose themselves forcefully on our consciousness, unmistakably invading the terrain of popular entertainment such as Hollywood cinema. The late 1960s and early 1970s appears to be such a time.

These were years of quite extraordinary upheaval and drama in American society.[4] Far from everyone in America was directly involved in the events sketched above. Many probably continued to live their lives more or less unchanged. But these events had an undoubted impact on American culture, if only through their pervasive coverage in the media. Single issues such as Vietnam and Watergate were potent enough in themselves. What is most striking about the period, however, is the sheer number of crises and upheavals. Their cumulative impact in a relatively short period of time is what gives grounds for assuming a further-reaching challenge to some American values and assumptions. Images of America as a place of freedom and democracy were dented, if not more seriously damaged.

How, though, were these events reflected in the films of the Hollywood Renaissance? A major ingredient of many of these films is a foregrounding of youthful alienation and/or rebellion. *Bonnie and Clyde* is, essentially, the story of two handsome, if rather mixed up, people who seek escape from the limitations of small-town life. Their chosen pursuit, bank robbery, appears to be a means to this end, rather than an end in itself. Neither seems to be in it for the money, little of which appears to be accumulated. They do it for the hell of it, for the freedom, celebrity and sheer style offered by a life of crime. Nods are made in the direction of a 'Robin Hood' agenda. The point is made that Bonnie and Clyde rob the same banks that are foreclosing against poor farmers. They become popular heroes, but more for the fantasy of escape they enact than for any very specific action. Relevance to the youth rebellions of the 1960s is implicit rather than explicit, the upheavals of the 1930s and the Depression a loose surrogate for those of the later decade.

*The Graduate* draws more directly on the 1960s culture of youthful alienation. The target is not banks and law-enforcement officers, but the consumer-oriented world of 1960s suburbia. Benjamin appears to have it all: looks (more or less), intelligence, youth, physical prowess and a world of family friends bearing connections and employment opportunities. But exactly what is he offered? 'Plastics', recommends Mr Robinson (Murray Hamilton). A career in plastics, the epitome of all that is fake, unnatural and superficial. The world of his parents is presented as a plastic world, as bright, shallow and unreal as the interior of the fish-tank in Benjamin's bedroom, through the glass of which his figure is sometimes framed to underline his alienation. Benjamin eventually breaks free, swapping a one-dimensional sexual relationship with the middle-aged Mrs Robinson (Anne Bancroft) for 'true romance' with her daughter Elaine (Katherine Ross).

The satirical portrait of conformist suburbia offered by *The Graduate* is in keeping with broader images of 1960s rebellion, although Benjamin Braddock is hardly a fully-fledged hero of the counterculture. For all his escape from the world of his parents, he remains a rather 'straight' individual. His hair is about early Beatles length, a dark bob with a parting: long enough probably to annoy the generation of his parents, but modest by the standards of the late 1960s. He is clean-cut, dressed conservatively in jacket and collar. As such, Benjamin is perhaps not untypical of contemporaries who embraced some of the decade's more radical criticisms of authority. Many came from similar backgrounds, the cosseted university-educated products of the middle classes who had the time and opportunity to 'drop out'. Benjamin is too naïve and otherwise preoccupied to be much like the student 'outside agitator' suspected by his landlord during the pursuit of Elaine in Berkeley. But he could easily shift in that direction. The social movements of the 1960s and early 1970s were diverse, often overlapping but also filled with contradictions. Leftist radicals in the student or anti-Vietnam movement and black leaders of various kinds had important points in common with the 'hippie' movement, for example. They shared some of the same targets. But there were also plenty of divergences. How much would the escaped Benjamin Braddock have in common with the central figures of *Easy Rider*, the paranoid Billy (Dennis Hopper) and the laid-back Wyatt (Peter Fonda)? Not much, perhaps, but who knows what change another two years of the counterculture might effect?

*Easy Rider*, in a sense, takes up the story where *The Graduate* leaves off. It offers a paean to the freedoms of life on the road, 1960s style, fuelled not so much by gasoline as by marijuana, LSD and the anthems of contemporary music. The film has plot and narrative development, but its appeal is close to that of a musical. Its heart is in the regular and frequent 'numbers' in which Billy and Wyatt cruise across America, especially the open landscapes of the south-west, to the accompaniment of acts such as Steppenwolf, The Byrds and The Band. The presentation of the numbers is a celebration of the counterculture reduced again,

1. The counterculture goes Hollywood: on the road, 1960s-style, in *Easy Rider*, © Columbia Pictures, 1969. Ronald Grant archive

primarily, to a freewheeling spirit of freedom, motion and style. The landscape traversed by Billy and Wyatt is undoubtedly that of the 1960s. The commune in which a group of city kids attempt sincerely, but somewhat desperately, to create a pastoral idyll in semi-desert. The southern small-town café where a group of teenage girls are bursting with attraction to the passing bikers while the adults are all crew-cuts, innuendo and menace; an outpost of the redneck world whose flarings of racial violence were regularly thrust onto television screens across America in the 1960s.

The core of the film celebrates the counterculture, the primary source of its appeal to the youth audience Hollywood belatedly began to court. There is also a more cynical edge, however. Billy and Wyatt are on a binge of freedom, but their lives are not exactly without clutter. Their gas-tanks are stuffed with dollars, the proceeds of a cocaine deal. Wyatt is most of what we might hope for in an attractive 'hippie' character: mellow, easy-going and generous. Billy is very different: edgy and hostile, suggesting perhaps the down-side of overindulgence in re-creational drugs.

The texture and appeal of *Easy Rider* and *Bonnie and Clyde* lies to a large extent in their evocations of freedom. Both are clouded, however, by a sense of doom. The protagonist of *The Graduate* achieves a gradual emancipation. Released from one of the last trappings of his suburban inheritance – the rich kid's red sports car, which runs out of fuel – he and Elaine escape aboard a bus. Bonnie, Clyde, Billy and Wyatt all end up dead, victims of the forces of repression and reaction. Bonnie and Clyde die, balletically, amid a vigilante hail of bullets. Billy and Wyatt are cut down more unceremoniously, arbitrary targets of a redneck shotgun. If the highway is the avenue to freedom in these films, it is also the place of death, of bleeding bodies left on the verge.

It is not hard to read these violent endings in terms of the shifting dynamics of the later 1960s, even if both films were released before the high season of assassination, 1968, which witnessed the killings of Robert Kennedy, Martin Luther King and the revelation of the massacre at My Lai. The events of the 1960s were filled with currents and eddies, not all of which moved in one direction, but there was a distinct sense of escalating violence, and at times absurdity, in the latter part of the decade. The end of *The Graduate* is largely the stuff of romantic fantasy, although a certain sense of unease lingers over the final images of Benjamin and Elaine on the bus, overlaid by Simon and Garfunkel's 'The Sound of Silence' ('hello darkness, my old friend'), the song used to underpin the sense of alienation created in the film's opening sequence. Those of *Easy Rider* and *Bonnie and Clyde* are examples of an important aspect of the films of the Renaissance: a recognition of dark forces that threaten the more utopian or idealistic aspirations of 1960s social movements. (Another strain of films from the early 1970s marked a violent backlash against the counterculture itself, or that for which it supposed to stand, especially a cycle of right-wing vigilante films such as the *Death Wish* and *Dirty Harry* series.)

It is possible, at the risk of some simplification, to divide the social context of the Hollywood Renaissance into two main currents. One, as we have seen, celebrates aspects of 1960s rebellion. The other explores or manifests elements of a darker mood in which alienation leads towards fear and disillusion. If the counterculture, 'flower power' and 1967's proclaimed 'summer of love' represent one side of the equation, Vietnam

and Watergate are pervasive reference points for the other. The two
are not entirely separate, of course, either in the history of the period
or in its reflection in Hollywood. Vietnam, especially, was a major
catalyst for a host of oppositional currents, a key factor in whatever
coherence is found in the various strains of 1960s alienation and
radicalism in America. Landmark films such as *Bonnie and Clyde* and
*Easy Rider* contain elements of each, appearing almost on the cusp
between one mood and the other.

Many films of the Hollywood Renaissance lean more heavily in the
direction of cynicism. Exactly how far the influence of the Vietnam
war was felt is not easy to determine. Except for the jingoistic drum-
beating of *The Green Berets* (1968), a film that argued a case for American
involvement, the war itself was rarely confronted directly until the late
1970s. The closest to a substantial Hollywood treatment was *M\*A\*S\*H*
(1970), an irreverent black comedy the Korean setting of which was
clearly a substitute for Vietnam. The presence of the war is felt in the
background of numerous other films, including *Alice's Restaurant* (1969),
a portrait of countercultural lifestyles over which hangs the threat of
the draft. Traces of Vietnam and its fallout have been identified in
various other films of the period, in genres ranging from the western
to horror and those featuring the alienated returning veteran. The
traditional assumptions and conventions of the western came under
critical scrutiny in numerous films, as will be seen in chapter 4. The
horrors of films such as *Night of the Living Dead* (1968) and *The Texas
Chain Saw Massacre* (1974) have also been associated with the broad
climate of the Vietnam and post-Vietnam eras.[5]

Watergate, along with some of the previous secret machinations of
the Johnson and Nixon regimes, is usually credited with the development of a specific sub-genre in the 1970s: the paranoid conspiracy
thriller. Watergate is treated most explicitly in *All the President's Men*
(1976), the story of how two journalists pursued a trail that led to the
resignation of President Nixon. A sober account that presents its
protagonists as dwarfed by the scale of the conspiracy, *All the President's
Men* is not, however, the best representative of the Watergate-era sub-
genre. Woodward and Bernstein are seen to prevail. Their task might
be difficult, but not impossible. Heroic endeavour, largely in the form

of dogged persistence, is sufficient to uncover the conspiracy. Demons are exorcized.[6] A similar sense of resolution is offered by *Executive Action* (1973), which offers a version of the kind of right-wing conspiracy that might have led to the assassination of JFK.

The most interesting examples of the conspiracy genre, from the point of view of a 'Renaissance' of more challenging filmmaking, are those in which no such solutions are found. *Executive Action* is notable for the dullness of a very flat, matter-of-fact exposition, an approach perhaps deemed necessary at the time for the imagination of so heinous a crime. *All the President's Men* follows a linear narrative form, methodically charting the gradual uncovering of secret deeds. Some other films of the period offer spirals of intrigue, deceit and misunderstanding. Two prominent examples are *The Conversation* (1974) and *The Parallax View* (1974). *The Conversation*, directed by Francis Ford Coppola, focuses on Harry Caul (Gene Hackman), an audio surveillance expert. Caul is the best in his field, yet far from a typical Hollywood hero. Balding and habitually garbed in a cheap plastic mac, Caul lives primarily for his work ('I don't have anything personal; nothing of value'). He is obsessive about his security – that of his workplace, his San Francisco apartment and a self kept equally under lock and key. At work, in a large, impersonal warehouse-type building, he has a strict policy. His concern is for the quality of eavesdropped recording, not what is said ('I don't care what they're talking about. All I want is a nice fat recording'). One case begins to get beneath his defences, however. He starts to wonder what it is all about. Why are the couple whose conversation he seeks to reconstruct from a variety of taped sources seemingly in fear of their lives?

So far, this could be conventional enough. The taciturn expert has a heart after all. The uncommitted suddenly finds commitment. He smells a rat and refuses to turn over the tapes. He gets involved. This is the stuff of potentially mainstream narrative: the transformation of a prickly, awkward and passive individual into active protagonist, hero. Caul remains a grey and unromantic figure, but one who refuses to be used, as he turns investigator rather than mere recording device. But there is a problem. He gets it all wrong. As a technical expert, his work appears to be flawless, legendary in the field. When it comes to interpretation, he is hopelessly mistaken. The couple are not under threat, but part of a murder conspiracy. The incessant replaying of Caul's recordings on the soundtrack of the film focuses on an initially hidden phrase. 'He'd *kill* us if he got the chance', is how Caul hears it. This is what sparks his conscience. Events prove the emphasis wrong. It should be: 'He'd kill *us* if he got the chance', a protest not of fear but in defence of pre-meditated murder.

Caul's realization comes too late, only after the bloody remains of the act overflow, in horror film imagery, from the toilet bowl of a hotel room. He is left powerless to act, his tapes having been stolen. Worse still, the privacy on which he sets so much store is invaded by the conspirators. His own apartment is bugged. He tears it apart, slowly, obsessively, down to the bare plaster of the walls, in search of the device. The films closes with Caul finding refuge only in a womb-like retreat, playing his saxophone, the camera panning back and forth across the ruined apartment with a mechanical repetitiveness that itself suggests the implacable presence of a security camera recording his every breath.

*The Parallax View* begins in positive and familiar fashion. A conspiracy of political assassination is suggested, but to be combated by a hero who looks the part, not the least because he is played by Warren Beatty. Joe Frady is a reporter, the profession to be immortalized in *All the President's Men*. Events move him rapidly from scepticism to belief in the existence of the conspiracy. He is doubted initially by his editor, as is the normal fate of such characters. He begins to penetrate the shady Parallax Corporation, posing as the type of character it seeks to recruit: a social misfit. A twist reveals to us that the corporation is on to him. The editor is poisoned, leaving Frady on his own. This produces a dramatic frisson, but no great departure from convention. Heroes are expected to face 'unexpected' setbacks, the greater to highlight their eventual success. Frady continues on his mission, trailing one of the conspirators to a hall where a political rally is being rehearsed. He pursues his quarry into the shadows of the gantries and walkways high above the hall. Shots rings out and the candidate is assassinated.

Does Frady capture the assassin and/or expose the truth? No. The reverse happens. He is mistaken for the killer. We might still expect him to prevail, but as he attempts to escape through a doorway he is shot dead. Not only does he die, but he is also made to take the fall. He has been set up, thoroughly traduced. Precisely when he thinks he is closer to proof of the conspiracy he is tying himself in its knots. His efforts to expose the truth help to secure the lie. *The Parallax View* closes with the repetition of an image seen after a previous assassination, witnessed by Frady, at the start of the film. The findings of a tribunal of inquiry into the assassination are delivered by a panel of anonymous figures sitting in line beneath a massive wooden façade, from which the camera slowly retreats: a monument to cover-ups, real or imaginary, from the assassination of John F. Kennedy to Watergate. Frady is found to have acted alone. Conspiracy is denied and, by implication, continues. Heroism and democracy are negated, very much against the norms of Hollywood.

From counterculture to Watergate, the events of the 1960s and early 1970s seemed to have a distinct influence on the films of the Hollywood Renaissance. It is never easy to make direct connections, however, or to establish precisely how the traces of historical events or social currents find their way onto the screen. Many films defined as part of the Renaissance might be linked with their social or historical context in a more diffuse manner. The term suggests more than just films 'about' youthful alienation, the counterculture or the impact of Vietnam and Watergate. Other dimensions of these films also need to be explored. Qualifications need to be made even in what appear to be the more obvious cases. *The Conversation* and *The Parallax View* appeared in 1974, the year Nixon resigned and two years after the Watergate break-in that led to his downfall. This might be the perfect time-scale for the production of features drawing on the mood created by ongoing events. But it is not that simple. What is the exact provenance of these films? When were they initiated? Did they draw on the history of Watergate and its aftermath, or were they already in the pipeline. Are their links with Watergate real or largely a matter of hindsight?

The full scale of the conspiracy of which Watergate was a part emerged slowly, which would make a strong connection between these films and the specifics of Watergate very hard to demonstrate. Full-blown Watergate conspiracy was not revealed in time to have shaped films made in 1974. The closer we look, the less clear-cut these matters appear. The idea for *The Conversation* was developed in 1967. Its genesis has a link to Watergate, but an oblique one. The scenario was inspired by an article about a sound expert who was later to be called in to examine the White House tapes during the Watergate investigations.[7] The film is also strongly indebted to *Blow Up* (1966), directed by Michelangelo Antonioni, an allusive tale in which evidence of murder is inadvertently uncovered by a fashion photographer in 1960s London.

On release, these films might have entered into the discourse of the moment, becoming part of the Watergate-era mood. Brief mention of Nixon's difficulties is inserted at a key and nightmarish moment in *The Conversation*, during a television broadcast Caul uses to drown out the sounds of murder from a neighbouring hotel room. The broader political context is introduced by association. A distinction can be made between where films like these *come from* and what they become *part of*. Some films might qualify as products of 1960s or 1970s movements on both counts. *Easy Rider*, for example, draws on aspects of the counterculture and contributed to a wave of further youth and counterculture oriented filmmaking. Neither *The Conversation* nor *The Parallax View* have their roots in Watergate as such, unlike *All the President's Men*. It is generally harder to make firm connections with specific events than with less clearly defined or amorphous objects such as the counterculture or a general '1960s' radicalization or later 1960s and 1970s paranoia. Numerous events of the 1960s had the potential to undermine traditional concepts of heroic agency. The plot of *The Parallax View*, for example, based on a 1970 novel by Loren Singer, has its roots in the political assassinations of the 1960s, a major aspect of the more general atmosphere of the time. The wider culture of bugging and clandestine operations implied by *The Conversation* was far from limited to Watergate, having been used by Nixon against other political opponents and by the CIA and other agencies against overseas enemies from Cuba to Vietnam.

Films often reflect something of the time in which they were made or appeared, but they rarely do this in a simple manner, even in so heightened a context as the events of the 1960s and 1970s. Films do not *just* reflect or express the *zeitgeist*, the spirit of the times. They may do so, to varying extents, but not directly. Hollywood films, especially, remain the products not just of their culture and society but of a specific industrial regime. The extent to which particular social currents find outlets in Hollywood is strongly shaped by this industrial context. The industrial context of the Hollywood Renaissance was one in which a number of potentially far-reaching changes had taken place, changes that played an important part in helping to determine the kinds of films that were produced.

## Crisis and new freedoms: the industrial context of the Hollywood Renaissance

In 1946 weekly cinema attendance in the United States was about 90 million. By 1950 it had plunged to 60 million. In 1960 the figure was 40 million. A low of some 17 million was reached in the early 1970s, after which numbers recovered to about 20 million in 1980 and 27 million in 2000.[8] The reasons for this catastrophic fall in the number of people going to the cinema have been much debated. Television is often assumed to be the main culprit. But the rise of television was only one aspect of a wider process of social change that undermined and shifted the social and cultural position of cinema. The post-war years saw an economic boom in America. Not everyone was invited to the prosperity party, as studies of continued poverty and inequality revealed, but many Americans were better off than before.

Increased prosperity is not good news for all. Not for the cinema in this case. Cinemagoing is relatively inexpensive and requires no great investment of time or resources. Higher earnings and shorter hours enabled many people to pursue other leisure activities that required both. The 1950s saw a large increase in participation in other activities, especially sport and pursuits centred around the home, as rivals to cinemagoing. Another major factor was a movement of population that was close to epochal in scale. Huge numbers of Americans moved to the suburbs in the 1950s. This had an impact on cinema attendance for a number of reasons. Relatively few cinemas were located in the new suburbs at this time, before the development of the shopping-mall based multiplex of later decades. The most prestigious cinemas were in the city centres that were losing much of their population to the suburbs. New homes in the suburbs brought their own leisure attractions. These included television, but also other activities such as gardening, do-it-yourself and back-yard barbecues. Added to these developments was the 'baby-boom' of the post-war years, which saw a rise in the number of couples with young children and less able to get out to the cinema at night.

Hollywood in the 1950s was faced with large-scale social forces that represented a significant threat to the industry. It was also hit by major blows closer to home. The most significant was the enforced break-up of the vertically-integrated studio system. The dominance of the major studios was secured by their control of the entire film industry, including distribution and exhibition as well as production. This system began to be put in place in the late 1910s and early 1920s. By the 1930s the industry was dominated by the 'big five' major studios: Warner Brothers, Loew's Inc. (which owned MGM), Paramount, Twentieth Century Fox and RKO. Each had substantial holdings in all stages of the business: producing films, distributing them (at home and overseas) and owning cinemas in which to show them. Alongside the 'big five' were the so-called 'little three' – Universal, Columbia and United Artists – which did not have fully integrated operations but generally worked with the majors.

The production end of the business attracted most of the attention, the glamour and the mythology of Hollywood as the 'dream factory'. But it was control of distribution and exhibition that was crucial to the way the system worked. Distribution is not a glamorous, 'sexy' or even a very visible activity. It is an essential part of the business, however. The major studios had large national and international distribution networks that formed a vital link in the chain. Any production company wanting to get its films seen had to go through this avenue. The overseas distribution networks developed by the majors were particularly important, enabling Hollywood to dominate most of the world's markets as early as the 1920s.[9]

Exhibition, in the studio era, was seen as the most profitable end of the business. It represented by far the largest investment of the majors. The huge production facilities and star salaries accounted for only about five per cent of the total, according to figures cited by Douglas Gomery. Distribution accounted for one percent. Something like 94 per cent of investment during the 1930s and 1940s was tied up in ownership of cinemas across America.[10] Even at this level of investment, the 'big five' did not own the majority of cinemas. Tino Balio suggests that of 18,000 cinemas in the United States in 1943, the majors owned or directly controlled only 3,000, little more than 15 per cent.[11] What mattered was not sheer numbers, but the kinds of cinemas they owned.

The most important cinemas were the major first-run theatres in the big cities, the movie palaces. They accounted for some 70 per cent of the entire box-office. It was here that the majors gained much of their power. They owned or controlled most of these prestige cinemas. This gave them a large slice of the box-office receipts, but also a form of control that spread more widely. The higher budget pictures produced by the majors would open in the first-run cinemas, where they would be established as the prestige hits other cinema owners needed if they were to make money. The majors were able to dictate the terms on which they made these films available. Independent cinema chains would only be allowed to show the big films if they agreed to take a string of less attractive movies, a system known as 'block booking', which gave the studios an almost guaranteed outlet for even their least desirable products.

The big studios worked together to ensure their own success and to freeze out any potential competition.[12] At the level of exhibition, they competed against one another in the big cities, but not elsewhere. The 'big five' bought cinema chains in different regions of the country, effectively carving it up among themselves. In smaller cinemas across the United States they showed each other's films and gave them preferable treatment over any other products. The result was that a big success for one studio benefited all at the box-office. One of the great myths surrounding the Hollywood of the studio era was that it was a highly competitive business. It was not, really, certainly not among the majors. Neither was it quite the frantic, inspired, crazy world often implied in portraits that focus only on the world of production ruled over by charismatic studio heads. Competition did not even exist to any great extent at the level of production, where the studios often loaned one another stars or other talents on easy terms not made available to anyone outside this cosy relationship.

What the studio system amounted to was not strictly a monopoly – control by a single entity – but an oligopoly, control by a few. It was an effective system, ensuring largely stable control of the film industry for three decades. It always existed under the shadow of legal threat, however. An earlier attempt to control the film business through near-monopoly organization had been declared illegal under American anti-trust laws against monopoly practices. The Motion Picture Patents Company, created in 1908, was dissolved in 1915 after legal action, although a number of other factors had already rendered it ineffective. Action against the major studios was launched in 1938. Ten years later, after a series of decisions, delays and appeals, the case reached the Supreme Court, which ruled that that studio system was an illegal monopoly.

Various restrictions were imposed, the most significant of which were that the studios were obliged to sell off their cinema chains and the block booking system was outlawed. This removed two key sources of stability for the majors. A place in the exhibition market could no longer be guaranteed for the whole production slate. The enforced sale of cinema chains freed up capital in the short term but it also removed the principal source of collateral against which the studios had gained finance for production, a development that was to have implications for the future shape of Hollywood considered in the next chapter, 'eventually forcing the studios to find other sources of capital through arrangements (mergers, for example) with better-capitalized, better-diversified companies.'[13] The timing could hardly have seemed worse. The Supreme Court ruling came just as box-office attendance began to nose-dive. Hollywood was also under pressure from the McCarthyite anti-Communist witch-hunt and from post-war restrictions on the export of films to some overseas markets. Important elements of the system appeared to be unravelling. Two major sets of changes can be identified as a result. Each helped, potentially, to create some space at the industrial level for what was to become known as the Hollywood Renaissance.

The production system changed. Falling audience numbers and the loss of the security provided by ownership of key cinemas made the old factory-style system no longer viable. It was not worth tying up resources on huge permanent staffs and in-house departments. The majors scaled down their operations, making large numbers of staff redundant and selling resources. Studio space was hired out for independent productions, in which the majors were directly involved to varying extents. Independent production was not entirely new within the studio system. The studios had maintained relationships with a number of independent producers who had provided some of their most successful box-office attractions. The most prominent of these figures was David Selznick, a former executive at MGM, Paramount and RKO, who produced high prestige films such as *Gone With the Wind* (1939) after founding his own Selznick International Pictures in 1935.

The difference in the 1950s was that independent production became increasingly the norm rather than the exception. Films were put together on an ad hoc package basis. The necessary ingredients of production were assembled film by film, or in small portfolios. A producer, or increasingly frequently an agent, would take responsibility for the organization of a project. A script would be written or rights secured for the adaptation of a property in another form. A director, stars and other key personnel would be assembled. These would constitute the basic 'package', for which finance would then be raised. This system created potential freedoms, but also its own constraints. The freedoms are of direct relevance to the Hollywood Renaissance. The constraints will be considered at length in the following chapter.

Potentially, at least, there was more scope for fresh ideas, approaches and innovation in this changed industrial context. Production did not fragment entirely. The studios remained powerful bases for production, with key producing and creative talent often locked in to individual studios through multi-picture agreements. But films were no longer just the product of a few giant machines ruled by a small number of executives. The whole system was potentially more open. Finance still had to be agreed, of course, and could be a major stumbling block, as could access to distribution. But it could be a good deal cheaper to make films in this way. Independent one-off productions might have lost some of the economies of scale available to the production-line system, but they did not have to carry the overheads of running a large permanent establishment. It took some time for the potential freedoms of this new system to be realized. Until the mid-1960s the studios remained in the grip of an ageing generation, including legendary names such as Jack Warner at Warner Brothers and Darryl F. Zanuck at Twentieth Century Fox, figures who appeared increasingly out of touch with the large baby-boom generation coming of age during the decade, an audience often catered to more effectively by low-budget outfits such as AIP.[14]

The system of film production became more fragmented. So did Hollywood's conception of its audience. The films of the studio era had, in general, been targeted at a wide-ranging audience. It is not true to say that they were aimed at a single entirely undifferentiated 'mass' audience. Recent studies have argued, convincingly, that such claims had more to do with the industry's attempt to present itself as a fount of democracy, a strategy designed at least partly to deflect attention from its restrictive industrial practices.[15] The studios, especially at the exhibition end of the business, were conscious of divisions in the audience and targeted films accordingly. A particular distinction was made between films aimed at 'sophisticated' or 'unsophisticated' audiences, a division often made along geographical lines, between major cities and small town or rural locations. Other distinctions were made according to age and gender.[16] The ideal production would succeed in appealing across a range of audience groups, but many were targeted more specifically.

All the films of the studio era shared a certain horizon of possibilities, however, shaped by the confines of the Production Code drawn up in 1930. Films might have been targeted at specific groups more than others, but they were expected to be suitable for viewers of all ages. To gain distribution and exhibition, each film had to carry a seal of approval from the Production Code Administration (PCA), a body created in 1934 by the Motion Pictures Producers and Distributors of America (MPPDA). This mechanism of self-regulation by the industry was designed to avoid the threat of censorship by others, as suggested in the introduction, ranging from local authorities to the Catholic church's powerful Legion of Decency. The PCA often acted in collusion with such bodies, however, its primary motivation being to avoid bans or boycotts that might threaten the commercial prospects of individual films or studios.[17] Self-regulation also added another dimension to oligopoly control by the big studios. The ability to award or withhold the seal was a source of considerable power.

This system of regulating the content of Hollywood films came under increasing pressure from the 1950s. Audiences were being lost in droves and Hollywood was keen to stem the flow. Many films continued to be targeted at a broad constituency, potentially that of the idealized 'family audience'. But some were not. Some were targeted at the growing 'youth' audience. Others aimed more challenging or explicit material at an 'adult' market. The films of the Hollywood Renaissance were, in a sense, targeted at a combination of the two: relatively youthful viewers thought to be receptive to a harsher and more questioning portrayal of aspects of American culture and society. The audience for Hollywood films was generally becoming younger, more educated and in some cases more radical in its views than that typical of the studio era. If some films of the 1960s and 1970s foregrounded aspects of the youthful counterculture, in other words, this was not simply a reflection of social context. It was also part of a deliberate audience-targeting strategy. The Production Code system began to creak under a variety of strains.

The break-up of the vertically integrated studio system threatened to erode the power of the PCA, which was based on studio control of the entire process of distribution and exhibition. A less centralized industrial landscape could dilute or evade its power. *The Moon is Blue* (1953), a comedy about sex and seduction directed by Otto Preminger, was released by United Artists despite being refused a seal of approval. The code specifically prohibited the use of seduction as a subject for comedy.[18] The film was banned in some places but picked up for successful exhibition by two big cinema chains.[19] The same company and director repeated the procedure with *The Man with the Golden Arm* (1955), a story of drug addiction, another forbidden topic. Both films were profitable, partly as a result of the controversies they sparked. Controversial films held the lure of pleasures forbidden in other media, especially television. This was a significant element of their appeal to the industry at the time.

The success of *The Man with the Golden Arm* led to a revision of the Production Code in 1956. 'Responsible' treatments of drug addiction, prostitution and inter-racial sexual relationships were permitted.[20] Other barriers gradually fell in the late 1950s and during the 1960s, including restrictions on representations of 'illicit' sex, particularly the suggestion that adultery or sex outside marriage could be attractive. The Production Code was further revised and shortened in 1966 before being abandoned entirely in 1968 in favour of a ratings system. The ratings system institutionalized the process of targeting films at particular audience groups. A formal system of classification was used to determine the suitability of films for one age group or another. The bounds of possible expression were widened, although at the risk of restrictions on the permitted audience.

The principal motivation for the development of the ratings system was commercial, the box-office potential of more 'adult' material having been demonstrated by the success of a number of foreign and American independent features that pushed at the boundaries of the permissible during the 1960s. Extending the limits of what could be represented in the mainstream also enabled the studios to compete with the sex film industry, a low-budget sector that boomed for five years from 1968, with films such as *Deep Throat* (1972) and *The Devil in Miss Jones* (1973) outperforming many big-budget studio productions. Tighter local regulation of the kinds of films that could be shown in 'legitimate' theatres was introduced as a result of Supreme Court decisions in 1973, a development that left the more mainstream 'adult' market in the hands of Hollywood.[21] The success of the studios in adapting to changed circumstances was, again, partly the result of learning from more marginal and independent competitors, including in this case, Jon Lewis suggests, 'how to market a product and how to use artistic freedom as a means toward better identifying that product in advance of release'. This lesson was to prove central to the New Hollywood of the corporate blockbuster explored in the next chapter.[22] The ratings system, created and administered by the Motion Picture Association of America (MPAA), the successor to the MPPDA, also reasserted studio control over entry into the marketplace, an MPAA rating, like the previous PCA seal, being required for success in the commercial mainstream.[23]

The breakdown and eventual replacement of the Production Code was a development of great significance to the establishment of the Hollywood Renaissance. Few of the films associated with the Renaissance could have existed within the confines of the regime policed by the PCA in the forms that made them so striking, precisely as something new and innovative. Drug-taking could not be shown at all, let alone celebrated as part of the counterculture. The sexual 'liberation' of the 1960s could not have found its way to the screen unless soundly condemned, and even then without any nudity or unpunished enjoyment. Neither could the explicit violence of certain key films, or the depiction of criminals as heroic, justified or victims of oppression.

Few if any of the films examined so far in this chapter could have reached the screen in such circumstances. The violence in a film such as *Bonnie and Clyde* could have been toned down, made more implicit, but that would change fundamentally the nature of the film. Much of its impact lies in its sudden mood swings between explicit violence, lyricism, comedy and drama. Remove one element from the mix and the effect would be lost. *The Graduate* is not exactly a celebration of adultery, given the angst generated by Benjamin's relationship with Mrs Robinson, but it tackles the subject with a wit and style foreign to the allowable world of the PCA. *Easy Rider…* Well, it hardly needs saying that the film could barely even have reached the drawing board.

If many films of the Hollywood Renaissance explore areas beyond the confines of the Production Code, this is also true in less specific ways. Sex, violence and drug-taking were among a host of particular issues carefully controlled by the PCA. More generally, the Code sought (not always successfully) to impose a kind of moral certainty on Hollywood films. Dubious activities or characters could be depicted, but should always be clearly labelled as such. The more interesting products of the Hollywood Renaissance often undermine this requirement. Moral ambiguity and complexity are two of the primary virtues of many of these films, marking them out from the usual melodramatic Hollywood fare based on more simplistic oppositions between 'good' and 'evil'. *Taxi Driver* (1976), directed by Martin Scorsese, is a good example.

*Taxi Driver* would have failed the tests of the PCA on innumerable grounds, ranging from its portrait of an adolescent prostitute played by Jodie Foster to its violent bloodbath climax. More pervasive, though, and ultimately more disturbing, is its refusal to take a clear stand towards the central character Travis Bickle (Robert DeNiro). What are we supposed to make of this figure, his obsessions and his final outburst of bloody mayhem? Bickle is clearly not a well-adjusted man, but why exactly? He claims to have received an honourable discharge from the Marines in 1973, which would make him a veteran of the war in Vietnam. This is not made explicit, however. There are no Vietnam flashbacks or references to the conflict in his voice-over commentary. These might have provided a clear frame of reference for his behaviour, but they are absent.

Are we meant to identify with Bickle? Clearly not in some cases. His naiveté is at times excruciating to witness, particularly when he takes the 'angelic' woman he idolizes from afar, Betsy (Cybil Shepherd), to a pornographic film show. At the end of the climactic shoot-out, the camera offers a detached perspective, a direct overhead shot that provides a god-like objectivity and retreats portentously from the scene. The camera performs similarly detached movements on several other occasions. In one case, Bickle is on the phone to Betsy, trying to renew contact after their disastrous date. The camera tracks away sideways. We can hear Bickle's voice still on the phone, but the camera abandons him, coming to rest at the end of a passageway to the street. Bickle eventually catches up, finishing his call and walking into view and away from the camera, but the intervening moments are strange and disorienting. A similar movement occurs earlier in the film when Bickle first visits the taxi company. Camera and character part company before he walks out of the underground garage. Bickle moves out of frame to the right as the camera executes a slow pan to the left, across the garage, the two being reunited as Bickle reaches the entrance. The effect, again, is quietly disorienting.

At other times, however, we are invited to occupy a position closer to Bickle's subjectivity. One memorable shot tilts down into a fizzing glass in which a tablet is dissolving. The movement continues until the interior of the glass fills the screen. All sounds are excluded except the fizzing noise, an apt metaphor for the character's disconnected and volatile psychological state; a state we are thus invited to share, if only vicariously. Intense proximity or unsettling withdrawal. The power of *Taxi Driver* resides to a large extent in these shifts of perspective. The viewer is not offered a single stable relationship with the character, or a clear point of judgement.

Does Travis Bickle end up a hero, as the newspaper cuttings on his wall suggest? His final acts of violence are only loosely motivated. Why exactly does he plan to assassinate the political candidate Charles Palantine (Leonard Harris). Just because he is rejected by a woman who works for him? Thwarted by the presence of security agents, his violence is redirected towards a pimp and his associates. He has sought to rescue Iris (Foster) from the pimp's clutches, but the action towards which he is propelled seems disproportionate. Some have criticized the film for apparent incoherence, but this is the source of much of its power. Travis, and the viewer, is denied the final redemptive death that might be expected in the shoot-out. Instead he survives, lauded in the press because one of his victims turns out to be a minor Mafia figure and because Iris is returned home to the dubious comforts of the family she had escaped. The film's coda, a brief scene in which Bickle remains distanced in a final encounter with Betsy, leaves open many of the questions raised by the film. Has Bickle changed? Has something significant happened to his character, or was it all an arbitrary series of events that leave, him much the same as before? No ready answers are available.

Broad changes at the levels of both the production and consumption of films helped to create *space* for the Hollywood Renaissance. It is still not clear that these changes alone would have permitted the particular outbreak of innovation witnessed by the late 1960s and early 1970s. The bounds of possibility were widened, but possibility is not the same as actuality. One additional element needs to be considered if we are to understand what happened. The decisive factor in ensuring that this potential was realized to some extent was the financial crisis in which the major studios found themselves in the mid-to-late 1960s.

Hollywood had tried to respond to falling audiences by targeting films at a variety of smaller and more specialized audiences, including the 'adult' market. But it also resorted to a very different tactic. Huge resources were spent on lavish productions intended for a much bigger audience, a tendency to which we will return in the next chapter. The success of *The Sound of Music* (1965) appeared to vindicate this strategy. Made on a budget of $8 million it earned $72 million in the United States and Canada alone.[24] The lesson taught was to be a dangerous one. The majors, and especially Twentieth Century Fox, poured money into a series of musical extravaganzas designed to replicate the earnings of *The Sound of Music*, including *Doctor Dolittle* (1967), *Star!* (1968) and *Hello, Dolly!* (1969), none of which earned more than a fraction of its cost at the domestic box office.[25] Fox was plunged into near collapse. Too much money was being gambled on borrowed money. Too many films were being made. Three new companies had entered into the business, including the broadcasters CBS and ABC. Increased competition pushed budgets higher. Expansion was driven partly by the new source of profits found in the sale of blockbuster films to television. The television bonanza came to a temporary halt in 1968, however. The networks had met their needs for the coming three years and also preferred to invest in their own productions.[26]

The combination of these factors created a serious economic crisis from 1969 to 1971. The industry went through a period of retrenchment and restructuring. Spending was curtailed, temporarily at least. All of this was to the enormous benefit of what was to become the Hollywood Renaissance. The success of *Bonnie and Clyde*, *The Graduate* and *Easy Rider* could not have come at a better moment. Lower budget productions with a contemporary edge were shown to be far less risky in this context than unwieldy spectacles that seemed to belong to another era.

A number of industrial factors combined to make possible the Hollywood Renaissance. A specific set of industrial circumstances enabled aspects of the social and historical context to find expression in Hollywood. To understand the particular manner in which the flavour of the period was sometimes translated onto the cinema screen in these circumstances we also have to look elsewhere. The Hollywood Renaissance was also shaped by the influence of the stylistic experiments of a new generation of filmmakers outside Hollywood.

## An American 'New Wave'? The stylistic context of the Hollywood Renaissance

The fizzing glass of water in *Taxi Driver* is an expression of Travis Bickle's state of mind, itself perhaps some unspecified product of its time. It is also a direct borrowing from a film by one of the key figures of the French New Wave, *deux ou trois choses que je sais d'elle* (*two or three things I know about her...*, 1966), directed by Jean-Luc Godard. In *deux ou trois choses* the camera descends to the surface of a cup of coffee during a lengthy disquisition by one of the characters. The films of the Hollywood Renaissance abound with such borrowings.[27]

The jump cuts in the opening of *Bonnie and Clyde* are strongly indebted to the French movement, especially Godard's *A Bout de Souffle* (*Breathless*, 1959), probably the single most influential film of the New Wave. *A Bout de Souffle*, itself inspired by the Hollywood B-movie and dedicated to the low-budget Monogram studio, is filled with departures from classical editing regimes. Like *Bonnie and Clyde*, it opens with a series of close and medium shots in which no establishing shot is provided. Later, the shooting of a motorcycle cop by the central character Michel (Jean-Paul Belmondo) is rendered in a few rapid and highly compressed shots that flout the 180 degree rule. An initial series of shots establishes that the officer approaches Michel's stationary car from the left. Michel reaches inside the vehicle for a gun, conforming initially to this spatial relationship. Cut to a closely framed pan down across the side of his face, now facing in the opposite direction. Another close-up pan takes us to the right, across his hand holding the gun. Cut rapidly to another close pan along the length of the gun, from chamber to barrel. In each of these shots the gun is pointed out of frame to the right. A shot is heard, although not actually seen, as we cut to the cop already falling dead. He seems to fall as if shot from *his* right, which would violate the relationship established the previous group of shots, although the brevity of the image and a general lack of directional clarity makes this uncertain. We then cut to Michel already fleeing on foot across a field.

The sequence is telegraphic and disorienting, reflecting the arbitrary nature of the killing. A similar effect is created, to a lesser extent, in a

2. Reflection in a broken lens: an overt reference to *A Bout de Souffle* in *Bonnie and Clyde*, © Warner Bros., 1967. Ronald Grant archive

series of shots and reverse shots that underpins the shock of the first moment of graphic violence in *Bonnie and Clyde*, the shooting in the face of a bank clerk who jumps onto the running board of the getaway car.[28] Another reference to *A Bout de Souffle* appears in the single-lens broken sunglasses worn by Clyde Barrow at the film's climax, mirroring an identical image of Michel. It comes as no surprise to learn that two key figures of the French New Wave, Godard and Francois Truffaut, were at one point invited to direct *Bonnie and Clyde*, or that several of Truffaut's suggestions were incorporated into the screenplay.

*Taxi Driver* owes a number of debts to the films of Robert Bresson, one of the subjects of a study by the screenwriter, Paul Schrader. The voice-over narration from a diary kept by Bickle is based on *Journal d'un Curé de Campagne* (*Diary of a Country Priest*, 1950). His diet of bread soaked in brandy and the fear that he has cancer are more specific references to *Journal*, the protagonist of which subsists on a diet of bread soaked in wine because of his cancer.[29] Martin Scorsese has acknowledged the extent to which his work has been influenced by the films of Godard, Truffaut and Alain Resnais. Early in *Mean Streets* (1973), he uses three rapid shots, cutting in progressively closer towards the central character, Charlie (Harvey Keitel), a striking device lifted from Truffaut's *Tirez sur le Pianiste* (*Shoot the Piano Player*, 1960) and which Scorsese once said was in every film he had made.[30]

Other Truffaut films have been credited with influencing the use of a number of techniques in Hollywood Renaissance-era films. The lyrical bicycling interlude and freeze-frame ending of *Butch Cassidy and the Sundance Kid* (1969) bear the mark, respectively, of *Jules et Jim* (*Jules and Jim*, 1961) and *Le Quatre Cent Coups* (*The 400 Blows*, 1959). *Jules et Jim* has also been seen as one source of the prevalent use of slow motion in Hollywood films of the period, along with Akira Kurosawa's *The Seven Samurai* (1954), the latter an influence particularly on the use of slow motion in violent sequences. The combination of slow and normal speed footage used to achieve maximum impact in the climactic massacre of *Bonnie and Clyde* was directly inspired by *The Seven Samurai*. The list goes on. As Robert Ray suggests, the final shoot-out in the snow in *Shoot the Piano Player*, 'with its absence of establishing shots, frequent 180° crossings, long shots, and fizzy off-center compositions' is translated into the climax of the unconventional western *McCabe and Mrs Miller* (1971), directed by Robert Altman. 'The 360° pans of *Breathless* and *Weekend* (1967) (both accompanied by Mozart) were repeated in *Five Easy Pieces* (1970) (accompanied by Chopin).'[31] And so on.

What should we make of all this? Are these just superficial borrowings, the trappings of what might be considered hip and trendy at the time, to please the filmmakers themselves and the relatively small number of viewers likely to pick up the references? Or is something more serious at stake? Something of each, perhaps. Departures from the conventions of dominant or 'classical' Hollywood style do carry a serious and radical potential. Style is no innocent matter. The conventions of continuity editing generally serve to focus attention on the story, or narrative, rather than on technique. The implications of this are considerable. The impression given is that the world in front of the camera unfolds naturally and effortlessly. We are given what usually appears to be immediate access to the fictional world of the film. The fact that all of this has been carefully fabricated, down to every last camera position and cut, is obscured.

Paying close attention to the devices of the classical style takes a great deal of effort and is difficult to sustain for any lengthy period of time. So familiar have these devices become that they are usually taken for granted, rendered all-but invisible. But why should this matter? The point is that a particular view of the world is constructed, as in any artistic or cultural product. The world represented by a Hollywood film is not neutrally recorded. Instead, it is actively created. Not only created, but created according to particular assumptions that have social, political and ideological implications. The conventions of continuity editing, for example, tend to imply a world that is ordered and comprehensible. They offer the viewer in most cases a 'safe' and comfortable position from which to understand the world presented on screen. This is why departures from these conventions can be so effective. They create a sense of discomfort and uncertainty.

Continuity editing creates a coherent impression of space and time, and the connections between one and the other. Jump cuts and breaches of the 180 degree convention upset these coherencies. Initially unexplained or abrupt flashback insertions can have a similar effect. Their use in Resnais' *Hiroshima, Mon Amour* (1959) is credited with sparking a Hollywood trend starting with *The Pawnbroker* (1965). Flash-forwards are even more unconventional, used to create spiky and unsettling scene transitions in *Easy Rider* and *Petulia* (1968). Such devices make spatial and temporal relationships uncertain.

Another technique found in some American films in the Renaissance period is the use of zoom lenses, instead of cuts or tracking shots, to move through space. This is a device drawn partly from 1960s documentary filmmaking (and from television), to create an impression of spontaneity in front of the camera; a sense of reacting to, rather than carefully staging, events. It can also be used expressively. An unexpected zoom is used in *The Graduate* to underpin the moment when the relationship between Benjamin and Mrs Robinson is irrevocably ended. Two separate close-ups of their faces, linked by an eye-line match, imply an initial spatial proximity. A zoom back from Mrs Robinson to include Benjamin in the frame suddenly opens up a gulf between the pair, the change of focal length creating a shift in perspective that makes literal the reduction of the former to a diminutive figure in the background. Departures from dominant conventions might not be recognized explicitly. Most filmgoers are unlikely to be able to identify a breach of the 180 degree rule as such, to describe what exactly is different. But they may be aware that something seems 'not quite right'. The familiarity of the dominant conventions is such that they become notable primarily in the breach.

Two major outcomes are possible from such breaches of convention. One is simply a feeling of disorientation, which can be exploited to potent effect. The viewer of *Bonnie and Clyde* does not need to know anything about continuity editing or jump cuts to be given an impression of edginess and impatience by the opening images. The same is true of *A Bout de Souffle*, which repeatedly uses jump cuts to create a sense of unease and of the provisional nature of the lifestyle of its protagonist. Even fairly minor departures from the dominant conventions can be sufficient to give a film, or a group of films, a sense of freshness and innovation, a major ingredient in any films deserving to be labelled as part of a 'New Wave' or 'Renaissance'.

Non-conventional techniques can also have more radical effects, shattering the carefully fabricated illusion that the fictional world merely unfolds in front of the camera. Explicit attention might be drawn to the process of construction usually concealed by the classical style. This might be the case in the shooting of the motorcycle cop in *A Bout de Souffle*. Godard appears to be playing with, even mocking, continuity conventions, as if deliberately to bring them to our attention. The same could be true of the unconventional camera movements in *Taxi Driver*. We become more aware of the existence of the camera when it does something unusual or unexpected. A camera focused on the central character from a familiar angle and distance is likely to recede from our attention. One that takes up a strange position, or wanders off on its own, seemingly detached from the action, is more likely to be noticed.

Drawing attention to the way a film is constructed makes us aware of its status *as* a construct. Film viewers are perfectly aware, on one level, that films are constructs. We do not very often mistake the film for 'reality'. We are encouraged to do this, on another level, however, during the process of viewing. Classical conventions *invite us*, much of the time, to surrender to the pleasurable illusion that we are merely witnesses at the scene, rather than that the scene has been fabricated for us. The abandonment of familiar conventions can be a denial of this pleasure, with potentially political implications. If we become consciously aware of the constructed status of the image we might also become aware of the *basis* on which it has been constructed. To undermine dominant conventions can be to question dominant ideologies.

The dividing line between these two effects is important, but not always easy to establish. On one side, departures from classical conventions can be seen as expressive devices. They break the 'rules', but in a manner that is contained. They are 'motivated' by matters of character or narrative. As such, they remain within the influential definition of the classical style given by David Bordwell.[32] For Bordwell, a defining characteristic of the classical style is that matters of style are subordinated to narrative. Stylistic flourishes or unconventional imagery serve narrative purposes rather than existing for their own sake. The opening images of *Bonnie and Clyde* give expression to the mood of character. The errant camera of *Taxi Driver* expresses something of Travis Bickle's disconnection (and, conversely, the use of classical reverse angles and two-shots in one sequence involving Travis and Betsy might emphasize the extent to which, on this occasion, he is trying hard to act 'normal'[33]). A sustained period of 'experimental' techniques – including rapid discontinuous montage editing, the use of a distorting 'fish-eye' lens, unstable 'subjective' camera-work and non-realistically motivated sound effects – is used in *Easy Rider* to convey the impressions of an acid trip.

Films of this period sometimes offer a seemingly contradictory mix of the 'expressive', a heightened use of stylistic devices to convey subjective experience, and the 'realistic', with its claims to objectivity. Similarly unconventional shooting and editing styles can in some cases fall into either or both categories. Departures from continuity editing can be expressive, in a stylized manner. They can also suggest, along with hand-held camerawork, the immediacy of unplanned or *verité* footage, shot on the hoof, to give an impression of freshness and spontaneity, distinct from the carefully-staged effect that might result from use of the full panoply of expensive studio apparatus. Lessons were learned from the work of documentary filmmakers such as Richard Leacock, D.A. Pennebaker and David and Albert Maysles, who used cheap, lightweight hand–held equipment to capture a flavour of contemporary reality on the streets. Elements of this style contribute to the edgy quality of films such as *The French Connection* (1971) and *Mean Streets*, the latter a particularly effective blend of *verité* and expressive techniques. A similar combination is found in some films of both the French New Wave and the Hollywood Renaissance. At what point, though, do any of these devices translate into a less easily contained break from the classical style? A distinction has often been made between their use in Hollywood and in the New Wave or other products of the European 'art' cinema of the 1950s and 1960s. The fizzing glass shot from *Taxi Driver* offers one useful point of comparison.

Scorsese uses this device to capture a sense of Bickle's subjective state. The sequence is brief and to the point, lasting in total only about 20 seconds, the effervescent surface filling the screen for only about a quarter of that time. Godard's original is similar in some respects but also radically different. The coffee cup sequence in *deux ou trois choses* also takes us into the interior state of a protagonist. Immersion in the cup, like that of the glass, shuts out the ambient sounds of the café. It lasts a good deal longer, however, and is used as the basis for a weighty meditation. The sequence extends for more than two minutes, much of which is spent in extreme close-up on the black surface of the coffee. Voice-over narration is the stuff of heady French existentialism, one line of which even seems relevant to the theme and style of *Taxi Driver*. 'I cannot escape crushing objectivity or isolating subjectivity', muses the character, a pair of oppositions akin to the perspectives the viewer is offered on Travis Bickle.

The Godard character's thoughts range across the impossibility of revolution, the threat of war, the uncertainty of capitalism and the retreat of the working class; science, the proximity of the future, and the creation; the limits of language, death, vagueness and a rebirth of consciousness. The surface of the coffee seems a perfect backdrop for such intellectual pondering. At first it swirls, blackly, clouded patterns suggesting the shape of galaxies forming in the void. Something closer to stasis sets in as the last bubbles of froth break on the surface. An even closer shot begins in silence and further abstraction, heaving blackness and the glint of reflecting lights. Whatever we make of this – profundity or pretentiousness? – it is a far greater intrusion into conventional narrative filmmaking that anything found in *Taxi Driver* or any other films of the Hollywood Renaissance. The device is not a passing expressive moment but a major interruption, increasingly typical of the films of a director working towards a radical deconstruction of Hollywood-style conventions *and* capitalist ideology.

Similar distinctions might be made in the narrative dimension. Some films of the Hollywood Renaissance do depart, to an extent, from mainstream narrative conventions. The narrative of *Taxi Driver* fails to establish any clear-cut motivation for Travis Bickle's action. The reticence of Harry Caul in *The Conversation* is motivated to some extent by a previous operation in which he was the unwitting cause of death. His utter failure of comprehension is devastating, however, particularly because the viewer (or, in this case, auditor) is made to share the misunderstanding. The placing of the emphasis on the key line ('He'd kill us if he got the chance') changes in the moment of final revelation, suggesting retrospectively that the version we have heard several times during the film was filtered not just through Caul's audio equipment but also through his own subjective interpretation. Broader motivation and explanation is in short supply in *The Parallax View*, which never gives us a clear sense of what the Parallax Corporation is, where it comes from and what agenda it might have.

These are interesting departures from the Hollywood routine, but they are also limited in scope and contained by other frameworks. Like many Hollywood Renaissance films, these examples remain largely within the bounds of familiar generic structures. *Taxi Driver* can be read as an example of 1970s film noir. *The Conversation* and *The Parallax View* are versions of the detective thriller. Generic frameworks offer considerable scope for innovation, sometimes radical, as will be seen in chapter 4. But they also impose limitations on, and motivations for, less than conventional narratives. The truth does emerge in *The*

*Conversation*, even if it is only grasped belatedly by the central character. Truth is also uncovered in *The Parallax View*, albeit limited and at the cost of Frady's life. The gloomy or inconclusive endings of these films are themselves motivated to some extent by the conventions of the emerging form of the conspiracy-thriller. As with departures from conventional editing regimes, the unconventional touches in the narrative structures of some Hollywood Renaissance films appear rather modest when compared with more radical instances from European 'art' films. We gain a reasonably clear sense of who committed the murder, and probably why, in *The Conversation*. Almost all of this is withheld in *Blow Up*, the film on which it is partly based.[34] No Hollywood products approach the elliptical style and narrative enigma of the likes of Alain Resnais' *La Dernier Anné a Marienbad* (*Last Year at Marienbad*, 1961).

The Hollywood Renaissance witnessed a number of stylistic innovations. This is most apparent when comparison is made with the dominant tendencies of the commercial mainstream, rather than the European 'art' cinema. These did not amount to anything like a wholesale abandonment of the 'classical' style, even in the more radical or interesting products of the period. Large parts of films such as *Bonnie and Clyde*, *Easy Rider* and *Taxi Driver* conform to familiar conventions such as those of continuity editing and narrative motivation, providing a ground against which elements of innovation can be measured. Hollywood demonstrated its ability to absorb stylistic elements from other cinemas without being significantly transformed. It had done this before. Aspects of styles as radically different from classical Hollywood as Soviet montage and German expressionism were taken on board during the studio era. The montage sequence became an effective way of compressing a series of events into a brief sequence contained within a conventional narrative. Expressionistic canted-camera angles and lighting were absorbed by the horror film and film noir.[35]

Classical Hollywood style contains a considerable degree of flexibility. It can embrace a wide range of devices, provided that they are given a distinct rationale, usually in terms of character, genre and/or other aspects of narrative. This does not mean that departures from the norm are devoid of any power to disturb or unsettle, merely that these are unlikely to upset the entire edifice. They may appear bold and innovative at one moment. Soon, however, they can become just another part of the repertoire.

Freshness and innovation within a framework of more conventional forms and structures might be the best way to characterize the formal dimension of most products of the Hollywood Renaissance. The same goes for their subject matter. A flavour of the times is captured in many, often with an implicitly critical note. The films of the Renaissance tend to question the bland reassurances offered by many Hollywood products. Some are openly critical of dominant myths and ideologies. This is the case especially with anti-westerns such as *Little Big Man* (1970) and *Buffalo Bill and the Indians, or Sitting Bull's History Lesson* (1976), which will be considered in chapter 4. Many Renaissance films remain within the compass of dominant mythologies, however, even if they are given a new twist.

*Bonnie and Clyde* and *Easy Rider* are, to a significant extent, updatings of the old mythology of the frontier. Journeys into open spaces, now on the road, continue to supply the possibility of romantic escape from the confines of 'civilization'. The fate met by such figures is more grim than that of the protagonist of the classical western, but the latter is also portrayed as ultimately doomed in some cases, gaining only temporary respite from the inexorable movement of 'progress'. The Hollywood hero has typically been represented as the rebellious individual standing out against institutional forces of one kind or another. The subversive potential of films such as *The Conversation* and *The Parallax View* is to deny any possibility of success to the hero, or even the compensation of heroic doom. Even here, however, the diagnosis is entirely negative. No alternative is offered. Diagnosis is not accompanied by any prescription for change. To do so would be to make the political implications explicit rather than merely implicit and muddied by genre conventions.

Explicit political comment of any radical nature is extremely rare in Hollywood. This is not just a matter of the political leanings of those in power in the industry. Political controversy is generally avoided because of its divisive potential. Hollywood prefers to smooth over its conflicts. Room is often left for a variety of readings, in order to appeal to the largest possible audience. This is less true of some films associated with the Hollywood Renaissance, which were aimed at audiences that might be more open than usual to relatively radical perspectives. Few take up the more explicitly political aspects of 1960s social movements, however. Films such as *The Strawberry Statement* (1970), based on student rebellion at Columbia University, and *Medium Cool* (1969), which culminates amid the Chicago riots of 1968, are exceptions, to some extent. The complacency of a detached television news cameraman in the latter is challenged by some of those with whom he comes into contact, a challenge offered also to the audience in scenes in which their objections are played direct to camera.

Major issues of class, wealth, inequality and structural racism are generally absent from the picture in the films of the Renaissance, however. Where potentially radical issues are raised they are usually subordinated to a focus on the dynamics of the relationships between individuals, a respect in which these films often differ little from the rest of Hollywood cinema. *Medium Cool* is, again, something of an exception, demonstrating the ability of some films of the period to depart from the glossy Hollywood norm. The potential sentimentality of a relationship developed between the protagonist and a woman with a teenage son is avoided by the use of a detached documentary-style and a downbeat ending.

Far from all the films produced in Hollywood in the period from the late 1960s to the mid-to-late 1970s exhibit the characteristics of the films considered in this chapter. The Hollywood Renaissance is merely one tendency within a period in which the box office continued to be dominated by more conventional fare. *The Graduate* was the biggest hit, heading the box-office chart for 1968 (after being released in the latter part of 1967). *Easy Rider* was a major success, but relative to its low budget as much as in absolute terms. It came 11th in 1969, a year in which the top-grossing film was *The Love Bug*. *M\*A\*S\*H* was the third most successful film of 1970, when top place was taken by *Patton*. Other number-one hits of the period included *Love Story* (1971), *The Godfather* (1972), *The Poseidon Adventure* (1973), *The Sting* (1974), *Jaws* (1975), *One Flew Over the Cuckoo's Nest* (1976) and *Star Wars* (1977); mostly films with few radical pretensions.[36] Precisely where the boundaries of the Renaissance lie remains a matter for debate. Many more titles could be added to those cited in this chapter. They would still constitute only a small proportion of the output of the decade. These films have gained disproportionate attention, which should not be surprising. Relatively small groups of films that stand out from the mainstream have always tended to attract more critical attention than might strictly be merited in terms of their broader significance. The films of the Renaissance are not unique in this respect. Nor are they the first films to have offered some of the qualities considered above.

Youth rebellion was a popular topic for a number of films in the 1950s. Doubt, cynicism and bleak endings characterize many examples of film noir produced in the 1950s and 1940s, as well as some gangster films of the 1930s. They have also been found in a number of films produced since the 'end' of the Renaissance, usually dated quite specifically to 1979. Unconventional stylistic devices were incorporated into some of these films, especially film noir. *Verité* style, using an earlier generation of lightweight equipment, is used in a number of post-war thrillers. Some of the stylistic borrowings of the films considered in this chapter are in fact taken from products of studio-era Hollywood, if often from the work of mavericks within the system. The direct overhead shot in *Taxi Driver* owes a clear debt to Hitchcock. The giant lips of Faye Dunaway are reminiscent of those of Charles Foster Kane (Orson Welles) uttering his dying 'Rosebud' in *Citizen Kane* (1941), an enormous influence on many filmmakers coming to prominence in the Renaissance period. Many borrowed freely, not just from the French New Wave. If montage techniques, shorn of the dialectical intent of the Soviet filmmaker and theorist Sergei Eisenstein, could be made over into narrative flourishes in the studio era, *Bonnie and Clyde* could also have its bespectacled bank clerk shot in the face in a manner reminiscent of the death of a woman in the famed Odessa Steps sequence of Eisenstein's *Battleship Potemkin* (1925).

An upsurge of more-complex-than-usual Hollywood filmmaking was also noted by numerous commentators in 1999 and 2000, including examples such as *American Beauty* (1999), *Magnolia* (1999) and *American Psycho* (2000). Why, then, should what has become known as the 'Hollywood Renaissance' be marked by so grand a term? Perhaps it should not. Whether, on balance, novelty outweighed convention sufficiently to justify the term, or to suggest a common basis for the assessment of a range of very different products, is uncertain. As a body of work, these films have come to be defined from two directions. Initially, they were marked out according to differences from the norms of the studio era. That, at the height of the movement, seemed the most relevant criterion. More recently, and increasingly, the Hollywood Renaissance has been defined by its difference from the version of New Hollywood that has largely replaced it and that was beginning to take shape at the time.

Worthy of the term or not, the Hollywood Renaissance was the outcome of a conjunction of forces: social, industrial and stylistic. It was in many ways the product of a period of transition. The 'Old' Hollywood was struggling. New industrial frameworks were still finding their optimum form. A measure of freedom was available in the interim. Today, the Hollywood Renaissance has become the stuff primarily of fond nostalgia, which may not be surprising given some of the characteristics of what has since become the dominant version of New Hollywood: the era of the corporate blockbuster, the subject of the next chapter.

# New Hollywood, Version II
## Blockbusters and Corporate Hollywood

> The notion of the New Hollywood... underwent a strange mutation.
>
> Murray Smith[1]

A monster movie. A monster *of* a movie. Or just a monstrosity? Production cost: approximately $120 million. Big, noisy and unsubtle, both off-screen and on. The monster invades Manhattan. The movie takes on the entire country, opening on an unprecedented 7,363 screens in 3,310 cinemas across America. Expected to devour an equally record-breaking $100 million at the box office on its opening holiday weekend. Massive promotion and publicity. Hundreds of product tie-ins and spin-offs. 'Size does matter' was the tag-line for *Godzilla* (1998), an irresistibly appropriate phrase for both the film and the industrial strategy of which it is a prominent example.

*Godzilla* is a perfect illustration of the contemporary Hollywood blockbuster and a version of 'New Hollywood' that seems a million miles away from the edgy products of the Hollywood Renaissance. The notion of New Hollywood did, indeed, undergo a mutation every bit as strange as that which created the giant lizard star of *Godzilla*. Godzilla is the product of nuclear fallout. *Godzilla* is the product of an industrial regime that has come to dominate Hollywood, the world of giant media corporations into which the industry has been absorbed. How, though, did we get from one version of New Hollywood to the other? From *Bonnie and Clyde*, *Easy Rider* and *The Graduate* to the likes of *Godzilla* and other 'franchise' movies such as *Star Wars* (1977), *Batman* (1989), *Toy Story* (1995) and *X-Men* (2000)? This chapter will seek an explanation primarily in terms of the industrial context of New Hollywood. Other dimensions of the corporate blockbuster, including its formal qualities, will be considered in later chapters. First, though, it is worth a closer look at some of the distinguishing features of the New Hollywood blockbuster.

Most obviously, blockbusters are usually 'big' films, like *Godzilla*. They tend to consume large amounts of money. They feature spectacular on-screen events that often include expensive displays of the latest in special effects technologies. Blockbusters are also heavily promoted and advertised, often well in advance. The first teaser trailers for *Godzilla* appeared in cinemas and on the film's website a year before the film itself. Large sums of money are devoted to saturation television advertising at the time of cinema release. The contemporary blockbuster is also likely to be opened simultaneously in a large number of cinemas, the theatre record set by *Godzilla* having been exceeded since by *Scream 3* (2000: 3,467 theatres), *Wild Wild West* (1999: 3,342) and *Austin Powers: The Spy Who Shagged Me* (1999: 3,312).[2]

Another crucial feature of many blockbusters is that they are 'pre-sold', based on properties already familiar to a potential audience. They might be adaptations of products known in other forms, or sequels to other films. *Godzilla* trades on audience knowledge of the original Godzilla, or Gojira, a long-running star of a series of films made in Japan and the familiar stuff of TV screenings in America and elsewhere. Blockbusters also tend to be relatively conservative in their political or ideological implications.

This kind of filmmaking is very different from that associated with the Hollywood Renaissance, or early uses of the term 'New Hollywood'. It seems odd that the same term should have been used to describe the two. But the features of the corporate blockbuster can be explained by some of the same underlying changes that provided space for the Hollywood Renaissance. Similar tendencies can have some very different outcomes. To understand the development of the blockbuster format that dominates Hollywood today we need to look again at some of the background examined in the previous chapter, including responses to falling audience numbers and the break-up of the old vertically integrated studio system.

## From 'niche' to 'event': reconstructing the 'mass' audience

Hollywood lost much of its previously regular and reliable audience in the post-war decades. One response was to target films at a variety of smaller, more specific or 'niche' audiences, a factor that contributed to the appearance of the Hollywood Renaissance. Another was the exact opposite. The Hollywood studios, in their modified form, produced big and usually expensive films in the hope of regaining something like the larger audience that had been lost. This is what the blockbuster scenario is all about. The successful blockbuster is one that attracts a huge audience.

Overall cinema attendances are much lower than those of the 'golden age' of classical Hollywood. More than four billion admissions were reported in 1946, the post-war high-point. The figure dropped to below one billion in 1970, although it has since recovered some ground, reaching 1.42 billion in 2000.[3] The most successful films generally attract audiences larger than those of the past, however. The all-time record for admissions is still held by *Gone with the Wind* (1939, 199 million) and *Snow White* (1937) also ranks in the top ten (eighth, at 109 million). Otherwise, the list of most highly attended films is dominated by blockbuster productions of the New Hollywood era, in its broadest historical conception, from *Star Wars* (second, at 178 million) to *The Sound of Music* (third, at 142 million), *E.T.* (fourth, at 135 million) and *The Ten Commandments* (1956, fifth, at 131 million).[4]

Fewer films are made today than in the studio era. Up to 200 are released each year by the main companies, compared with 350–400 in the 1940s to mid-1950s.[5] This again represents a relative recovery, the total having dropped as low as 130 or fewer during the 1970s.[6] The major studios deliberately cut their level of production during the 1970s in order to concentrate on a smaller number of more expensive would-be blockbusters. Many of these do not fare particularly well at the box office. The financial health of the industry depends to a large extent on the success of a relatively small number of blockbuster-scale productions. Hollywood's box-office income is not spread at all equally across its range of product. A few films each year account for a disproportionate share.

Different figures are cited by different commentators, but something like 10 per cent of films can account for up to 50 per cent of all business (on big screen and small). The big studios tend to concentrate their efforts on films seen as likely to achieve this kind of success. The aim of these films, ideally, is to attract an audience that goes beyond the confines of regular movie-goers. The ultimate achievement is to gain the status of an 'event' movie, like *Star Wars* or *Titanic* (1997). An event movie is one that gains prominence in the wider culture, beyond the cinema screen; one that everyone seems to be talking about, that is almost impossible to avoid. One of the most recent examples is *Star Wars: Episode One – The Phantom Menace* (1999), seemingly adorning the cover of every magazine and penetrating into every crevice of popular culture, a quality likely to greet the next films in the *Star Wars* series due for release in 2002 and 2005.

Blockbusters or would-be 'event' movies tend to be large-scale spectacular affairs because such qualities are usually seen as the most effective way to tempt people back to the cinema. They play on the kind of effects that work best on the big screen, that make use of its sheer size and scope. This accounts to a large extent for the prominence of genres such as action-adventure and science fiction. They lend themselves to a spectacular cinematic experience sold as something bigger and better than the experience of rival media such as television.

This tendency is far from entirely new. Scale and spectacle have been important ingredients of Hollywood productions dating back to the earliest days of the studio system or before. Some of the roots of the contemporary blockbuster format can be found in the 1950s, the decade in which the industry was forced to come to terms with a changed social and economic environment. The typical spectacular blockbusters of the 1950s were biblical epics, musicals and inflated versions of the western. Money continued to be poured into such extravaganzas during the 1960s. The financial crisis of the late 1960s led to a temporary reduction in this kind of production, but not for long. A periodic self-criticism for excessive spending is a regular feature of the economic soul-searching that goes on among studio executives. One or two really big successes are all that are needed to restore confidence in the blockbuster strategy. The 1970s had perhaps more than its share, a decade that saw significant refinements in the blockbuster strategy, to which we will return shortly. Periodic mutterings about reducing budgets and offering a more balanced slate of releases have continued ever since. The temptations of blockbuster production are hard to resist, however, for a number of reasons explored in this chapter.

*Godzilla* was designed to be an 'event' movie. Along with *The Mask of Zorro*, it was one of two pictures on which much of the success of Sony Pictures appeared to hang in the summer season of 1998.[7] Films such as these have become known as 'tentpole' pictures, their success capable of propping up the fortunes of an entire studio. *Godzilla* did achieve 'event' status, although not quite in the manner intended. It performed disappointingly at the US box office and came in for a great deal of criticism. The film became a by-word for all that appeared to be wrong with contemporary Hollywood in general, and the blockbuster format in particular.

This all sounds like a rather unstable way to run an industry. Gone are the sheltered securities of the studio system. The success of individual films could not be guaranteed even then, but the overall stability of the industry was generally secured by the system of vertical integration. Today, it seems, enormous piles of money are invested in expensive blockbusters whose behaviour at the box office is as unpredictable as any rampaging mutant lizard. Some make vast profits. Others fail to recover their costs at the box office. But the New Hollywood of the corporate blockbuster is not quite the crazy and unpredictable beast it sometimes seems. Even the most notorious box-office disappointments are not always the financial disasters they might first appear. A number of strategies are used to minimize risk. These take us a step further in helping to explain some of the ingredients of the blockbuster recipe.

## Pre-selling, advertising and saturation releasing: restoring stability

*Jaws* (1975) is a key landmark in the development of the contemporary version of the blockbuster format. *Jaws* was pre-sold, based on a best-selling book. The same goes for a number of successful films that helped to pull Hollywood out of financial difficulties in the first half of the 1970s, including *Airport* (1970), *The Godfather* (1972) and *The Exorcist* (1973). In some of these cases the books were not published, or even completed, during initial production of the film, but were seen as attractive properties that could be released ahead of and/or in conjunction with the film in order to create prior audience awareness and anticipation. The potential benefits of pre-sold properties are considerable. Money can be invested with some confidence that an audience already exists. Pre-sold properties have credentials and a track record; they appear less risky. Hollywood has always produced films based on successful books, stage plays or well-known historical events, including many of the more expensive 'prestige' productions of the classical era.[8] This practice became especially attractive in the more fragmented production environment of the New Hollywood, from the 1950s, in which each project was sold to a greater extent on its own merits. Existing tendencies to play safe were reinforced. Entirely new, separate or original projects always carry an extra degree of risk and unpredictability and are harder to finance. They have to be sold afresh each time.

Best-selling books are only one source of pre-sold properties on which the corporate blockbuster has drawn. Many areas of popular culture have been mined for exploitable potential. Comic book characters have proved one of the most popular sources. Figures ranging from Superman and Batman to Judge Dredd, Tank Girl and the X-Men have all featured in science fiction extravaganzas. Classic television shows have also been plundered, recent examples including *The Addams Family* (1991), *The Flintstones* (1994), *Mission: Impossible* (1996), *Lost in Space* (1998), *The Avengers* (1998) and *Charlie's Angels* (2000). And then there are the sequels, including sequels to many products that were pre-sold in the first place, such as *Superman* (1978), *Batman*, *The Addams Family* and

*Mission: Impossible.* The sequel to an already pre-sold property might be the quintessential stuff of the contemporary Hollywood blockbuster, doubly hedged with what are hoped to be built-in reassurances of some kind of success.

*Jaws* was one of many box-office successes of its time to be pre-sold. In two other respects it marked a significant change in the blockbuster strategy. *Jaws* was the first big-budget Hollywood film to be given both saturation television advertising and to be released from the start in a large number of cinemas. Both are now standard. At the time, this was a strategy usually reserved for cheaper and less reputable 'exploitation' films that did not always deliver quite what was promised by salacious titles and publicity. The aim was to squeeze the maximum profit from a film quickly, before poor reviews or bad word-of-mouth had time to inflict any damage. From *Jaws* onwards the strategy has been adopted as one of a number of ways of attempting to reduce the risks of expensive blockbuster production. If *Easy Rider* marked a point in the Hollywood Renaissance at which productions associated with industrially marginal exploitation material were taken up in the mainstream studio arena, *Jaws* demonstrated another way in which the studios learned, and stole some of the thunder, from the low-budget exploitation sector. Like *The Exorcist* and a number of other blockbuster hits of the 1970s, it was the stuff of exploitation given the glossy high-budget treatment.

*Jaws* opened in more than 400 theatres, a small total by recent standards but almost unprecedented for a big-budget picture at the time.[9] This is a significant change from the traditional release patterns established during the studio era. The norm was to release films gradually. Big films would be opened in a relatively small number of 'prestige' cinemas in the major cities. The opening would be treated as a special and selective event, underlining the high status of the film. Films would gradually work their way through a hierarchy of cinema chains, from the 'movie palaces' to small-town fleapits. The aim was to milk the maximum possible revenue from each film. Higher-run cinemas charged higher admission prices and generated the biggest share of profits. Films would be kept in these cinemas, protected from competition by zoning arrangements, for as long as demand held up. Then they would move down a stage, to medium-run cinemas that charged less but more than those on the bottom rungs of the ladder. Filmgoers had a choice. If they wanted to see a film while it was new and fresh, they had to pay top dollar. If they wanted to see a film cheaply, they had to wait.

This system was very effective in the studio era, when finance was spread across a large slate of production with guaranteed outlets and key assets such as stars were tied down by long-term contracts. It is less well suited to the New Hollywood context, in which films are packaged and sold individually and under greater pressure to pay for themselves. Films are still produced in studio slates to a significant extent, but these have become both smaller and less well balanced. Each film took a considerable time to go through the layers of the run-zone-clearance system, even if the lion's share of box-office receipts was taken in the first-run theatres. Quicker returns are sought in the more fragmented production system of New Hollywood, especially as blockbuster budgets escalate. Films are sometimes financed with borrowed money on which interest is payable, usually the high rates charged on relatively short-term loans. The sooner a film's profits can be realized, the sooner loans can be repaid and interest saved; or the sooner returns can be gained on in-house capital investments from the reserves of the majors or their corporate parents. Hence the appeal of a fast 'smash and grab' approach to distribution and exhibition.

Films opened successfully in large numbers of cinemas can cover their costs rapidly. A demonstration of the merits of this strategy was given by *Batman*, which opened on more than 2,000 screens in the summer of 1989. It grossed $40 million on its three-day opening weekend, a figure equivalent to a production budget estimated at $30–40 million. By the end of the first week it had taken $70 million, more than the total incurred in production and promotional costs, the latter estimated at around $10 million. Within 11 days it had reached the $100 million mark, a point at which production would be likely to go into net profit after the subtraction of the share taken by exhibitors and distribution.[10] The heady figures anticipated for *Godzilla* were based on studio hopes of beating the previous record opening performance of *The Lost World: Jurassic Park* (1997). *The Lost World* opened in 3,281 cinemas and took $92.7 million over a holiday weekend, more than its production budget of $73 million.[11] The two prongs of the wide-release/

saturation advertising strategy are mutually reinforcing. A film opened widely across America can be supported by a single nationwide advertising campaign. This is easier and more efficient that attempting to arrange a complex network of campaigns linked to more gradual and varied release patterns. The growth of the internet as a source of publicity on an even wider scale is one factor (along with efforts to combat digital video piracy) currently pushing the studios towards the simultaneous release of key films on a *global* scale.

The system of big releases has created a distinctive culture in Hollywood today. Films handled in this manner are under pressure to make money quickly. They usually have a week or two at most to make an impression at the box office. The returns of the opening weekend come in for intense scrutiny by studio executives. These figures can shape the entire future prospects of a production. Films that do badly are liable to be pulled rapidly from circulation, or have their support reduced. In some cases, a poor opening performance will lead to a positive re-think of, and investment in, marketing strategies, in an effort to recover the situation. But this is not typical. Extra advertising is more likely to be devoted to films that are already doing well.[12] Little space is left for films to build an audience gradually, through staged patterns of release or the development of 'word-of-mouth' recommendation. This, in turn, helps further to shape the kinds of films that get made. Huge releases and advertising blitzes are best suited to blockbusters or other formulaic products aimed at a mass audience. A more modest and graduated approach is appropriate for smaller or more unconventional films, for which good reviews and slowly accumulated word-of-mouth recommendation play a more important part. This approach is still used in some cases. A good example is *American Beauty* (1999), a critical hit budgeted at $15 million that took a total of $130 million at the domestic box office after opening in just 16 theatres and building to 1,500 over a period of two months. Filmmakers often complain that carefully modulated strategies such as this are increasingly hard to achieve in face of the steamroller logic associated with the blockbuster release.

Widespread opening and saturation television advertising are responses to potential financial insecurity and increasing budgets. They are designed to protect investments. Advertising is seen essentially as 'support' for a film, rather than leaving it to fare for itself in the harsh world of box-office competition. Saturation advertising on national television creates a high level of audience awareness of a film's existence at the local multiplex. The trouble is that these strategies also exacerbate some of the problems they are designed to alleviate. Both are expensive, contributing substantially to the escalation of budgets. A familiar feature of the contemporary blockbuster is the cost of advertising, especially on television. The promotional budget for *Jaws* was $2.5 million.[13] Advertising budgets increased from an average of $3.54 million in 1980 to $24 million in 2000.[14] The cost of prints rose over the same period from $790,000 to $3.30 million. The total cost of prints and advertising (known as P&A in the business) reached $27.31 million in 1999, half as much again as the average negative cost (the cost of getting the production completed on film, including studio overhead) of $54.8 million. And these are *average* figures. P&A costs are generally much higher for would-be blockbusters, estimated by industry sources as close to $50 million for *Godzilla*.[15]

With all of the major companies pursuing the same strategies with their key blockbuster products, a diminishing return might be expected. Saturation advertising and promotion might be effective, but what if rival blockbusters are given the same treatment? Huge sums might be spent only to cancel out one another. This happens to some extent, but efforts are made to stagger the release of blockbusters in the key summer, Christmas and Easter holiday seasons. A blockbuster vacuum was created around *Godzilla*, for example.[16] So awesome were the promotion and expectations that no-one wanted to risk opening a high-stakes production directly against it. The only other film scheduled to open against *Godzilla* was *Fear and Loathing in Las Vegas*, directed by Terry Gilliam from the cult novel by Hunter S. Thompson and positioned as 'counter-programming', to appeal to a smaller audience less likely to be attracted by the heavyweight blockbuster.[17] Direct head to head competition by major would-be blockbusters, such as that between *The Patriot* and *The Perfect Storm* on the 4th of July holiday weekend in 2000, has become newsworthy in the trade press in its own right. More importantly, the saturation release/advertising strategy makes it extremely difficult for anyone outside the big companies to compete.

3. Heavy handed, on screen and off? Seeking to crush the opposition in *Godzilla*, © TriStar Pictures, 1998

Like all Hollywood extravagance, heavy investment in promotion and release constitutes another 'barrier to entry' that helps to maintain the dominance of a small number of very large players.

But was not the old industry dominated in this way supposed to have been unravelled along with the studio system? Why do we continue to speak of the dominance of a few big companies amid the greater freedoms of the 'post–studio' era in which the old suspects were obliged to sell off their cinema chains?

## 'It's distribution, stupid…'

The studio system is dead. Long live the studio system! A great deal changed in the way Hollywood was organized industrially during the 1950s and after. But much stayed the same. Major continuities exist between Hollywoods 'Old' and 'New'. The production system became more fragmented. Factory-style production-line filmmaking gave way to a system in which films are made in packages or relatively small portfolios, often involving independent production companies. But the Hollywood system as a whole has not become fragmented. The big studios were forced to get rid of their cinemas during the 1950s. This was designed to reduce their dominance of the industry. It did not. The major studios remain overwhelmingly dominant. How come? The answer is that the legal action taken against them missed a key point. It forced the studios out of exhibition, but it left them in charge of the system of distribution. Distribution, subsequently, has become the key strategic source of control over the industry. The enforced sale of cinemas can be seen from one perspective as a 'blessing in disguise'.[18] Cinemas tied up large amounts of capital and incurred substantial overhead costs throughout the year. Peak profits, however, are made on a seasonal basis. By removing themselves from exhibition, the big studios were freed from these large fixed costs. They could still control the industry through distribution, without having to meet such expenses. Their removal from exhibition also coincided with a period during which that sector of the business underwent major and expensive change, leading to the construction of new generations of multiplex and shopping-mall theatres, as a result of the movement of populations out of urban centres and into the suburbs

Production and exhibition were fragmented as a result of the Paramount case. But not distribution. Why? As Nicholas Garnham suggests, a key factor was the control of international distribution networks. These enabled Hollywood to dominate the globe. The US government took action against Hollywood dominance at home. As far as the overseas market was concerned, the government took a very difference stance. The promotion of American economic and cultural influence abroad took priority over any squeamishness about the niceties of fair competition. An act passed in 1918 permitted the studios to collude overseas. They were allowed to act together, to carve up foreign trade in a manner that would have been in clear breach of anti-monopoly laws in the United States. Numerous different collaborations have been formed since. Paramount and Universal combined their overseas operations in 1977 to form Cinema International Corporation, which changed its name to United International Pictures (UIP) in 1981 when it expanded to include the overseas business of the smaller studio MGM/ United Artists.[19] Sony/Columbia, Warner and Fox have joint venture deals in Europe and Latin America.

Global distribution networks are expensive. They require offices and staffs around the world. Collusion between the major studios in this arena made it extremely difficult for anyone else to compete. No-one else could operate on the scale required, and even if they could they faced the prospect of a market that had effectively been sewn up in advance.

The overseas market became increasingly important to Hollywood in the post-war decades, as audience numbers declined at home. Revenues from overseas gradually increased as a proportion of overall earnings. During the 1950s and 1960s the market outside the United States accounted for about half of Hollywood's box-office revenue. Differing rates of growth (and fluctuating exchange rates) reduced this to just over a third during the 1980s. The relative importance of the overseas market increased again in the 1990s, fuelled by developments such as the collapse of state communism in eastern Europe, with foreign returns surpassing domestic rentals for the first time in 1994.[20] For some studios in the late 1990s, particularly Fox and Disney, the split was about 60:40 in favour of overseas revenues, the result of increased penetration of studio films into foreign markets rather than a reduction in the size of the domestic audience. This is one way the studios have sought to make up the shortfall caused by a rate of increase in box-office spending in the US well below that in costs of production/ marketing (7.9 per cent and 26.6 per cent, respectively, in 1997).[21] Hollywood has recently had an envious eye on the potentially vast market of China.

In some cases the overseas market plays an even bigger role, especially in the case of action or star-centred blockbusters that tend to translate particularly well onto the international stage. The overseas market contributes an increasing proportion of the revenues of successful blockbuster productions.[22] Market success overseas is even more concentrated on a small number of big hits abroad than it is at home, where more films are released: the top ten films of 1998 accounted for 27.3 per cent of the theatrical market in the US, 35.1 per cent in the

UK, 30–45 per cent in much of Europe and 51 per cent in Japan, Hollywood's single most important overseas market.[23]

The domestic box-office gross of *Godzilla* was ultimately disappointing, if substantial, at about $135 million. Add overseas earnings and the picture becomes rather more positive. Around the world *Godzilla* grossed in the region of $220–250 million, making a total of up to $385 million. The majors have maintained control over this large part of the market. This provides them with the necessary resources to operate in a more stable manner than would otherwise be possible at home and abroad.

Far from everything has fallen apart in Hollywood. The major studios remain the major players. They control distribution. Revenues from distribution enable them to continue to play a dominant strategic role at the level of production. The big studios today have two primary roles. One is distribution. The other is financing. The studios have effectively become bankers to the film business. Stable revenues from distribution are what enable the studios to fund expensive blockbuster productions, or to gain access to credit from elsewhere. They operate at a sufficient scale to be able to balance-out some of the shorter term fluctuations created by the unpredictability of the film industry. The financing of production has not become quite as fragmented as might have been imagined.

As producers, financiers or distributors, the studios have varying degrees of investment in individual films.[24] Some films are financed, produced and distributed entirely in-house by the studios' own integrated production labels. Others are produced elsewhere, but funded and distributed by the majors. Some of these are wholly funded by the majors, some only partly. Many films are produced by independent or semi-independent production companies tied to particular studios by a number of different kinds of arrangement. In some cases they are provided with development funds and facilities on the studio lot in return for giving the studio first refusal on any projects developed, an arrangement known as a 'first-look' deal. Some are more substantial and enjoy more autonomy than others. On occasion two of the major studios will share the costs, especially with particularly expensive ventures such as *Titanic*, funded jointly by Twentieth Century Fox and

Paramount. This has become an increasing tendency in recent years, as part of a strategy of seeking to hedge bets in the ultra-high-budget category. The studios involved will usually split the distribution rights, one taking the domestic market, the other overseas.

The majors also distribute a range of features produced and financed elsewhere, another strategy that has been used to reduce risks associated with the most expensive productions. From the mid-to-late 1980s, the studios entered into partnerships with substantial independents such as Carolco (TriStar), Castle Rock (Columbia) and Morgan's Creek (Warner), in deals that usually involved partial financing, domestic distribution and lower than usual payments by the studios for distribution rights.[25] Such arrangements give the majors access to blockbuster films without making huge investments of their own, Carolco in particular having specialized in expensive action-oriented productions: 'After aligning with TriStar, Carolco delivered three big-budget blockbusters in a row, *Total Recall* (1990), *Terminator 2: Judgement Day* (1991) and *Basic Instinct* (1992).'[26] One reason why TriStar and Columbia struggled in the mid-1990s was the loss of their relationships with Carolco and Castle Rock (TriStar and Columbia were part of the same corporate empire, as will be seen below).[27]

In 1997, the year in which *Godzilla* was shot, production at Sony Pictures broke down into three main categories. The largest involved ongoing deals with separate production companies and in-house subsidiaries, which accounted for approximately 40 per cent. The remainder was divided between projects co-financed and those produced entirely in-house, the latter claiming a slightly larger share than the former.[28] The breakdown between such categories varies considerably from one studio to another, however, and is also volatile from one year to another, depending on changes in the broader global financial climate.

A high percentage of all films that make it into the mainstream in America, and much of the world, are distributed by one or more of the majors, a figure usually put at between 80 and 90 per cent. As distributors, they take a slice of box-office returns. This is usually 30 per cent of gross domestic rental, 40–45 per cent overseas (rental being the sum retained after deduction of the exhibitor's share). The distributor's share of the cake is taken at an early stage, enabling the majors to profit as distributors from loss-making films (the distributor will also take between 50 and 80 per cent of any net profits left after the deduction of production, marketing and other costs[29]). It comes as no surprise to learn that the share taken by the distributor in the split between distributor and exhibitor has increased since the break-up of the earlier system of vertical integration. The majors are able to use their continued control over access to desirable products to demand favourable terms.

Sony initially demanded 80 per cent of the box-office gross for *Godzilla* in the opening weeks – the period when it was (correctly) expected to do most of its business – prompting indignation from exhibitors. Larger cinema chains signed deals closer to the blockbuster norm in which the studio received 70 per cent of the gross for periods ranging from the opening two to four weeks.[30] Exhibitors, generally, have been squeezed. They are forced to accede to demands for payment in advance, or guaranteed minimum payments. To gain access to *Star Wars: Episode One – The Phantom Menace* (1999), cinemas had to guarantee runs of at least two or three months on the best screens (although in this case control was kept mainly in the hands of the producer, George Lucas).[31]

Deals such as these are all very well if the film turns out to be a hit, as was always likely to be the case with *The Phantom Menace*. They are bad news for exhibitors if an expected blockbuster turns out to be a dud. They are locked into showing films they might prefer to pull from the screen, in a manner reminiscent of how independent exhibitors were treated under the studio system.[32] As distributors the studios earn substantial revenues without incurring great risk. Their fees and expenses are usually the first items to be paid out from box-office takings. The studios also tend to get preferential treatment when they contribute to production costs. Studio investments are usually made on terms that ensure they will be first in line to be repaid.

The commitment of the majors varies from one film to another. Most is at stake in the entirely in-house productions. Here, the studios stand to make profits or losses as financiers and producers as well as taking their slice for distribution. Next in line are films that they finance wholly or mostly. Additional spending and support is usually distributed according to this hierarchy. Enormous resources were lavished on the opening and promotion of *Godzilla* because it was an expensive in-house production for Sony Pictures and therefore worth extensive support, to protect the initial investment and in the hope of producing windfall profits. The budget for the US launch alone has been put at $50 to $60 million, with a similar sum spent on overseas marketing and promotion.[33]

*Godzilla* performed disappointingly. It took $55.5 million over the four-day Memorial Day weekend of 1998: a handsome sum but below the very high expectations encouraged by the studio. The real problem was the film's lack of 'legs', its inability to sustain a high level of attendance. Marketing and promotion can do much to boost a film on opening, but word-of-mouth, over which the studios have little if any control, tends to take over in the following weeks. Criticism of the 'excessive' hype that preceded the opening of *Godzilla* may be misplaced: without it, the film might have fared badly without even the benefit of a healthy opening weekend. Advance 'awareness' of the film, a quality eagerly measured by studio surveys, registered a very high level of 95 per cent.[34] Box-office figures for blockbusters often decline considerably after the first week, but for *Godzilla* the fall was precipitous. The gross for the second weekend was in the region of $18 million, which declined to $9.7 million and $6.2 million in the subsequent two weekends.[35] The film was not withdrawn or its release drastically scaled back, however. The number of screens on which it opened remained steady throughout these weeks. Too much was riding on its fate – both economically and in terms of the pride of the studio and the fate of senior executives – for it be treated to such indignities.

The status of *Godzilla* as an in-house production also accounts for its prime release date. The Memorial Day weekend is a key slot, a high-profile holiday occasion in which cinemas are often crowded, and considered to mark the start of the important summer season. Another lesson taught by *Jaws* was the potential benefit of an early summer release that could enable a successful blockbuster to dominate the entire peak season. The majors use their power to reserve the best dates for the pictures in which they have the biggest stakes. This is another aspect of their continued control of the industry. In the studio era, when the majors had a big stake in exhibition, their output was spread more evenly across the year. The production end of the business was committed to supplying exhibitors with a full year's slate of product.[36] Cutbacks in production, and the emphasis on smaller numbers of more expensive potential blockbusters, led to a much more selective focus on the peak summer, Christmas and Easter holiday seasons, which now contribute a disproportionately high share of box-office receipts for the entire year. The majors can ensure the presence of their key films in the best and most profitable cinemas at the best and most profitable times of the year. No-one else is able seriously to compete for these slots. Exhibitors remain dependent on the majors for the films that earn their profits – in terms not just of box-office returns but of the lucrative margins on sales of food and drink that constitute a large part of their income – and are able to put up only limited resistance to their demands.

## Corporate empires

The big studios remain in charge of Hollywood today. But what exactly are the big studios of the corporate New Hollywood era? *Godzilla* was produced by Sony Pictures Entertainment. Not a name familiar from the classical studio era. Copyright in the film is held by TriStar Pictures, one of the filmmaking divisions of Sony Pictures. The other is a much more familiar name: Columbia Pictures. Columbia has a pedigree dating back to the early days of the studio system. It was founded in 1924 and became one of the 'little three' that existed in the shadow of the five majors. Sony Pictures Entertainment is part of the giant Sony Corporation, a household name in the realm of electrical goods such as hi-fi equipment, televisions, video machines and PlayStation games. These corporate relationships can become confusing and sometimes hard to untangle, not the least because the regularity with which they seem to change.

This is not an aspect of New Hollywood that usually appears to be among the most sexy, interesting or exciting. It is the stuff of the business pages rather than art or entertainment. An understanding of this dimension of Hollywood is crucial, however. It plays an enormous part in shaping the kinds of films that reach the screen. A defining characteristic of contemporary Hollywood is the fact that the major studios are located within the landscape of large media corporations.

The major studios today – in approximate pecking order – are Warner Bros., Disney, Twentieth Century Fox, Paramount, Universal, Sony Pictures/Columbia and the newcomer, DreamWorks. The largest players are mostly familiar names from the past, although with one or two changes. Columbia and Universal have been 'promoted' from the lower division. Disney has gone from small animation specialist to major player. So, where are the rest of the majors located? Warner Bros. is part of AOL Time Warner. Twentieth Century Fox is owned by Rupert Murdoch's News Corporation. Paramount is part of Viacom. Universal is owned by Seagram/Vivendi. Disney is allied with Capital Cities/ABC. These relationships were established in a series of take-overs, mergers and expansions that began in the 1960s and continue today.

Initially, some of the studios were taken over by extremely large and unwieldy corporations with no particular focus on the entertainment business. In 1967 Paramount became part of Gulf + Western, a conglomerate with wide-ranging interests including financial services, publishing, sugar, zinc, fertilizer and real estate. United Artists was taken over by Transamerica, an insurance and finance corporation. In 1969 Warner Bros. – at the time, Warner-Seven Arts – became part of Kinney National Services, the primary activities of which were car rental, car parks, construction and funeral homes. The initial phase of take-overs came at a time when the Hollywood studios were in need of finance and stability. Resources such as the back catalogues of their films were under-valued, which made them tempting targets for corporate predators. Ownership of a Hollywood studio was also seen as a way of adding a touch of glamour to grey corporations and perhaps increasing their appeal to investors.[37]

Subsequent rounds of manoeuvring and reorganization left the studios within large but less sprawling corporations, more coherently organized around a number of media and related industries. Gulf + Western 'downsized', selling off more then 50 companies in the 1980s and re-creating itself as Paramount Communications, focused on the entertainment industry, which was bought by Viacom, Inc. in 1994 (Viacom expanded its media tentacles in 1999, achieving what was at the time biggest media merger in history when it bought the television network CBS). Kinney Services became Warner Communications, which scaled itself down to more manageable proportions in the early 1980s. This environment has proved a fertile one in which to develop a form of domination arguably greater than that achieved by the 'big five' at the height of the studio era.

Two major benefits come from what might be termed the 'corporatization' of Hollywood. First, it helps to increase stability and minimize risks, especially those associated with the production of expensive blockbusters. A $100 million movie represents a huge investment to an ordinary or even a fairly large business. It does not take many failures or disappointments for such a company to be threatened with destabilization or closure. This is less likely to be the case if the company is part of a much larger organization. A giant corporation with a range of interests has enough resources and flexibility to even out some of the unpredictable ups and downs of the film industry. The studios can also benefit from access to substantial capital or credit reserves, including the possibility of internal investment. Capital from one part of a corporation might be invested elsewhere at lower cost than money obtained from outside, a particular advantage at times of high interest rates such as the period from the mid-1970s to the mid-1980s.[38]

A large corporation cannot be relied on for charity, of course. This brings us to the second benefit to be gained from the location of Hollywood studios within larger media conglomerates. It can be an ideal way to maximize profits for all concerned. This takes us to the heart of the way Hollywood operates commercially today. The big studios have become part of corporations with interests in a range of media through which film products can be exploited. The cinema screen is just the start of the process. Apparently 'secondary' sources of income are more important, in the longer term, than initial box-office returns. The development of ancillary markets has been a key aspect of recent Hollywood strategy; a way of increasing revenues that became increasingly important from the 1980s to the early 2000s, a period in which growth in box-office income was outstripped by escalating production and marketing costs and an increasing share of gross profits was claimed by key creative talent.[39] A whole new world of revenue was opened up, as were many questions about the implications this might have for the kinds of films produced and/or given the biggest investments in areas such as promotion and marketing. The best way to understand this is not in the abstract but by examining some concrete examples. What, then, of Sony Pictures and *Godzilla*?

*Godzilla* is a source of potential profits for Sony from a number of in-house sources beyond the theatrical box office at home and abroad, the ease of securing a deal for the rights to the Godzilla franchise having been increased in the first place by an existing relationship between its owner, Toho Pictures, and the Japanese-based multinational.[40] Video has become an increasingly important aspect of the economic equation, as we will see in chapter 7. Sony Pictures owns its own label, Columbia TriStar Home Video, and so is able to exploit this avenue directly for itself. The *Godzilla* video is distributed by Sony Music Operations, part of the Sony Corporation's music division, Sony Music Entertainment. It earned $8.04 million in rentals in its first week in the United States, the biggest video opening at the time since *Titanic*. The soundtrack album featuring bands such as the Foo Fighters, Jamiroquai and Rage Against the Machine achieved sales of more than one million: it was released on Epic Records, a label owned by Sony Music Entertainment. Sony Pictures also has extensive interests in television production through the Columbia TriStar Television Group. To a roster including hit shows such as *Wheel of Fortune* and *Jeopardy* was added the animated *Godzilla: The Series*. A Sony PlayStation game based on *Godzilla* is yet to emerge, but there is an on-line computer game produced by Columbia TriStar Interactive and two games have been developed for the GameBoy platform.

A film such as *Godzilla* is more than just a single, free-standing product. It is a *franchise*, a property that can be exploited in numerous other ways. A franchise is usually owned by a particular studio or its corporate parent, a product brand to which it has obtained copyright-controlled access (unlike a repeated framework such as a genre or a short-term cycle, on which all producers can freely draw), a quality highly desirable in the corporate media environment. The cumulative profits realized from a successful franchise can be enormous. A large measure of stability is provided by the knowledge that an expensive production that might not do as well as expected in the cinema can move into profit elsewhere, laterally or further down the line. Expensive films that appear disappointing or even disastrous on initial release can produce decent profits in the end, if more modest than might have been anticipated. *Godzilla* is one prominent example. Another is *Waterworld* (1995), which was deemed a failure and another indicator of Hollywood excess after earning less than half of its estimated $175 million cost at the domestic box-office. *Waterworld* is thought to have entered into profit when the overseas and ancillary markets are included. As a Universal production, it was also able to supply a popular attraction at the Universal Studios theme park in Los Angeles.

In-house sources of exploitation are especially attractive, but the process does not stop at the corporate boundary. License fees can be earned for numerous tie-ins produced elsewhere. This was the case with a range of *Godzilla* toys and books. The prospect of a blockbuster hit also attracts a swarm of attention from other companies keen to get in on the act. Taco Bell, for example, spent $60 million on a *Godzilla* tie-in promotion campaign linked to its 'Gordita' line of tacos. This is free advertising for the film. Further earnings were secured from product placement deals in which items such as Kodak cameras and Swatch watches featured prominently on screen.[41]

It is not hard to see why the Hollywood studios are attractive prospects for corporations with interests in other aspects of the media and related industries. The films they produce, distribute and/or finance are engines that can drive streams of profitable sources of revenue. The communications industry as a whole was the fastest-growing sector in the US economy from 1994 to 1999 and was expected to remain so for the next five years; spending on filmed entertainment was expected to grow at a rate of 5.8% from 1999 to 2004.[42] The studios are sources not so much of free-standing films as of 'software' that can be exploited in numerous forms. Sony's $3.4 billion purchase of Columbia Pictures Entertainment (as it was then called) in 1989 was a classic illustration of this process. Sony is best known as a global manufacturer of electronics hardware. It made good business sense to buy into providers of software, properties that would keep the hardware supplied with attractive materials (especially after the lesson learnt through the failure of Sony's Betamax video system, launched in 1975). The take-over of Columbia included ownership of a library of more than 2,700 films and 23,000 television episodes.[43] Such catalogues are by far the most important assets of most film companies, suggests Martin Dale, worth an industry total in the mid-1990s of some $6–8 billion.[44]

Each side of the business is of potential benefit to the other. Sales of hardware depend on a demand for the software programming it plays. Sales of software depend on hardware on which to play it. A similar process had worked for Sony in the music field, where its interests include the manufacture of hi-fi equipment and ownership of four record labels. Sony was followed into Hollywood by another Japanese electronics giant, Matsushita Electrical Industrial Company, which bought the parent of Universal pictures, the Music Corporation of American (MCA), for $6.9 billion in 1990 (80% of MCA was subsequently sold to Seagram in 1995, a drinks and chemicals concern that merged with the French conglomerate Vivendi in 2000). A favoured industry term for these relationships is 'synergy', the idea that complementary activities can be brought together to create something more than just the sum of their parts: one-plus-one in the right combination includes a magical extra ingredient that makes the total add up to three.

Hollywood remains an integrated business, on more than one axis. Old-style vertical integration exists in the combination of production/ finance and distribution. Something closer to the original format has also been reinstated, with a number of studios moving back into exhibition during the 1980s, largely as a result of the Reagan admin- istration's lax attitude towards industrial regulation. The industry has only rarely faced opposition from the Federal Trade Commission or the Federal Communications Commission to cross-media operations that appear to be in breach of laws against anti-competitive practices. The 350-screen Loew's Corporation circuit came into the hands of Columbia in the mid-1980s, via its purchase of TriStar. A subsequent merger left Sony with a 39.5 per cent stake in what became Loew's Cineplex Entertainment, with 2,870 screens in 450 city locations in the USA, Canada and Europe. MCA/Universal, Paramount and Warner Bros. all followed Columbia's example.[45]

The term 'horizontal integration' is often used to characterize the broader range of industrial strategies used in the corporate era, although this process displays some basic features of vertical organization. Either way, the aim is to maximize control. This might be defensive, in the interests of stability, or in more offensive pursuit of greater profits. Success is far from guaranteed. Matsushita, in particular, had an unhappy experience with MCA before selling to Seagram. But a cross-media platform can be an effective way of hedging against risk, either for particular products or entire corporations. *Godzilla* refused to meet high expectations at the domestic box office. This might have had a knock-on effect in some other arenas but the franchise still generated very substantial revenues, with total profits over the lifetime of the film estimated at $350–400 million by Sony forecasts.[46]

Sales of *Godzilla* merchandise were reported initially to have been disappointing. Toy retailers complained that sales were hampered by excessive secrecy which meant their products could not be unveiled until the film had opened. According to Sony, however, retail sales of consumer products other than videos and music accounted for more than $400 million.[47] Merchandising was designed to play not just on the film but also on the animated series and the original *Godzilla* films, another way of widening the net beyond the new production. Sony's link with *Godzilla* and its merchandising has continued, demonstrating the potential longevity of such brands even when they encounter initial difficulties. In 1999 the company acquired rights to seven classic Japanese features not previous seen in the United States. It also distributed Toho's *Godzilla 2000: Millennium*. Plans for the development of its own sequel were said to have been scaled down rather than abandoned, to aim at a more specific niche audience.[48]

The relatively disappointing performance of *Godzilla* at the box office is reflected in Sony's annual report for 1999, which refers to 'less successful theatrical releases' compared with the previous year (which had been a particularly good one for Sony) and an anticipated knock-on effect 'expected to reduce sales from the home video and pay television markets resulting in lower total sales for the Motion Picture group in the fiscal year ending March 31, 2000.'[49] In the 2000 report, the film is noticeably absent from examples cited of films from the previous year that 'performed well in different markets and formats'.[50] More generally, the film or media divisions of the large corporations are by no means immune from the broader fluctuations of fortune characteristic of corporate capitalism. Sony invested billions of dollars in Columbia after the 1989 take-over. Sony Pictures performed satisfactorily until 1993 but lost $3.2 billion on its film business in 1994 and announced that it would never recover its investment.[51] As Tino Balio puts it: 'Sony's two Hollywood studios soon returned to profitability, but not to top-tier status. The reason: Sony had neither forged connections with cable television nor had it acquired theme parks or consumer product chain stores to extend the franchises developed by its studios.'[52]

Two lessons emerge from the problems faced by Sony, at these different levels. One is that the success of individual films still matters. The other is the desirability of even wider-ranging corporate ties and ancillary operations. *Godzilla* was far short of the disaster it was some-times painted to be. But neither was it a triumph on the scale many had anticipated. For whatever reasons, it was generally not well received on release. As a result, it failed to generate the momentum to perform to maximum potential in subsequent arenas.

Cinema exhibition accounts for a relatively small proportion of the revenues earned by Hollywood features, a total of about 26 per cent in the late 1990s and early 2000s, according to *Screen Digest*.[53] This does not mean cinema exhibition is unimportant, however. Release in the cinema remains the biggest stage on which to display Hollywood's wares. It is the most prestigious part of the life-cycle of Hollywood entertain-ment. Success in the cinema is what usually translates into the greatest levels of success further down the chain. It creates the impetus that keeps the entire machine running. This is why so much is often invested in initial advertising and promotional campaigns that can act as loss-leaders. Their costs can be a sound investment in the longer term value of the product, measured against more than just the initial box-office returns. Big hits at the box office are usually the titles that fill walls in video rental and retail outlets and earn the biggest fees for release to cable, satellite and terrestrial television; a factor that helps, in turn, to entrench the emphasis on blockbuster production. Films are often sold to television in packages of 10 to 20 at a time, a system reminiscent of block booking in the cinema. The value of a package is established largely by the value of the lead films. Successful blockbusters act as 'locomotives' to drive the rest of the slate.[54] They are the films most likely to be converted into video or computer games and to sell vast quantities of other merchandise.

*Godzilla* stumbled somewhat at the start, reducing the total that could ultimately be earned off its back. Within just a couple of weeks Sony was forced to lower its expectations as far as a sale to television was concerned. It had hoped for $35 million, reports Peter Bart, 'but at one meeting after another, the Sony representatives were rebuffed. Word of mouth was weak, they were told, and box office was dropping off quickly.'[55] The company settled for 'a less-than-thrilling' offer of $25 million from NBC for five showings over five years. Columbia's major hit of the previous year, *Men in Black* (1997), was sold to the same network for more than twice as much.[56] *Godzilla* earned considerable sums from its merchandising, but not as much as top-performing predecessors *Star Wars* and *Batman*.

George Lucas retained all merchandising rights to the *Star Wars* films as part of his original deal with Twentieth Century Fox and, as is part of New Hollywood legend, profited on billions of dollars of revenue, far more even than the vast sums earned by the ongoing series at the box office. *Batman* took $250 million at the US box office and is believed to have made four times as much in spin-off merchandise. *Batman* was produced by Warner Bros., another of the Hollywood studios to have found a large corporate home. If *Batman* was more successful than *Godzilla* in both box office and merchandising (especially relative to its costs), it was also the product of a corporate environment even more conducive than Sony to exploitation of movie-based products through multiple in-house profit centres.

The *Batman* franchise offers an illuminating route through the various avenues of some of these conglomerate formations and a particular strong example of the construction of an in-house blockbuster property. The 1989 film was very much a product of the particular corporate environment in which it was shaped to maximize profits and efficiency.[57] *Batman* was a pre-sold property, a character familiar to audiences from comic books, television series and earlier film treatments. The first film in the series was made by Warner Bros. in 1989 under the aegis of Warner Communications. The rights to the character already belonged to Warner as part of its acquisition of DC Comics in 1971. A new comic book version of *Batman* was released by DC Comics, Eileen Meehan suggests, as a way to test the market for the dark version of the character envisaged for the film.[58] The success of the comic led to additional in-house publications. These were profitable in themselves and helped to build an initial core audience for the forthcoming film. The film itself was accompanied by two records produced on the Warner label, earning additional income and providing promotion for the film. The title was released on video by Warner Home Video in November 1989, just six months after its theatrical release, bringing in revenues of $179 million in the domestic market.

New avenues of in-house exploitation for *Batman* were created in January 1990 by a merger between Warner and Time, Inc., creating the giant Time Warner conglomerate. Time Warner became the second largest provider of cable television services in the United States, including the premium channels HBO and Cinemax on which *Batman* appeared.[59] Licences for the merchandise based on the film and its sequels were handled by another in-house division, the Licensing Corporation of America, created to manage and protect the copyright on a stable of Warner Bros. characters ranging from Batman and Superman to Bugs Bunny. Trademark products can be bought directly from Warner retail stores across the globe. Coverage of the *Batman* films appeared in prestigious Time Warner publications such as *Time* and *Life*. Time Warner has certainly had strength in areas seen by Balio as lacking in the case of Sony, notably in cable television and retail outlets. Each new merger brings with it new potential arenas in which to exploit new and existing products. In 1995, Time Warner expanded its empire by taking over Turner Broadcasting, the assets of which included CNN, other cable channels and the MGM film library.

## Dominating into the digital age

January 2000: the first month of what was celebrated as a new millennium. A propitious moment, perhaps, for a deal that stood out as a landmark in the history of Hollywood's recent corporate history. The media conglomerate Time Warner was at it again. This time it announced a merger with America Online (AOL), the world's leading internet service provider. The deal, which came into operation in January 2001 after being approved by the Federal Communications Commission,[60] was one of the largest in history, creating a company worth $327 billion at the time it was announced, the fourth biggest in the world. It also marked the most significant union at the time between one generation of media industries and the next; between the relatively 'old' media of film and television and the 'new' media of the digital age. The attitude of the Hollywood studios to the internet is typical of their response to many new technologies offering potential new channels for the delivery of films.

Like cable television and video when they first appeared on the scene, the internet is sometimes seen as a threat to Hollywood's ability to control the exploitation of its properties. The unlicensed downloading of digital copies of films from the internet is seen as a particularly damaging form of piracy, in terms of both difficulty of policing and potential quality of pirate copies. The studios are also wary of the power of unofficial advance reviews on the internet to contribute negatively in some cases to the ephemeral 'buzz' surrounding film releases – another dimension to which unusual importance is attributed in the case of large-scale blockbuster openings. But the studios, and their corporate parents, have not been slow to move onto the internet themselves. The Time Warner-AOL deal provided the most dramatic evidence of a growing tendency.

The internet is of value to the studios as another way to promote their existing film products. It also holds the potential to create new products designed specifically to be distributed online. The internet is one of the fastest-growing forms of communication and is especially popular among some of the younger, higher media-consuming and better educated groups that constitute key audience constituencies for Hollywood films. Most new films have their own websites, a new dimension in global advertising and promotion. The industry's recognition of its importance is demonstrated by the fact that the statistics gathered by the MPAA in its annual *US Economic Review* now include a whole section on the internet. The benefits to Time Warner from its merger with AOL are not hard to imagine. Time Warner products, including its films and their spin-off products, can gain access to the huge AOL network of subscribers. They might be advertised, or featured, on AOL's home page or in its entertainment listings. Reciprocal benefits are also likely for AOL, access to Warner products helping to draw customers into AOL's network and thus increasing the rates it can charge for advertising on its pages.

A number of studios, including Warner Bros. and DreamWorks, have announced plans to produce short films to play directly over the net. These could be the forerunners of a major new distribution channel. The video retail giant Blockbuster, part of the Viacom group that owns Paramount Pictures, has announced deals with companies including AOL to develop video-on-demand-type services over the internet.[61] The media corporations have also established links with major telephone companies in order to buy into another key aspect of future home delivery systems on the so-called 'information superhighway'. Viacom has worked with Nynex; Time Warner with US West.[62]

Media convergence is the current name of the game, with the lines between one form and another becoming increasingly blurred. Cable television, wide-band telephone lines and computer networks have particular potential to merge, which is why cable is seen as so important an ingredient in the corporate media profile as a potential source of access to the homes of consumers. Another convergence occurs between DVD, the internet and other computer-based media. This is another arena in which Time Warner has been prominent. The company helped to develop the DVD format, in a joint venture with Toshiba. For Warner, DVD represents a new format in which to exploit its library of some 5,700 feature films. Warner Home Video joined forces with Sony in a promotional campaign in 2000 to expand DVD sales in Europe, a typical example of the way such corporate rivals work together to mutual benefit overseas. Sony's PlayStation 2 includes a DVD drive, as does Microsoft's X-Box console.

Digital technologies are also penetrating into the more conventional business of watching films in the cinema. *Toy Story 2* (1999) was the first film to be both produced and exhibited digitally. It was made, like its predecessor, using computer-generated animation. Potentially more revolutionary is the prospect of digital distribution and exhibition. *Toy Story 2* is one of a small group of Hollywood films to have been screened digitally in selected cinemas. Digital projection is achieved without the need for expensive celluloid prints; without film itself, in other words. Films can be screened directly from computer disk. Digital projection offers a number of benefits, not least being an end to the scratched old prints often shown in less prestigious theatres. It could also reduce distribution costs, especially in the case of wide blockbuster releases. A study by *Screen Digest* in September 2000 predicted a complete transition to digital screens within 20 years, bringing savings of more than 90 per cent on print production and distribution.[63]

Technological changes such as this are sometimes heralded for their potential to open up industries like Hollywood to change, including new competition. This was the case with the development of outlets such as video and cable.[64] They were seen initially by Hollywood as a threat to box-office returns, but welcomed by others as potentially liberalizing the industry by creating new and lower-cost means of getting films in front of viewers. Hollywood soon came to embrace such potential rivals, however, including them within its corporate orbit. This is already happening in the case of the internet. There is little to suggest that a wider use of digital distribution to cinemas will be any different.

Digital distribution and/or exhibition is unlikely to reduce the grip of the major studios on the industry. They are well placed to control such innovations. Some savings will be available, but a change of technology will not lead to the evaporation of the global networks through which the studios ensure their domination. Physical distribution of films might become much less expensive but it is not one of the largest costs, even for the biggest and most widely opened blockbusters. Barriers to entry are likely to be maintained by other factors including the far greater cost of marketing and promoting blockbuster films. The exhibition end of the business may be forced to carry most of the costs of conversion while the distributors stand to be the chief beneficiaries.

The entanglement of Hollywood studios in the business of larger corporate entities involved in the development and exploitation of new technologies is not new. Strategic links with large corporations have influenced the studios in the past, including as epochal a move as the coming of sound during the 1920. The initiative came not from the studios themselves or from audience demand, but from the corporate giants AT&T/Western Electric and RCA/General Electric, which were seeking to exploit technologies developed in the spheres of telephone and radio.[65] Links forged in this process led to a number of the major studios buying into the music and radio businesses, establishing the beginnings of some of the synergies on which a new generation of corporate domination built decades later.

What is distinctive about the New Hollywood version is the increased centrality and importance of this aspect of the business. Hollywood has become more thoroughly integrated within a broader media landscape ruled over by a small number of large media corporations. None of this guarantees success at all levels. Time Warner suffered from a heavy debt burden, before the merger with AOL, and its performance was considered disappointing. Conglomerates such as these are powerful and influential, but far from omnipotent, as we have seen. They have reshaped the landscape in which Hollywood is located, however, and largely to the benefit of the big studios. The contours of this landscape have helped in turn to shape the kinds of films that get made, especially those that receive the 'full treatment' in terms of heavy promotion and prime windows of distribution/exhibition. Some suggest that the weight of external demands, such as marketing and promotion or providing products that can be profitable in other media, has come to threaten the very existence of Hollywood film as a distinct and coherent entity, an argument to which we will return in chapter 6.

The films of the Hollywood Renaissance were the product of a specific set of historical and industrial circumstances. These were unlikely to last far beyond the mid-to-late 1970s. Change was happening at the socio-cultural level. American politics and social attitudes underwent a broad turn to the right towards the end of the decade. This was reflected to some extent in the implicit politics of the corporate blockbuster. Formal experimentation and potentially radical content are generally avoided, in this arena, in the interests of attracting large audiences rather than through specifically ideological motivations. If Hollywood's blockbuster productions tend to be politically conservative, as numerous commentators have argued, this is primarily because they are designed to resonate, in various ways, with dominant and familiar social attitudes. The aim is not to alienate potentially significant audience groups. This does not make the films any the less political in their implications. But it makes them less *explicitly* or recognizably political: a key distinction as far as Hollywood is concerned. Films dealing more or less directly with contentious contemporary issues tended to be overshadowed by works operating in the modes of fantasy or wish-fulfilment.

The films of the Renaissance were targeted at specific audience groups likely to be attracted by some gesture towards an element of radical critique. They risked offending others, but this was seen as a gamble worth taking. The aspiring 'event-movie' scale blockbuster cannot usually afford to take such risks, which is why it tends (with some exceptions) to gravitate towards the middle of the ratings scale: neither too juvenile-seeming to alienate audiences aged from teens to 20s and 30s upwards nor too 'adult' to lose any possibility of reaching 'family' audiences. It seeks a broad audience profile, even if the record-breaking success of films such as *Star Wars* and *Titanic* can be boosted significantly by the phenomenon of multiple 'repeat business', in which relatively small numbers of enthusiasts exert a disproportionate influence on box-office returns. The nature of the core audience, around which larger constituencies are built, was also changing in the late 1970s, Thomas Schatz suggests. The demographic profile moved towards a new generation less influenced by the radical aspects of the 1960s, 'shifting from the politically hip, cineliterate viewers of a few years earlier to even younger viewers with more conservative tastes and sensibilities.'[66]

Changes in the industrial landscape further limited what space had been available for less conventional Hollywood production. Renewed stability and the growing success and entrenchment of the blockbuster strategy removed any need to give much leeway to those operating further from the commercial mainstream. These tendencies were exacerbated by the fact that some of the filmmakers associated with the Renaissance were heavily implicated in the development of the new generation of blockbusters. The most striking contrast is found in two science fiction films directed by George Lucas: the bleak, dystopian *THX 1138* (1971) and the now-archetypal comic-book blockbuster

*Star Wars*. The world of corporate cross-media control strongly favoured the latter. Some films associated with the Renaissance might have been capable of generating profitable spin-offs, especially in the case of recorded music. But even the biggest box-office hits of the Renaissance were not suited to the intensive multimedia and merchandising exploitation favoured by the corporate giants that took shape in the 1980s and 1990s.

This is not to say that what I have described in this chapter as the 'corporate blockbuster' is the only kind of film produced in Hollywood today. New Hollywood cannot be reduced to the characteristics of the corporate blockbuster any more than it was previously defined exclusively by the products of the Hollywood Renaissance. The two 'versions' of New Hollywood outlined in the opening chapters of this book are rather polarized extremes, reflecting two dominant senses in which the term 'New Hollywood' has been used. The industry remains large enough, and sufficiently idiosyncratic in its operations, for other kinds of filmmaking to exist between these two poles, including more modestly 'traditional' and more challenging and innovative types of production.

The industry continues, periodically, to question the wisdom of relying as much as its does on expensive blockbuster production. Concern is sometimes expressed in the trade press about a shortage of smaller and medium-budget films that can help to balance the unpredictable box-office performance of lumbering monsters such as *Godzilla*. Warner's *Fact Book* for 1999, for example, reported a reduction of its release slate to 20–25 films a year from its usual 25–30, along with an increase in the number of co-financed productions. The company also 'plans to have a more diversified mix of genres, talent and budgets.'[67] Several big pictures were reportedly put on hold in the wake of *Godzilla*'s relatively disappointing performance.[68] The mega-budget blockbuster is hardly likely to disappear or become much less central a feature of the Hollywood landscape, however, given the vast profits available from the most successful examples and their strategic location at the centre of a wider economic regime. Warner's note of caution was soon accompanied by the announcement of plans for not just one but two sequels to *The Matrix*, its biggest hit of 1999: a new blockbuster franchise in the making.

A similar strategy of planning sequels and second sequels in advance has been adopted for other brands, including *X-Men* (2000), for which Twentieth Century Fox had some key performers locked into a three-picture deal, *The Mummy* (1999, Universal) and New Line's *Lord of the Rings* series, future instalments of which were being trailed for three successive Christmas seasons from 2001.[69] Other major franchises-in-the-making in 2001 included the translation onto film of the enormously successful Harry Potter novels (Warner acquired rights to the first, *Harry Potter and the Philosopher's Stone*, for a reported $1.5 million, with a commitment to making a sequel and options on the first four instalments of a seven-volume series; *Harry Potter and the Sorcerer's Stone,* as the first film was titled in the USA, took a record equalling $90.2 million in its three-day opening weekend in November 2001) and, in competition, a four-film, book and cross-media deal in which the author Clive Barker stood to receive $8 million for creating a teenage girl equivalent as a new in-house property for Disney.[70] Plans such as these reflect a tension in Hollywood production between large-scale investment in franchise properties and the desire to reduce costs through the economies of scale involved in planning or shooting sequels more than one at a time. Pre-contracted sequels have the advantage of avoiding some of the excessive costs often incurred in sequel production, which tends to involve higher budgets than those for the originals (partly as a result of generous gross-profit deals required to keep major stars attached). A continuing commitment to single mega-budget productions was marked by Disney's decision to green-light *Pearl Harbor* (2001) on a budget of $145 million, the highest ever to be agreed in advance.

Far from all of the high hopes invested in franchise movies are realized. Even the more disappointing can usually cover their costs one way or another, however, and it only takes the occasional full-scale event-movie triumph to turn around the fortunes of a studio when it is at a low ebb, as was the case with Sony/Columbia and the success of *Men in Black* in 1997. After another two years of mediocre performance in 1999 and 2000, Sony Pictures turned to a slate heavy with sequels, including the inevitable *Men in Black 2* and follow-ups to *Stuart Little* (1999) and *Charlie's Angels*.[71]

One factor remains inescapable for all kinds of Hollywood production, blockbuster or otherwise. Corporate Hollywood sets certain
limits on what can be achieved. Space for less obviously commercial or
more challenging material is determined to a significant extent by the
success of the mainstream blockbuster. A period of sustained success
creates more scope for such indulgences (although more subtle or
complex films can also, on occasion, generate blockbuster-worthy
revenues, such as the $293 million and $130 million taken at the US
box office by *The Sixth Sense*, 1999, and *American Beauty*, respectively).
Relatively more troubled times are likely to encourage the kind of
retrenchment marked by Sony's renewed focus on sequels from 2001.
Even the more innovative and apparently 'independent' end of the
spectrum has to a large extent become absorbed within the corporate
maw. Some of the studios have developed subsidiaries of their own to
make or distribute 'arty' or up-market features, examples including
Sony Pictures Classics and Fox Searchlight. Two of the largest and
most influential independent distributor/producers were taken over
by the majors in 1993, Miramax being acquired by Disney and New
Line by Turner Broadcasting, itself soon to become part of the Warner
empire.[72]

This is another aspect of the broad studio strategy of seeking to cover
all the bases, to seek to leave no potential opportunity for profit
unexploited. The independent sector has gained increased prominence
since the late 1980s, fuelled initially by a short-lived boom in production
generated by the rapid growth of the video market. Some 'art' or independent films have crossed over into mass-market success on very low
budgets, none more dramatically than *The Blair Witch Project* (1999,
distributed by the independent Artisan Entertainment), which took
$140 million in the domestic market on an initial budget of just $35,000,
the kind of performance on which the majors do not like to miss out.
'Independent' or 'art' film divisions enable the majors to cherry-pick,
to seek to benefit from the relatively few films of this type that break
through to larger success. They can be good for the image of the studios,
a matter of some significance given their potential vulnerability to federal
regulation. Access to a world further from the Hollywood mainstream
is also a valuable source of new, fresh and original material from which

studio executives might otherwise be insulated by the corporate cocoon. The 'independent' sector is home to some of the more distinctive and individual filmmaking talents; the principal carriers of the legacy of the Hollywood Renaissance. A figure like Steven Soderbergh, director of the seminal independent hit *sex, lies and videotape* (1989), is valued for his ability to produce 'classy' mainstream star-vehicles such as *Out of Sight* (1998) and *Erin Brockovich* (2000) and more innovative-but-reasonably-commercial and Oscar-nomination-winning works such as *Traffic* (2000). Which brings us to the subject of the next chapter: the role of, and space for, the director as 'author' in New Hollywood.

# From Auteurs to Brats

## Authorship in New Hollywood

> What matters to me is that I get to make the pictures – that
> I get to express myself personally somehow.
>
> Martin Scorsese[1]

> New Hollywood directors develop their own recognizable
> style because it increases their market value.
>
> Warren Buckland[2]

A film by Martin Scorsese. A Steven Spielberg production. A Tim
Burton film. A film directed by Spike Jonze. Robert Altman's... The
practice of labelling films according to the name of a single filmmaker,
usually the director, has become widespread in Hollywood. Statements
such as these often feature prominently in the opening titles and in
posters, trailers and other publicity materials. The line on Spike Jonze,
in the advertising for *Being John Malkovich* (1999), is unusual in making
a more modestly literal statement. Names of directors are used as more
all-encompassing hooks for studies of films ranging from daily journalism
to academic works. The first mention of a film is often followed, in
brackets, by the date in which it was made or released and the director's
name, as if the latter were an undisputed mark of authorship.

How appropriate is all this? To what extent can the products of
New Hollywood be defined by the name of the director? Are
Hollywood movies the expressions of individual filmmakers as authors?

Or are director's names just used as another way to sell a more standardized commercial product? The Hollywood Renaissance has been understood partly in terms of the 'artistic' expression of a new generation of filmmakers. The New Hollywood dominated by the corporate blockbuster appears less conducive to the freedom of the individual director. 'Name' directors remain important to both versions of New Hollywood explored so far in this book, however. Exactly how and why will be examined in this chapter. A number of qualifications will also be suggested, particularly in terms of the rival influence of industrial and social-cultural contexts.

## Auteurs

Questions about issues of authorship have been asked of the whole of Hollywood cinema, 'Old' and 'New'. The issue is of particular relevance to New Hollywood because it was at the start of this era that it became a major influence on the study of popular cinema. The notion that some films can be seen as the distinctive products of individual film-makers can be traced further back. Individual figures such as D.W. Griffith were celebrated early in the twentieth century for an artistic 'genius' seen to transcend the confines of an increasingly high-cost industry. Others have also been singled out, including the likes of Orson Welles and Alfred Hitchcock. It was not until the 1950s and 1960s, however, that the practice of assigning authorship credentials to Hollywood directors became widespread.

Hollywood had been seen primarily as an industry, the role of the director being only one of many and usually subordinated to the constraints of factory-style production. A new critical trend was started in the French journal *Cahiers du Cinema* in the 1950s. This was to become known as the *auteur* theory. It was taken up in Britain by the journal *Movie* and popularized in America by Andrew Sarris. This approach started out less as a *theory* of authorship than as a polemical intervention by the critic-to-become-director, Francois Truffaut, arguing against what he saw as a dominant tradition in French cinema that gave the central creative role to writers, especially in adaptations of novels.[3]

So, what makes a filmmaker an auteur? Two main dimensions are usually considered. Distinctive thematic concerns have to be identified across a director's body of work. Particular issues or attitudes are detected. In many of the films of Stanley Kubrick, for example, we find a central theme of the alienation of humanity within a range of overpowering institutional frameworks, those of a technologically advanced future in *2001: A Space Odyssey* (1968) or of the military in *Paths of Glory* (1957) and *Full Metal Jacket* (1987).[4] The recurrence of similar themes is the first requirement if a director is to be considered more than just a hired hand working on material that has its essence elsewhere. (1)

(2) A distinctive film style is also required. A true auteur uses the medium in a manner that is identifiable from one work to another as his or her personal style. This serves, as Sarris puts it, as the director's 'signature'.[5] Ideally, the style should reflect the thematic concerns. So, in the case of Kubrick, a cool and detached style, in which the camera remains distanced from the protagonists, often underpins a theme of waning humanity. Style is seen by Sarris as a particularly important ingredient as far as Hollywood cinema is concerned. Under the studio system especially, directors had limited (if any) freedom to choose their own projects or to shape them at the development or script-writing stage. As a result, 'the director is forced to express his personality through the visual treatment of material rather than through the literary content of the material.'[6]

One of the main grounds for questioning auteurist approaches to Hollywood is the industrial nature of Hollywood filmmaking, a subject to which we will return shortly. Filmmaking in Hollywood has always been a heavily industrial and business–oriented process. Many different people are involved in shaping and constructing any individual film. The director has a central role, especially in the organization of the actual process of shooting. But the collaborative nature of the business has always put limits on the freedom of the director to claim the status of especially privileged author. This is true of almost all other than the most low–budget or 'independent' feature production, with some notable exceptions, including Kubrick, who manage to carve out wider degrees of latitude. It is especially the case in the heavily commercialized environment of mainstream Hollywood.

The point of Sarris's version of auteur theory is not to ignore this. Limitations are seen as a key factor in identifying the virtues of the auteur: 'The *auteur* theory values the personality of a director precisely because of the barriers to its expression. It is as if a few brave spirits have managed to overcome the gravitational pull of the mass of movies. The fascination of Hollywood movies lies in their performance under pressure.'[7] This is a Romantic approach, a celebration of artistic vision struggling to emerge from under the weight of industrial constraints. The concept of the auteur is often used evaluatively. Some directors are given the status of fully-fledged auteurs. Others are not. Sarris's principal work, *The American Cinema: Directors and Directions 1929–1968* (1968), is essentially a hierarchy. At the top are those admitted to the celebrated 'pantheon' of directors, including Chaplin, Ford, Griffith, Hawks, Hitchcock and Welles. Those found at the lower end are in some cases treated dismissively.

## Brats

The auteurist approach popularized by Sarris became a significant influence on the development of film theory in the 1960s, a period in which the study of film began to grow as a distinct academic discipline. As a result, it also had an impact on new generations of filmmakers, including many of those associated with the Hollywood Renaissance. A distinguishing characteristic of some of these figures was that they studied film at university or film school. Previous generations of directors had mostly come from the theatre or learned the job during apprenticeships within the studio system. One new generation, emerging in the mid-1960s, had been brought up in television production in the 1950s. This included some figures involved in films of the Renaissance, such as Arthur Penn, director of *Bonnie and Clyde*, and Robert Altman. Subsequent generations included growing numbers of film school graduates. This marked a significant shift. Among those in the first wave were luminaries of the Hollywood Renaissance such as Martin Scorsese (New York University) and Francis Ford Coppola (University of California, Los Angeles).

Filmmakers gaining their education in the 1960s benefited from formal study and from the increased availability of films from the international art cinema, a kind of production in which the vision of the director-as-artist is a major factor. One off-shoot of the break-up of the old studio system in the 1950s was that many subsequent-run cinemas closed, deprived of films to show by cutbacks in studio production. Some survived by converting into 'art' theatres screening films that had few outlets previously in the United States. Against this background, the writings of Sarris were an important influence on a film student such as the young Scorsese. They suggested that popular Hollywood filmmakers such as Howard Hawks could be taken as seriously as Ingmar Bergman or other figures from the European art cinema, opening up the possibility of some kind of combination of Hollywood and more esoteric influences.[8]

Auteur-based approaches were internalized by many products of film schools. It is hardly surprising that they should seek to pursue forms of filmmaking that included a strong measure of personal expression in matters of both style and content. The success of many Renaissance films, in turn, seemed to validate the claims of auteur theory. Some filmmakers were given increased freedom to shape their own products and pursue their own interests. The 1970s was hailed as the decade in which Hollywood became a 'director's cinema'. It was seen, as the subtitle of one influential book put it, as a period in which 'the film generation took over Hollywood.' The director John Milius proclaimed: 'Now, power lies with the filmmakers.'[9]

Many of the products of the Hollywood Renaissance lend themselves to analysis in auteurist terms to a greater extent than most Hollywood films. The 1970s films of Robert Altman, for example, offer a strong case for an auteurist interpretation in terms of themes (genre deconstruction and satirical portraits of a range of institutions), style (use of zooms, multiple and overlapping dialogue, loose narrative construction) and the deployment of something close to a repertory company of performers and other collaborators. The Renaissance is remembered in terms of the names of directors such as Altman, Coppola and Scorsese as much as the titles of individual films. Studies of the movement are very often organized on auteurist lines: a chapter on each of the above, along with Brian DePalma, George Lucas, Steven Spielberg and perhaps a few others. A number of constraints on the activities of the would-be auteur filmmaker had been relaxed. It was not primarily the power of filmmakers themselves that made this happen, however. The scope for this kind of filmmaking was to a large extent created by the particular industrial circumstances of the time, as we have seen. Any notion of individual authorship in Hollywood has always to be qualified by the consideration of industrial factors. This applies both to the specific factors associated with any particular historical moment, such as the Renaissance period, and more generally to Hollywood production as a whole.

The freedoms of the Renaissance period were given to filmmakers by the big studios. They could also be taken away. The industry was in difficulties and latched onto a new generation of filmmakers who held the promise of being able to attract a new and younger audience. Freedom was a product of uncertainty and transition. It did not last. By the end of the 1970s power was largely back in the hands of pro- duction executives, except in the case of one or two mavericks such as Kubrick (whose freedom was conditioned partly on his reputation for delivering films on budget, if not always very promptly), 'auteurs' who bought heavily into the commercial mainstream, or those who were prepared to work on the economic margins.

According to one version of what happened, this was largely down to the excesses of certain directors. Francis Ford Coppola and Michael Cimino are usually singled out most prominently for blame. They are accused of getting carried away with the freedom they were given at the height of the Renaissance. Past successes, especially in the case of Coppola, led to them gaining or being given too much leeway. The result was films like *Apocalypse Now* (1979) and *Heaven's Gate* (1980), enormous epics that overran their budgets and shooting schedules as the price of the indulgence of their visionary 'auteurs'. *Apocalypse Now* was also hampered by unforeseeable difficulties and eventually redeemed itself to some extent, after an agonizing shooting process in which the budget increased from $12 million to nearly three times as much. It covered its costs at the US box office and received a number of Oscar nominations but did long-term damage to Coppola's industrial standing.[10] The budget for *Heaven's Gate* ballooned from an original

$7.8 million to $40 million, not to mention the cost of promotion, and it died at the box office. The film has since gained legendary status, contributing to the decision of Transamerica to sell United Artists, sending the studio into a sustained period of crisis and instability.

The truth of what happened in this period is rather more complex than is suggested by the story of 'directors out of control'. The excesses of films like *Apocalypse Now* and *Heaven's Gate* were the product of a combination of factors. These cut across some of the characteristics of each of the versions of New Hollywood outlined in the first two chapters. The films can be located within the Hollywood Renaissance in many respects, particularly their claims to the status of artistic epics created by auteur directors. At the same time, they were caught up to some extent in the logic of the blockbuster. The real turnaround in the fortunes of Hollywood in the mid-1970s was the result of this kind of combination. The new style of blockbuster manifested by *Jaws* and *Star Wars* grew out of – if also away from – the Hollywood Renaissance, directed by key figures of the 'movie brat' generation, Steven Spielberg and George Lucas. Coppola and Cimino were not given freedom on *Apocalypse Now* and *Heaven's Gate* simply because the studio – United Artists in both cases – had ceded control to individual directors. The studio was using the status of the directors as part of its strategy to design and promote prestigious blockbuster productions. This backfired, especially in the case of *Heaven's Gate*.

Directors such as Coppola and Cimino were partly to blame, as Jon Lewis suggests: 'They had so upped the stakes and the costs – they had so focused on making big movies – that they had, in effect, collectively risked their status on each and every prestige *auteurist* package.'[11] But the studios were far from innocent victims. Little of their real underlying power was ever given to the filmmakers. Allowing a measure of freedom to a new generation of directors was a useful strategic move on the part of the studios in a time of difficulty. It enabled them to tap into currents that proved successful in reaching audiences, both specific (as in the case of the youth audience) and more general (in the blockbuster event movie, which was also built to a large extent around a core of younger viewers). It also enabled studio executives to protect their own positions, a major factor of day-to-day life in the Hollywood hierarchy.[12] When things started to go wrong, 'the studio executives were in a position to blame not only individual directors but also the very system the studios had formerly exploited. By supporting an American *auteur* cinema in the 1970s, studio executives maintained a position in which they could avoid culpability no matter when or how the *auteur* period fizzled out.'[13]

## Director's clout

If some directors were given additional freedom in the specific industrial conditions of the Hollywood Renaissance, the same can be said of the broader New Hollywood period dating back to the 1950s. The package system of putting movie projects together gives directors more power and influence than was usually the case in the classical studio era. The name of the director is an important ingredient in the package. Not as important as the star in most cases, as we will see in chapter 5, but significant nonetheless. The balance varies. A new, first-time or undistinguished director might not gain a great deal of power in this context. More established or celebrated directors can gain enormously. The package system generally tends to increase the power of anyone with existing clout in the business. Sold on a one-off basis, the movie package is constantly on the lookout for sources of security. These are needed to ensure the magical 'green light' go-ahead at a studio or finance from elsewhere. It is also important when it comes to selling the movie at the box office. A big name director can have a great deal of power in this context. His (there are few if any women directors with such power) name alone might be enough to get off the ground a project that would otherwise be unlikely to find backing.

An obvious example today is Steven Spielberg, the most powerful creative player in the business. A series of enormously successful films since the 1970s has given Spielberg the power to do almost anything he wants in Hollywood. A harrowing black-and-white film about the Nazi holocaust? Unlikely to get major backing in Hollywood. A Steven Spielberg proposal for the same? No problem: *Schindler's List* (1993), from Universal, with a budget of $25 million. Spielberg's name can secure backing for a project less likely to become a conventional blockbuster. It can also help to propel such material to success at the box-office. *Schindler's List* took $96 million at the US box office and achieved a blockbuster-worthy total world-wide gross of $317 million. The same could be said of *Saving Private Ryan* (1998), another film containing some genuinely disturbing material, particularly in the graphic and oppressive initial D-Day beach landing sequence: it secured a well above contemporary average budget of $70 million, took $216 million in the United States and a total of $440 million world-wide.

Spielberg is in many ways an exception. The extent of his clout is unusual. It illustrates a more general and fundamental principle, however: the importance of commercial success. Directors can be given considerable power and freedom in the New Hollywood framework. But this is always conditioned or qualified by their ability to deliver at the box office. Freedom to make large and expensive films is especially closely related to a director's track record. The same goes often for more modest productions, even if the success threshold is lowered. Woody Allen, for example, has gained a strong measure of freedom to pursue his own projects over a period of several decades because they have a consistent record of producing returns proportionate to their budgets. Allen's films constitute a distinct and identifiable body of work. They tend to make steady rather than huge profits. The figures involved are small compared with the excesses of blockbuster production and promotion, but such returns have their place in the overall scheme of studio strategies.

The studios or independent producers with which Allen has worked (most recently, DreamWorks) have been happy to continue funding productions budgeted at modest levels, without interfering greatly in his work. If he were to propose a significantly more expensive film, a very different response might result. Allen's name and reputation alone would be unlikely to carry sufficient weight to lever him into agreement for a film of blockbuster proportions. Other guarantees would be required: a big star, probably, or a highly marketable pre-sold property. Even here, such a project might be unlikely to get off the ground. A filmmaker's clout is based partly around the associations he or she brings to a production. Associations such as these are considered important in the process of gaining audience awareness and demand. Spielberg is associated with dynamic and emotionally loaded adventure-melodramas. Films like *Schindler's List* and *Saving Private Ryan* offer many of these qualities in addition to their less easily digestible components. They depart rather less than might at first be thought from the mainstream of Spielberg's output. Mixed associations can be interesting to some viewers and critics, but are usually regarded warily by the studios. Spielberg has the industrial weight to shake off any such doubts, a power shared by few others. Films that do not fit clearly into particular categories are generally seen as the most risky of all, a major factor likely to stifle any venture a Woody Allen might want to make into the world of the mega-budget blockbuster.

The scope of directors to exercise auteurist-type influence or control over their work is a factor of their power at the box-office. This was true even of most of the freedoms gained at the height of the Hollywood Renaissance. The movement was largely based on the financial success of a few initial forays, films like *Bonnie and Clyde*, *The Graduate* and *Easy Rider*. The ability of filmmakers associated with the Renaissance to keep making their own kinds of films was closely associated with continued success, or at least its promise, although critical reputation was also a factor. Robert Altman is a clear example. The blockbuster success of *M*A*S*H* was crucial to the existence of many of the films that followed.

Altman was seen as a worthwhile investment, although his output in the 1970s, during which he worked with a number of studios, was resolutely prickly and uncommercial. Even towards the end of the decade, when further success on anything like the same scale as *M*A*S*H* had proved elusive, Altman was able to secure a multi-film deal with Twentieth Century Fox, the producer of *M*A*S*H*. The relationship broke down after more commercial failures, culminating in the refusal of the studio to distribute *Health* (1979). In 1981 Altman sold his company, Lion's Gate Films, working for many years only in low-budget and independently distributed films and occasionally for television.[14] He has since managed to return to productions of larger budget and scope, including the Hollywood satire *The Player* (1992) and *Short Cuts* (1993), a very 'Altmanesque' multi-character affair based on the stories of Raymond Carver. Altman has also made a move closer to the commercial mainstream with *The Gingerbread Man* (1998), adding some distinctive touches to the unlikely material of a John Grisham thriller.

For Francis Ford Coppola it was the huge success of *The Godfather* that opened up vistas of apparent auteurist freedom. The blockbuster performance of *The Godfather* enabled Coppola to pursue the less commercial-seeming narrative structure of *The Godfather: Part II* – another box-office triumph, as it turned out – and the decidedly more 'artistic' visions of *The Conversation*, *Apocalypse Now* and *One From the Heart* (1982). The budgetary excesses of the last two, including the dismal performance of *One From the Heart*, led to a substantial reduction in both Coppola's wealth and his industrial clout. Coppola, like many others, has been obliged to mix 'personal' with more commercial projects, a blend illustrated by the contrast between two films made back-to-back in 1983 from teen novels by SE Hinton: the highly stylized and largely monochrome *Rumble Fish* and the more conventional and commercial *The Outsiders*. A blend of the two types of film was achieved to some extent in the mixture of elements of the art movie and blockbuster found in *Bram Stoker's Dracula* (1992).

Martin Scorsese is another prominent figure from the Renaissance whose ability to pursue his own personal visions has been mixed with an obligation to perform more mainstream directing duties. Scorsese has never had a single hit of the scale sufficient to carry him through a wave of more personal works. Most of his films have performed modestly at best, despite gaining critical praise – a quality of some, if not primary, relevance to the studios (an image of something other than naked commerce is seen as one way of forestalling threats of greater regulatory intervention in the industry). Scorsese has been able to pursue long-standing and controversial personal projects such as *The Last Temptation of Christ* (1988) and *Kundun* (1997), but only by combining them with more commercial fare such as *The Color of Money* (1986) and *Cape Fear* (1991). *The Color of Money*, a star vehicle for Paul Newman and Tom Cruise, was Scorsese's first real commercial success since *Taxi Driver*. The film is credited with 'rehabilitating' Scorsese's reputation in the higher echelons of Hollywood after the box-office failure of *New York, New York* (1977), *Raging Bull* (1980) and *The King of Comedy* (1983).

*The Last Temptation of Christ* offers a good example of the exigencies of auteurist production in New Hollywood. The film's auteurist credentials are clear enough, if qualified by the fact that it is based on a novel by Nikos Kazantzakis. Scorsese talks about it with reference to his childhood experiences of religion. The film resonates strongly with his background, interests and obsessions. Similar religious dimensions can be found in other Scorsese films, from *Mean Streets* to *Bringing Out the Dead* (1999). In discussing *The Last Temptation*, Scorsese refers to *Taxi Driver*'s Travis Bickle in terms of Old Testament bloodletting, implying some consistency of vision across a range of works.

The style of the film can also be interpreted in terms of its place in the Scorsese canon. Mobile camerawork is often used to express the energy and uncertainty of the central character. The Sermon on the Mount scene is shot close and hand-held, giving an edginess, a freshness and spontaneity, to what might otherwise be overly familiar material. Such devices are combined with more expressive touches, as elsewhere in Scorsese's work, including scenes bathed in the ominous red light found in *Mean Streets* and *Taxi Driver*. Familiar conventions of past biblical epics, such as full widescreen formats and heavenly choir music, are largely avoided in favour of a more gutsy and engaged approach.[15] Events from the life of Christ are presented in an idiom designed to appeal to contemporary American audiences and in a manner that helps to identify the film as a distinctly 'Martin Scorsese' production. As such, the film was not easy to get off the ground. Initially backed by Paramount, the project was dropped and rejected at several other studios before eventually being picked up by Universal. The price of Universal's commitment was Scorsese's agreement to give the studio a more commercial product in the future. This turned out to be *Cape Fear*, a noisy remake of the 1962 classic that went on to be Scorsese's biggest box-office success at the time.

Directors given space on the basis of initial success in the Renaissance era who failed to supply the goods again, or to compromise in more commercial forms of production, have tended to disappear from the scene. Many promising figures from the early years of the Hollywood Renaissance faded or disappeared from sight, including William Friedkin, Peter Bogdanovich and Hal Ashby. None went from boom

4. The Sermon on the Mount, Scorsese-style, close and hand-held, in *The Last Temptation of Christ*, © Universal Pictures, 1988

to bust more quickly than Dennis Hopper. Hopper was considered a hot, if somewhat unstable, property after the unexpected success of *Easy Rider*. He was given total control over the production of his follow-up, *The Last Movie* (1971). Universal gave Hopper a deal reflecting the mixed expectations of the studio: a whacking 50 per cent of the gross but a meagre salary of $500 a week. Hopper disappeared to Peru to shoot the film and demanded a year to edit it. The result won the Critics Prize at the Venice Film Festival but was otherwise poorly received by critics and died after just two weeks. The knock-on effect was already, at this early stage in the Hollywood Renaissance, to limit much of the freedom that might have been available to other upcoming directors.[16]

## Industrial stakes

Power and control sufficient for the exercise of auteurist tendencies is not always available merely through a reliable track record at the box office. Most New Hollywood filmmakers who have retained such power have gained stakes of their own at the industrial level. These take numerous forms. At the minimum, this might mean functioning as producer or executive producer as well as director. Many directors have formed their own production companies. In some cases this is primarily a matter of convenience and tax avoidance: lower rates of tax are paid on the profits of a small company than on Hollywood-level salaried payments. In others, however, these have become substantial film-producing entities. These range from the formation of short-lived, even disastrous, enterprises to the creation of a thriving new business and, in the case of Steven Spielberg, a whole new studio.

An important aspect of the Hollywood Renaissance was the appearance of a handful of production organizations that promised to open new horizons of control of filmmaking by filmmakers. The first, and at the time the most significant, was BBS, named after its three principals: Bert Schneider, Bob Rafelson and Steve Blauner. It was BBS, under its earlier name Raybert, that provided finance for the production of *Easy Rider*. The company was established with the intention of creating an environment in which talented directors could flourish. As Rafelson put it: 'What this business needs is not better directors, but better *producers* who are willing to give directors with the ideas a chance to do films their own way. It's not just final cut, it's final *everything*.'[17] The success of *Easy Rider* earned BBS a deal with Columbia to produce six features without interference, provided that the budgets remained less that $1 million, making it a centrepiece of the Hollywood Renaissance and counterculture. The fledgling company was given the right to final cut.[18] It went on to produce a number of other significant films associated with the Hollywood Renaissance, including *Five Easy Pieces* (1970, directed by Rafelson), *The Last Picture Show* (1971, Bogdanovich) and *Drive, He Said* (1972, Jack Nicholson).

The performance of *Easy Rider* also provided Francis Coppola with his first institutional base. Warner Bros. funded Coppola and associates including George Lucas to establish the alternative American Zoetrope studio in San Francisco. Warners supplied a stake of $600,000 in development funds in November 1969 in return for right of first refusal on any American Zoetrope products. For a modest investment, the studio aimed to tap into the youth market through a new generation of filmmakers based geographically at the heart of the counterculture.[19] The early 1970s saw the creation of the Director's Company, a joint venture between Coppola, Bogdanovich and Friedkin (director of *The French Connection* and *The Exorcist*). The Director's Company – an auteurist-sounding venture if ever there was one – was funded to the rather more substantial tune of $31.5 million by Paramount Pictures. Each of the three directors was contracted to make three films in a period of six years and to act as executive producer on at least one film directed by one of the others. The studio guaranteed production funds and a 50 per cent share of profits on condition that the trio worked exclusively for Paramount.[20]

Arrangements such as these appeared to offer some grounding for the notion of a cinema in which significant power and autonomy was granted to the filmmaker. Some striking films emerged, but all of these enterprises proved short-lived. The relationship between BBS and Columbia came to an end in 1974, the result of several factors. The studio, which had been in serious financial difficulty, underwent a shake-up at the top. The BBS films *A Safe Place* (1971, Henry Jaglom), *The King of Marvin Gardens* (1972, Rafelson) and *Drive, He Said* failed to repeat the success of *Five Easy Pieces* and *The Last Picture Show*. And the sixth film in the package turned out to be *Hearts and Minds* (1974), an anti-Vietnam war documentary which Columbia refused to distribute.[21] Warner pulled out of its deal with American Zoetrope after the money meant to have been put into the development of cheap films for the youth audience was spent on state-of-the-art equipment and the only projects pitched to the studio were the distinctly uncommercial-seeming *THX 1138* and scripts for *The Conversation* and *Apocalypse Now*.[22]

Next in line, the Director's Company produced only three pictures before the deal folded: *The Conversation*, *Paper Moon* (1973, Bogdanovich) and *Daisy Miller* (1974, Bogdanovich). Of these, only *Paper Moon* performed well at the box office. The arrangement had been suggested by Paramount's chief executive, Frank Yablans, in the belief that the bankability of the directors could be secured for the studio and that they would continue to create at least some films in the commercial mainstream. Not very many Godfathers or Exorcists would be required to make it pay. Coppola's *The Conversation* proved Yablans to have been mistaken in his assumptions, Jon Lewis suggests. Paramount soon withdrew from the deal.[23]

Francis Coppola had grander ideas to follow the collapse of the Director's Company. Still flush with his share of the enormous profits of the two *Godfather* films, he set out to establish a studio of his own. In 1980 he bought a production lot, the rundown former Hollywood General Studios, for $6.7 million. Zoetrope Studios, as the new enterprise was named, was intended to be a substantial base of auteur control in the heart of Hollywood. Just one feature was released before the studio was up for auction less than two years later: *One From the Heart*. The fate of Zoetrope Studios underlined the harsh economic realities facing anyone attempting to go their own way in Hollywood.[24] To buy and renovate the studio Coppola was forced into debt. The studio's prospects for survival were dependent on revenues from its first productions. To produce and distribute even one substantial film, however, Coppola remained dependent on the big studios. Zoetrope itself could not gain sufficient access to credit, which continued to be an important source of the power of the majors. Far from being a break into new freedom, Coppola's enterprise remained at the mercy of the usual suspects. Coppola himself appears to have acted as if this were not the case, helping to seal his own fate.

At an early stage in the life of the new studio Coppola announced that a large proportion of its revenues would be invested in the development of new electronic distribution and exhibition technologies. In future, he declared, films would be distributed electronically by satellite.[25] The rhetoric with which he trumpeted the potential of such technologies to alter the entire landscape of the industry was unlikely to endear him to the majors, jealous guardians of their control of any such processes. The studios had good reason to allow Coppola to fail. It did not require a great effort. As Jon Lewis puts it: 'Though it is tempting to wax conspiratorial here, there is no evidence of any accord among the studios to "get Coppola". But the production problems that plagued the film – all of which, more or less, had to do with capital secured through the major studio–big bank apparatus – seem at the very least to indicate an unstated industrywide decision to make the film as difficult to produce as possible.'[26] A distribution deal was made with Paramount, but one that enabled the studio to withhold funds until after completion and approval of the film.

Production of *One From the Heart* went ahead on sums of borrowed money that increased along with the budget of the film. Spending was lavish: a budget of some $25 million for a romance, including $4 million for sets and a similar sum, spent without the authority of Paramount, for the opening credit sequence alone. Paramount eventually dropped the picture, declining to distribute it. This undermined its chances at the box office and sealed the fate of Zoetrope Studios. Alternative distribution was arranged through Columbia, but only hurriedly, on a small scale and without success. Zoetrope hung on for another two years before its sale went through, a time in which Coppola continued to develop, produce and give his or the studio's name to the release of a number of varied and interesting products, including *Hammet* (1983, directed by Wim Wenders) and *Koyaanisqatsi* (1983, directed by Godfrey Reggio). A striking legacy, again, but another industrial-auteurist base that could not be sustained for more than a few years.

The price of success for auteurist control at the industrial level remains a simple one: either modesty or a large measure of mass-market mainstream conformity. Neither quality is generally associated with Francis Coppola. He could, quite probably, have sustained a largely independent operation at a lower level, without the trappings of his own production facility or visionary experiments in new technologies. His personal wealth and clout from the *Godfather* films was sufficient to have carved such a niche. Instead, Coppola gambled in a high stakes business in which even his millions were dwarfed. His timing was bad. Zoetrope Studios was launched in a period of high interest rates and at a time when the majors had been able to entrench their power in a number of directions.[27] He also continued to pursue complex and expensive film projects beyond his or any individual's means, condemning himself to dependence upon major studio finance and distribution while not producing material into which the studios were inclined to invest their best efforts. The filmmakers who gained the most sustained success in their own sizeable industrial ventures built their empires a good deal more soberly and more firmly around the mainstream blockbuster market.

Coppola's former protégé George Lucas provides a good example of the kind of filmmaker-led business that thrives in the New Hollywood landscape. Like Coppola, Lucas gained his industrial strength through the massive box-office success of a single franchise dating back to the 1970s. Lucas acquired enormous wealth from the success of *Star Wars*, especially through a deal that gave him ownership of the rights to merchandising and sequels. It was not squandered in grandiloquent gestures of the kind that seem irresistible to his mentor. Lucas invested more cautiously in the expansion of his companies Lucasfilm and Industrial Light and Magic, the special effects facility created to develop the effects techniques used in *Star Wars*. Although not without its own difficulties, Lucasfilm, founded in 1971, profited not just from the *Star Wars* films but also from the involvement of Lucas in the hugely successful Indiana Jones series.[28]

Zoetrope Studios was envisioned, variously, as a haven for new and older generations of auteurs, an artistic repertory company or as the personal preserve of Francis Coppola: on the commercial margins, either way. The best-known of the Lucas enterprises, Industrial Light and Magic, is positioned squarely at the heart of the economy of New Hollywood, having established itself as the premier business servicing a demand for new generations of special effects that could hardly be more central to the blockbuster business of the major studios. The Lucas empire also includes Skywalker Sound and the THX Group, which have had a similar impact on film sound design and reproduction.[29]

Coppola sought to push forward technological barriers, investing in research into electronic distribution/exhibition and in electronic 'previsualization' techniques in the shooting process itself. He may be proved to have been ahead of his time, but ended up lavishing resources on processes that were unable to produce returns because they did not fit in with the prevailing landscape. Lucas, in contrast, invested in dimensions such as special effects and improved sound that were of immediate and profitable benefit to the dominant blockbuster aesthetic and have made him a powerful player in the Hollywood landscape. Lucas also has his own licensing division, to handle the enormous merchandising business associated with the *Star Wars* franchise, and

LucasArts Entertainment, a major developer of computer games including, inevitably, a range of *Star Wars* offshoots.

Equally in the mainstream have been the industrial enterprises of Steven Spielberg. He formed his own Amblin Entertainment company in 1984, on the back of a string of all-time hit films including *Jaws*, *Close Encounters of the Third Kind* (1977), *Raiders of the Lost Ark* (1981) and *E.T.* (1982). Universal was happy to pay the $3.5 million cost of new facilities to house Spielberg on its lot, and to allow him what might have seemed the luxury of *Schindler's List*. This was the price of maintaining a relationship with so prolific a director. Spielberg could not be tied down entirely, however. His arrangement with Universal did not include an exclusive production agreement with the studio, a measure of his enormous clout. He made clear his intention to work with others, including Warner Bros.[30] In the next six years his Amblin duties included the role of producer or executive producer on 19 features, including major successes such as *Gremlins* (1984) and *Back to the Future* (1985), in addition to the films he directed. He also produced two television series, *Amazing Stories* and *Tiny Toon Adventures*.[31] The presence of his name on a project is seen by industry and public alike as close to a guarantor of quality and popular appeal.

In 1994 Spielberg achieved the kind of leap forward in the industrial arena that Coppola had attempted in 1980. He created his own new studio, DreamWorks, in a joint venture with the former Disney executive Jeffrey Katzenberg and the record mogul David Geffen. The enterprise absorbed Amblin Entertainment and became an instant multi-media corporation, involved in the production of feature films, television programmes, music and computer games, the biggest new entrant on the studio scene for some 60 years. Coppola's Zoetrope Studios was severely handicapped from the start by the debts incurred in its purchase and renovation and by its limited access to capital. DreamWorks was built on a much firmer foundation, a reflection of the commercially central position occupied by Spielberg and his partners.

The three founders each put $33.3 million into the studio. These were substantial personal investments. But the distinguishing feature of DreamWorks, in its ability to play seriously in the Hollywood arena, was a vastly greater scale of investment from outside sources. The

Microsoft co-founder Paul Allen invested $500 million, the Korean company Cheil Foods and Chemicals added another $300 million (its One World Media division gaining Asian distribution rights for DreamWorks products, excluding Japan). Loan commitments of up to $1 billion over a ten-year period were made by the Chemical Bank. The three founders still retained 67 per cent control of the company.[32]

A measure of the financial backing obtained by DreamWorks is that it could call on sufficient resources to continue operations despite a lack of success with its first batch of films and TV shows, a major point of contrast with Zoetrope Studios. One of the defining characteristics of a viable mainstream studio is precisely this capacity to maintain expensive production while riding out the less good times. It was not until *Deep Impact* and *Saving Private Ryan* in the summer of 1998 that the feature film end of the business tasted any great success. DreamWorks probably has a viable future – it enjoyed its best-yet year in 2000, with successes including *American Beauty* and *Gladiator* – but even an operation on this scale is not a source of complete independence. One difference between DreamWorks and the majors is its lack of an extensive library of past productions, a key source of stabilizing cash-flow revenue. Even with the deep pockets of its backers, the studio cannot be sure of sufficient resources to fulfil its ambitions alone. *Deep Impact* and *Saving Private Ryan* were co-produced with Paramount, for example, while *Gladiator* was a joint venture with Universal.

DreamWorks has been subject to repeated rumours that its independence might be curtailed by a merger or some kind of other arrangement with one of the majors, especially Seagram/MCA/Universal. DreamWorks and Lucasfilm both have limited domestic distribution capabilities but remain dependent to a significant extent on access to the powerful distribution networks of the established majors, DreamWorks forming a 10-year alliance with Universal/UIP to distribute its films in the overseas theatrical market.[33]

Notions of auteurism, or any cinema of 'personal' expression in Hollywood, always have to be qualified by consideration of the industrial dimension. Where freedom has been available, it has been the product largely of specific industrial factors. Any account of Hollywood filmmaking based on the assumption that the filmmaker is the principal author or source of the product also needs to be questioned on wider grounds, reaching out into the broader social and historical context. This also takes us into deeper questions about the assumptions underlying any notion of individual authorship of cultural products. These issues can usefully be explored through a focus on a single case-study.

## Auteurism vs. social-historical context: the 'Spielbergness' of *E.T.*

To what extent is *E.T. The Extraterrestrial* a product of Steven Spielberg? How far might it be seen instead as a manifestation of a particular social or historical context? A focus on a single example is a useful way to examine how different influences play across the products of New Hollywood cinema. A case can be made for the location of *E.T.* within a corpus of films bearing the distinctive stamp of Steven Spielberg, in terms of both thematic concerns and film style. *E.T.* can be read in terms of a theme that occurs in much of Spielberg's work: breakdown in the nuclear family, marked particularly by the absence of the father. This is combined with some movement towards reconstruction through the creation of a new or surrogate father figure. In *E.T.* the father of Eliot (Henry Thomas) is absent, estranged from the mother. Substitute father figures are found in the shape of *E.T.* itself – although the alien is also figured at times as child-like – and an empathetic scientist paired with the mother at the end. Similar thematic patterns are found in many of Spielberg's other films, from his first theatrical feature *The Sugarland Express* (1974) to *Jurassic Park* (1993) and many more in between.[34]

It is quite easy to relate the existence of these themes to details of Spielberg's personal background. Spielberg himself describes *E.T.* as 'a very personal story... about the divorce of my parents, how I felt when my parents broke up.'[35] Spielberg grew up learning not to idolize family life, his biographer Joseph McBride reports: 'But in the emotional void left by his family's dissolution, he could not help yearning for a substitute father figure.' This appears to be expressed in both his films and, for the biographer, in the career relationships formed with father-figures such as Sid Sheinberg at Universal and Steve Ross at Warner. The alien E.T. can be read as an embodiment of the alienation of the fictional Eliot. Both, in turn, can be read as figures of the alienation Spielberg himself experienced in the break-up of his parents and as a child of Jewish background who spoke later of being picked on after being moved to suburbia.

What about the stylistic dimension of *E.T.*? Identifying distinctive stylistic features in the work of mainstream directors is often less easy than picking out thematic consistencies. The style of directors operating closer to the commercial margins is sometimes easier to identify, the industrial location permitting greater scope to move away from dominant conventions. Devices that depart from the usual conventions are, by definition, usually easier to identify. They stand out from the norm. Spielberg's work can also be identified stylistically, however, if only in terms of the sheer skill and aplomb with which he deploys certain techniques available from within the dominant conventional repertoire. Such qualities are not always easy to pin down, the whole point of the classical style being its relative invisibility-through-familiarity.

Spielberg's style might be described in terms of a particularly fluent and dynamic use of classical conventions. His films tend to be filled with very smooth transitions and slick visual matches, coupled with dynamic use of continuity editing patterns.[36] One notable example can be taken from *Jaws* (1975), in a scene in which police chief Brody (Roy Scheider) is on a crowded beach anxiously on the lookout for a shark attack. Several figures walk between Brody and his view of the sea, disrupting his gaze. Spielberg cuts, repeatedly, on the movement of these figures in front of Brody and past the camera (although some of the credit should be attributed to the editor, Verna Fields, a typical example of the qualifications usually needed of auteurist assumptions). The effect is to both to heighten the tension of the sequence and to make the viewer share some of Brody's sense of frustrated vision. The shark eventually strikes, a point at which Spielberg uses a bravura effect to convey the shock of Brody's reaction. The camera dollies forward, abruptly, towards Brody. The lens is zoomed out at a matching rate. The effect is to maintain Brody's image at much the same scale within

5. Stand-in for the director? Eliot (Henry Thomas) investigates strange noises in his backyard in *E.T. The Extraterrestrial*, © Universal City Studios Inc., 1982

the frame while stretching the depth of field of the image. The background appears to recede alarmingly. The same device is used in *E.T.* A slower version of the zoom/dolly creates a more subtly disorienting effect in which an elevated vista of the landscape of suburbia seems to recede gradually, to suggest the unease created by the intrusive presence of a team of scientists on the alien's trail.

On thematic and stylistic grounds, then, there is scope for reading *E.T.* as the distinctive product of the individual filmmaker, Steven Spielberg. These readings can be challenged, however. Thematic concerns attributable to Spielberg can also be read from social, historical, cultural or ideological perspectives. Discourses about the threatened break-up of the nuclear family and the absence of the father were widespread in American society at the time the film appeared. Divorce and single parenthood were the subject of heated political debate in the early years of the Ronald Reagan era. The way such issues are handled in *E.T.* and other films directed by Spielberg can be interpreted as far more than just the concern of one individual. Indeed, for Robert Kolker: 'Spielberg's films constitute a factory of ideological production, the great imaginary of the eighties, full of images the culture wanted to see, images and narratives that expressed the culture.'[37]

Do these images come from Spielberg or from 'the culture'? What is the driving force here? To what extent are the thematic characteristics of films like *E.T.* 'rooted in' or 'possessed by' Spielberg or the Spielbergian? Is a mass-market filmmaker such as Spielberg the author, or just a mediator of such concerns? Do they come from him, or does he just plug into broader currents? These are complex questions. It certainly seems impossible to ignore the social-historical part of the equation, however strongly grounded some films might be in the background and concerns of the director. Steven Spielberg, as a filmmaker with considerable power to shape his own projects, remains a product of his own culture, just like anyone else. A coincidence of the personal concerns of the director and wider issues in the society might be one way of explaining the degree and consistency of box-office success enjoyed by a figure such as Spielberg.

Films such as *E.T.* do appear to 'tap into' issues of widespread social concern. They strike contemporary nerves, as well as providing glossy and emotional slices of entertainment. Their success can be attributed in part to the fact that they offer fantasies of recuperation in which real social issues are raised and then resolved at an imaginary level. Many of the films of Robert Altman display an equally consistent degree of box-office failure. This might be attributed to the fact that, while reflecting certain developments of their time, they usually deny precisely this kind of recuperative potential. Even the most hugely successful and ideologically resonant films do not spring fully-formed from the culture, however. They remain the outcome of multiple determinations, including the industrial framework, the work of individual filmmakers and the broader cultural scene.

Similar complications occur in the stylistic domain. Certain techniques can be viewed as the hallmark of a particular director. But these do not usually come out of nowhere. Individual filmmakers, whatever their auteurist credentials, draw on a repertoire of existing techniques and devices. The zoom/dolly used so effectively by Spielberg happens to have been devised by Alfred Hitchcock, a great influence on the movie-brat generation of directors, to convey the central dizzying impression of *Vertigo* (1958). The innovations that marked out a whole generation of filmmakers in the Hollywood Renaissance period drew heavily upon a range of influences, as was seen in chapter 1. The notion of the individual artist operating in a vacuum is a myth, even in spheres such as literature, painting or sculpture that might appear more conducive to personal expression.[38]

Hollywood filmmakers face all kinds of limitations on their freedom of personal expression, ranging from financial and logistical constraints to a requirement usually to adhere to something close to the basic conventions of the classical style. Here, as in other respects, the concept of the director-as-auteur is sustainable only if it is understood in a qualified manner. Particular social or industrial circumstances can allow individual filmmakers to ring the changes *within* the classical style. One of the characteristics of the classical style identified by David Bordwell is a redundancy that makes this possible.[39] The parameters of classical style include more than one way of achieving most ends. This leaves room for individual filmmakers to express themselves through the choices made within a set of options. A director who consistently makes certain sets of choices might thus establish something that could be termed an individual style. This is a significant measure of freedom, but within limitations. Exactly what can be contained within a broadly classical or mainstream stylistic approach is subject to historical change, as we saw in chapter 1 and will see in further examples in chapters 6 and 7. Innovation is possible. But, in anything close to the Hollywood mainstream, this is usually limited or motivated by factors beyond the realm of the individual auteur.

The issue of auteurism and Hollywood opens out into large questions about the possibility of the individual authorship of cultural products, questions with their roots in debates ranging across subjects such as literature and philosophy. In literature, a dominant tradition in the modern period has been to see the writer as the individual source of the text. This is a view that has been questioned by some critics and theorists. Roland Barthes, most famously, declared the 'death of the author' in an influential essay published in 1968. The text, Barthes declared, 'is not a line of words releasing a single "theological" meaning (the "message" of the Author-God) but a multi-dimensional space in which a variety of writings, none of them original, blend and clash. The text is a tissue of quotations drawn from the innumerable centres of culture.'[40] This description might be quite fitting for many of the products of New Hollywood, with its multiple re-writes of scripts and a development process designed to fabricate projects that draw on and rework earlier films and seek to include various elements to appeal to different audience groups. More generally, the point is to emphasize the extent to which all texts draw on multitudes of pre-established meanings and devices that are not all determined, controlled or limited by the creation of any individual author.

We are all shaped by the culture in which we exist, in various and multiply-determined ways. Any of us might, in an ideal world, be given the freedom to make a film of our own. Imagine a situation in which you were given complete control. Write your own script, get it shot on whatever budget is required. Final cut, no interference, access to unrivalled resources of marketing and distribution. It would be your own creation. But it would never *just* be that, and never could be. You might be an auteur, but in a manner that requires qualification. The ideas we have, and the shapes into which we put and express them, are drawn from all kinds of other sources. Certain horizons of meaning are created by the conceptual frameworks within which we exist. The same goes for languages, cinematic and otherwise. We cannot avoid the use of certain established tools and procedures. Even their abandonment is a tacit recognition of their presence and importance. We can inflect them in our own ways, with all kinds of interesting and significant results – as can many filmmakers – but only within certain bounds.

The stronger uses of auteur theory have come in for much criticism, both academic and from within Hollywood. Screenwriters have always been among its most vociferous critics, for obvious reasons. They tend to be granted far less status than directors, regardless of the true level of creative input they might have in any particular case. The overarching 'possessive credit', often claimed by the director, has become a source of antagonism. Industry executives tended to run scared of the concept of real freedom for the filmmaker by the end of the 1970s, except at the lower-budget end of the scale or in the case of directors with particularly impressive records at the box office (an example of the latter would be James Cameron, given an unusual degree of control over the production of *Titanic*, despite its enormous cost, in the combined roles of writer, director and editor). The identification of films by the name of the director has not significantly diminished, however. Why should this be the case? Several answers might be suggested. An implicit auteurism remains a convenience for journalism and other film writing and publication, the director being a handy tag on which to hang discussion or analysis that often fails to question the assumptions on which it is based. For the industry, too, the name of the director remains a potentially useful marketing tool.

## The 'Director's cut' and the commerce of auteurism

What is the status of the 'director's cut' version of the Hollywood film, the modified edition sometimes released in the cinema but more often found in belated video or DVD releases? Is the director's cut a return to the original vision of the auteur–director, freed from whatever compromises were involved in the initial release? Or just a cynical marketing ploy? It could be both. As far as the studios are concerned, the commercial dimension is likely to be paramount. What the phenomenon of the director's cut version implies, however, is the role a commodified version of auteurism continues to play in Hollywood's industrial calculations and marketing strategies.

The history of the director's cut version, in its current form, is usually dated to Spielberg's 'Special Edition' of *Close Encounters of the Third Kind*, a re-edited re-release that appeared three years after, and soon replaced, the original. The director's cut version of *Blade Runner* (1982), long awaited by fans, appeared in 1992. Many more have followed since, including Coppola's 'restored' *Apocalypse Now Redux* (2001), along with DVD versions of films that often include extras such as deleted scenes (like the 'spider walking' sequence from *The Exorcist*, available from 1999 and subsequently including in the cinema re-release of 2000) and alternative endings. There is an obvious commercial benefit from this kind of thing. Whatever Spielberg's personal or artistic motivations for re-cutting *Close Encounters*, the move was only funded by Columbia Pictures on the expectation of generating additional resources. To gain the $2 million required to make his changes, Spielberg was obliged to include scenes of the inside of the mother ship that became the major selling point of the advertising campaign.[41]

*Blade Runner* was undoubtedly 'improved', from a qualitative point of view, in the director's cut. An unnecessary voice-over was removed, along with a tagged-on happy ending. A dream sequence was added that raises questions about the human status of the principal character, Deckard (Harrison Ford). A number of compromises, made in the interests of greater mainstream commercial viability, appeared to have been excised. This is somewhat ironic, given the poor performance of the film on initial release and the revenues earned by the director's cut, the theatrical release of which achieved the highest per-screen grosses of its opening weekend.[42] The explanation is that the film had by this time gained a cult reputation among precisely the audience likely to see, buy or rent a supposedly 'more authentic' version of the film a second time around.

This audience might be defined, loosely, as a more knowing, film-educated or generally more film-literate audience, including in this case an audience of science fiction enthusiasts. Viewers such as these are a significant component of the audience for Hollywood films. They figure particularly among those who watch films on a regular rather than occasional basis. They are also likely to rent, and particularly to buy, tapes and discs at a higher than average rate. Such audiences are worth catering to. The release of various different versions, such as director's cuts or 'original' widescreen editions on tape or disc, can provide additional profits at no great cost. Consumers of these products might not constitute anything like the majority audience for the biggest films, but they spend disproportionately on all aspects of film viewing. The names of a few directors, such as Spielberg or Tarantino, might be recognized as selling points for a majority of filmgoers. Many other names, however, are likely to be picked up only by the smaller but generally higher spending constituency of enthusiasts. Hollywood does well to appeal to both kinds of viewer, in its general strategy of seeking to attract diverse coalitions to the cinema and/or video store.

The *Batman* series offers an interesting example. Few more clear-cut instances of the corporate-franchise construction of movie projects can be found. Where, then, does the figure of the director – as a distinctive presence – fit into this most heavily commercial context? *Batman* and the first sequel *Batman Returns* (1992) were directed by Tim Burton. The choice of Burton can be explained in simple terms of industrial track-record. Burton appeared a safe bet, having supplied Warner Bros. with healthy profits in the past with *Pee-Wee's Big Adventure* (1985) and *Beetlejuice* (1988).[43] But the presence of Burton also adds something distinctive and marketable to the films, for some sections of the audience at least.

The Burton-familiar viewer will anticipate, and receive, not just a mainstream comic-book caper, but some of the darker and quirkier dimensions of the developing Burton style, with its swooping camera movements orchestrated to the distinctive musical scores of Danny Elfman, a regular Burton collaborator. This is increasingly likely to have been an attraction in the sequel, as Burton's career progressed and a distinctive gothic-fantasy style rooted in his background in animation became more clearly identifiable. *Batman Returns* followed the appearance of Burton's more offbeat and 'personal' *Edward Scissorhands*

(1990). Some viewers, who like to position themselves as 'discerning', might be alienated by the heavy marketing hype accompanying the *Batman* films but attracted by the associations brought to the products by Burton's name. 'It is notable that after the disappointing performance of *Batman and Robin* (1997) Warner's plans for the revival of the franchise included hiring Darren Aronofsky, director of the low-budget cult hit π (1998) to co-write and direct *Batman: Year One,* in pre-production at the time of writing.'

Hollywood uses a variety of appeals in its attempts to maximize potential audiences. The name of a director may be trumpeted cynically, but it can reflect one distinctive element among the different components of a film. The name 'Tim Burton' is a contribution to the overall equation, helping to establish a set of expectations that can be analyzed through a qualified version of the auteurist approach. In other cases the associations sought through the identification of individual filmmakers may be rather less susceptible to such analysis. *Godzilla*, for example, was sold as 'from the creators of Independence Day', a reference to producer Dean Devlin and director Roland Emmerich. Associations with a style of blockbuster production, and its huge box-office success, were chosen in preference to the more auteurist implications of 'a film by Roland Emmerich'. This 'from the makers of' strategy is used quite frequently, as an attempt to build the expectations of one film upon the success of a predecessor. All sorts of links might be highlighted, however tenuous, if it is thought that they might gain extra business, including the names of producers, executive producers and even the usually unsung screenwriter.

The name of a director, and varying degrees of auteurist association, can be a considerable asset to the studios. The creation of such an identity is also a benefit to the individual filmmaker. The ultimate achievement for the New Hollywood commercial auteur is to become a distinct brand-identity, marketable on that basis. Stylistic traits and departures from classical conventions are encouraged, up to a point, as a way for the director to leave a distinctive mark or sign of authorship. For Timothy Corrigan, in the aftermath of the vicissitudes of auteurism in the 1970s, the commerce of auteurism is a phenomenon in which the director 'rematerialized in the eighties and nineties as an agent of a commercial performance of the business of being an auteur.'[44]

The business of being an auteur, in this context, is less a matter of personal artistic endeavour than of achieving a status that sells both the film to the viewer and the director to the studio. Hence the pheno-menon of the 'director as celebrity', famous partly just for being famous, a category that includes figures from 'movie brat' generations ranging from Francis Coppola to Quentin Tarantino (as well as some from the classical era, a notable example being Alfred Hitchcock). To play as a major 'auteur' in the commercial mainstream sometimes requires an investment in this larger-than-life dimension, unless one happens to have achieved the inordinate wealth and stability of success possessed by recessive figures such as Spielberg and Lucas. Coppola continues to bounce back, for example, emerging in 2000 with successes ranging from his California winery and a branded line of pasta, sauces and olive oil and a deal to supervise the production of a slate of pictures at United Artists; not to mention continued plans for his own long-standing future project, the typically ambitious sounding *Megalopolis*,[45] listed as being in pre-production at the time of writing.

# Genre Benders

Within the structured marketplace of myths, the continuity
and persistence of particular genres may be seen as keys in
identifying the culture's deepest and most persistent
concerns. Likewise, major breaks in the development of
important genres may signal the presence of a significant
crisis of cultural values and organization.

Richard Slotkin[1]

[T]he constitution of film cycles and genres is a never-ceasing
process, closely tied to the capitalist need for product
differentiation.

Rick Altman[2]

An edgy violent thriller. Stylish, blackly comic, not short of gratuitous
killing, even before the opening credits. A pair of hoodlum brothers
on the road after a robbery. A kidnapped bank teller without long to
live. George Clooney and Quentin Tarantino. One playing mean,
threatening and straightforward, the other quirky and a more than a
touch unbalanced. They hijack the motor-home of a disillusioned
preacher (Harvey Keitel) and two fresh-faced teenagers (Juliet Lewis
and Ernest Liu). Heading for the Mexican border, combined forces of
law and order on their trail. The quintessential nineties thriller, perhaps,
its principal features delineated within a few early minutes. A hip New
Hollywood version of *The Desperate Hours* (1955, itself remade in 1990),
a siege-thriller recipe in which desperate convicts hold ordinary citizens
at gunpoint.

6. Tooled-up for a genre-shift: Seth Gecko (George Clooney) ready to translate his penchant for violence into otherworldly realms in *From Dusk Till Dawn*, © Dimension Films, 1996. Ronald Grant archive

Our expectations are set. More edginess and violence can be anticipated, laced with dark wit, as we await a working out of the dynamics between two sets of major characters. The border safely crossed, they arrive at a cavernous truck-driver-and-biker bar and brothel to await a rendezvous the following morning. Busty showgirls provide the entertainment. An altercation between the brothers leaves several more bodies on the floor. Little surprise about that. But then something weird happens… The lead act among the showgirls (Salma Hayek) undergoes a strange transformation. The bodies rise, snarling. And somehow we are plunged into the middle of a vampire movie, the frame filled with pointed teeth and lurid gross-out effects.

What happens mid-way through *From Dusk Till Dawn* (1996) can be described as a shift of genre. From sadistic-comic thriller, with a bit of road movie thrown in, to vampire-schlock-horror. The principals seem to know the new conventions, at least: impromptu crucifixes and stakes are mobilized as they prepare for a long night's battle of the soul. Now we understand why we needed a priest, disillusioned or otherwise, and his previously pacific influence can be put to a use more in keeping with the violent instincts of the film. What are we supposed to make of this shift of cinematic conventions, though? What does it tell us about the function and uses of genre, both generally and in the specific contexts of New Hollywood?

Some have argued that genre conventions are used differently in New Hollywood, that a distinction can be made between 'classical' and 'post–classical' or New Hollywood uses of genre. One suggestion is that genre boundaries have become less stable than they were in the past. *From Dusk Till Dawn* might appear to offer support for this claim. As with other aspects of New Hollywood, however, such distinctions are easily overstated. Genre has been used in recent decades in a number of different ways, some with more in common with the era of classical Hollywood than is often implied. This chapter will begin by considering some general background on the form and function of genre in Hollywood before going on to look in more detail at the ways it has been mobilized in New Hollywood.

## Definitions of genre I: from industry to audience expectations

The concept of genre is one of which most filmgoers are likely to be aware at some level, or to use implicitly at least some of the time. The word is taken from the French term for 'kind' or 'type' and used in various ways to describe the categories into which films are placed. What constitutes a distinct genre? This is a question that turns out to be more complex than it might at first appear. We can begin, though, with a simple if rather circular definition: a genre is a type of film that has become recognizable as such because a sufficient number of films of that kind have been made, and identified in that manner, over a period of time. It is not hard to make sense of genre from an industrial perspective. Many Hollywood films can be located as products of one genre or another, or as combinations of distinct genre elements. The reason for this is quite simple. As primarily a business, Hollywood has tended to repeat formulas that prove successful at the box office.

If a film is made as a one-off, not fitting clearly into any particular genre, and it is a big success, it is likely to be copied or repeated. Similar films will be made. More will follow if these also succeed. If this proves to be a short-lived phenomenon it might be labelled a 'cycle', rather than a fully-fledged genre. The disaster movies of the 1970s or of the late 1990s might be defined in these terms. Or it might be a sub-genre, identifiable as part of an existing genre but with a distinctive twist. The vampire movie, perhaps, as a sub-category of horror dating back to the silent era. The difference between a cycle and a genre is largely one of longevity, although the borders are somewhat fuzzy. To qualify as a genre a film-type needs to be more than a passing trend or fad. It needs to last, to have some depth and resonance. A mainstream genre should be familiar and relatively easy to recognize.

The use of generic or cyclical typing is one way Hollywood has always sought to create commercial stability. Established genres or on-going cycles have a track record of gaining audiences that makes them appealing. Genre is one way movies have been pre-sold throughout the history of Hollywood. The studios have usually been reasonably confident that audiences of some kind exist for films that fit into the conventions of major genres, such as the thriller, the horror film, the romantic comedy, the literary adaptation, and so on, or for combinations of elements from familiar genres and cycles. They have worked before, on numerous occasions, and so are considered likely to work again. One-off films, which do not come with pre-established associations, are seen as particularly risky in the New Hollywood era. But they have never constituted a very large proportion of Hollywood output. Hollywood has always preferred to invest in products that can be described largely in terms of others that have proved successful in the past. Genre frameworks provide one source of this kind of replication.

The attraction of genre to the industry is closely linked to its presumed appeal to viewers. Filmgoers generally like to have a broad idea of what to expect from any individual picture. Genres are constituted not just by bodies of films but also by the established expectations of viewers. A sense of genre identity might be one of the factors that helps us decide what films to see. It is one of the things we reach for when attempting to describe or find out about a film. Some idea of genre location might be enough to enable us to decide to see a film. Or, of equal importance, to avoid it. For some the term 'science fiction' might promise enough. It might also have the opposite effect. The term 'musical' is sufficient to send some filmgoers running in the opposite direction. For the Hollywood studios, genre identity is one of a number of ways to hedge against the risks of investing money into expensive productions. For the filmgoer, it is a way of guarding investments not just in ticket or rental prices but in resources of available leisure time.

A genre label is an implicit promise. A horror film offers a particular set of pleasures, more appealing to some than others. A musical offers a different set. So does a thriller, a science fiction film, a war film, an action movie, a romantic melodrama, and so on. Films with clear genre locations offer specific pleasures according to the individual genre: the pleasure of being scared, uplifted, thrilled, brought to tears, or whatever. All genre films share one particular kind of pleasure: a blend of sameness and difference. Any film clearly belonging to a genre, sub–genre or cycle is in some respects similar to others in the same category. They share certain familiar and repeated characteristics, the nature of which we will consider shortly. At the same time, it needs to be different. Each individual horror film, musical or thriller offers its own element of originality. Some are more distinctive than others. But even the most mundane and unadventurous offer something new, if only a different set of names for the characters and the most superficial ringing of changes on the plot.

The mix of familiarity and difference offered by genre films appears to be pleasurable in itself. There is enough familiarity to generate a sense of comfort and orientation. We know our way around the conventions. The genre buff might have a great breadth of explicit knowledge of the rules and how they have been played out in the past. The casual viewer has a more general sense of the likely boundaries of what is permissible. Splattered gore and explicit violence are not just allowed but expected in the modern horror film. But not usually in the musical or romantic comedy. Our confidence that such expectations will be met is an important aspect of the enjoyment of mainstream films. Within these bounds, we are safe to enjoy something a little different. A fresh telling of familiar material, or just a minor twist in the way some of the elements turn out, is often sufficient to maintain our interest and enjoyment.

Too great a similarity may be tedious and overly predictable. Too much difference can be discomforting, undercutting our initial expectations of pleasure. Most genre films occupy a position somewhere between these extremes. It is in these terms that *From Dusk Till Dawn* is a useful example of the workings of genre. *From Dusk Till Dawn* does not stick to the conventions of the genre it appears to occupy for its first half. It undergoes a sudden shift, the effect of which is unsettling. On first viewing, or without any advance knowledge of what is to happen, the change of gear is liable to grate. Like it or not, the first half of the film obeys a particular set of conventions. These might not constitute a clear-cut genre but are those of a distinct crime-thriller format or sub-genre of the 1990s. One of the clearest conventions is that those who are shot dead at close range – which happens quite often and graphically in such films – do not subsequently get up and grow pointy teeth. One set of criteria according to which genres are defined is a regime of plausibility. Genres set limits on the kinds of events deemed to be believably acceptable within their confines. It is not usual for film characters to burst spontaneously into song. Unless they are in a musical. Ordinary domestic spaces do not usually conceal portals into other worlds or dimensions. Except in horror, fantasy or science fiction films.

Different genres can occupy very different ontological planes, with differing regimes of verisimilitude. Genre location legitimates much of what goes on. It provides motivation for varying degrees of departure from what is usually considered to be plausible in the real world, or in more 'realistic' fiction. Breaches of these aspects of genre conventions can be the most disturbing, upsetting the implicit 'contract' agreed between filmmaker and audience. If we agree to 'suspend disbelief', to some extent, to 'go along with' somewhat unlikely-seeming events, we do so to different extents in different kinds of films. *From Dusk Till Dawn* shifts its boundaries in mid-stream. It is not unusual for a leap in required suspension of disbelief to occur early in a Hollywood film. An initial situation of relative normality commonly precedes the most extraordinary on-screen events. What is unusual about *From Dusk Till Dawn* is that it devotes more than an hour of running time to the establishment of one set of conventions before switching to another.

The viewer does not have to dislike lurid vampire movies to find this move discomforting or a potential source of annoyance. Different viewers might react to the change in different ways. Some might prefer the vampire-movie half of the film. Some might enjoy the sheer audacity of the move: the transgression of genre boundaries might fit into the general spirit of transgressing cultural norms into which both generic locations play. Many, however, are likely to find it frustrating.

We usually 'buy into' a particular set of expectations. This happens economically, if we pay for a ticket or video rental, and also emotionally. We agree, tacitly, to go along with the conventions established mid-way into a film; unless, that is, we decide otherwise and stop viewing or remain more than usually detached, either of which are possible. A certain amount of emotion is usually invested in the events on screen: a complex range of identifications or allegiances with various characters, accompanied and shaped by the anticipation of what is likely to happen.[3]

One of the edgy-black-comic-thriller characteristics of *From Dawn Till Dusk* is a degree of uncertainty about likely sources of allegiance. The good guy is clearly Harvey Keitel's preacher, but his age and profession do not make him an obvious point of reference for the youngish-adult target audience of such a movie. Quentin Tarantino is a major 1990s movie icon for precisely this audience, yet plays a character who is dangerously unstable. George Clooney is a heart-throb actor; his character is not very likeable but appears to be more or less trustworthy. The character played by Juliet Lewis might seem the most obvious point of identification for many women viewers. How exactly we might wish to position ourselves in relation to this network of relationships is something the film promises to develop. The genre shift eliminates most of that tension, however, replacing it with an all-hands-to-the-pumps horror scenario in which differences are mostly expunged in the battle against an otherworldly common enemy.

## Definitions of genre II: social-cultural context and popular mythology

Genre films tend to repeat certain conventions, presenting similar characters, situations and issues over relatively long periods of time.

Similarity, from one film to another, sometimes seems to outweigh difference. It is hardly surprising, given these characteristics, that attempts have been made to understand genre in terms of its social or cultural implications. The fact that certain kinds of films prove to be popular time and time again can partly be attributed to industrial factors. Genre or cyclical frameworks continue to be used because they have been used profitably in the past. This is in some respects a self-fulfilling industrial process. Audiences get to a large extent what they are offered and their choices are limited. The popularity of films or film types does not directly reflect the social or cultural world in which they appear, as we have seen in other cases.

But films remain products of their social as well as their industrial context, especially those that demonstrate sustained popular appeal. It would be implausible to suggest that long-standing genres, or even more short-lived cycles, have no connection with their broader social, cultural or historical context. Genre frameworks can be seen as reflections or embodiments of their social contexts, even if mediated through the specific industrial operations of the film business. They can also be understood as playing a more active role in the reproduction of the mythic and ideological discourses in which our lives are embedded. Before getting further into this dimension it is useful to refine the definition of genre used so far in this chapter.

One particularly useful working distinction is outlined by Rick Altman: a distinction between the semantic and syntactic aspects of genre.[4] A *semantic* approach to genre focuses on the different elements that comprise a genre or an individual genre film. Semantics is the study of units of meaning, a term usually associated with the meaning of words. Any film or genre has its own elements of meaning. A classic western, for example, is likely to include elements such as cowboys, Indians (Native Americans), gunfighters, a hero, bad guys, the corrupt banker, the 'fallen' saloon woman and a nice schoolteacher woman who might make a wife for the hero, and so on. Other elements might include a particular setting, in this case various versions of the landscape of the American West. Semantic elements of a genre can also include more specifically cinematic features, such as the way a type of film is characteristically shot. The use of expressionistic lighting and shadows is usually seen as a feature of classic Hollywood film noir, for example, just as spectacular digital effects are often associated with the contemporary science fiction blockbuster.

Elements such as these play a major part in the identification of one kind of film or another. Semantic features identifying the initial genre location of *From Dusk Till Dawn* might include the arbitrary violence and bloodshed, the black suits/white shirts of the brothers and road-movie elements such as the south-western landscape and the world of back-road gas stations and motels. More specifically cinematic features of this self-consciously stylized form include a title sequence in which a cartoon-like device enables us to see through the side of the get-away car to the kidnapped bank teller in the boot and an effect in which the vehicle appears to chase one of the credits off the screen.

A semantic approach to genre is useful. But, as Altman suggests, it does not go far beyond being descriptive. It helps us to identify the elements that are present, but does not have much to say about how they are used or what their potential meaning might be. What Altman recommends is a combination of this and a *syntactic* approach. This takes us a stage further. Semantics is usually used in reference to the meanings of individual words. Syntax, in this context, refers to the grammatical structures of language: how the words are combined into particular patterns according to certain rules and conventions. A syntactic approach to genre seeks to do the same with the elements of meaning identified in types of film. A genre defined this way does not depend merely on the existence of the usual elements. It requires that the elements be organized in particular ways. The elements of long-standing generic frameworks might be patterned in ways that are repeated just as much as the individual elements themselves. Genres might begin as loose combinations of semantic elements, Altman suggests. But they can become more deeply rooted over a period of time through the patterns into which these elements become organized. This is one way of understanding genre in terms of social or cultural issues. Genres can be seen as frameworks within which films return repeatedly to the same underlying patterns, issues, questions and themes.

A number of writers have identified these kinds of patterns in the western, one of the most analyzed of Hollywood genres. The various elements of the classic western can be lined up according to a series of oppositions. At the broadest level, the western can be read in terms of an opposition between the world of settled civilization and that of the frontier wilderness. The familiar western townscape, according to this pattern, would exist not just alongside but in opposition to a surrounding landscape of open spaces, desert, mountain or forest. The banker or railroad mogul would be a representative of the more settled world further east, opposed often to the interests of the frontier farmer or cattleman. The Native American, or 'Indian', would be a representative of the wilderness at its most untrammelled. And so on.

Similar sets of oppositions can be identified in other genres. Science fiction films can often be read in terms of an opposition between humanity and the products of science and technology. Many horror films set up oppositions between rationality and the world of the irrational. The classical Hollywood musical is often organized around an opposition between instinctive spontaneity and more regimented and organized ways of life. Comedies, similarly, can be read in terms of oppositions between normal routine and the disruptive antics of the comedian.[5]

Genre films are often seen as offering some reconciliation of these thematic oppositions. The classic hero of the western is a figure who offers something of the best of both worlds. He (almost always male) usually stands as a representative of the world of the frontier, beyond what are seen as the stifling constraints of settled 'civilization'. Westerns tend to have a strong investment in a celebration of this world. The conventional ideal of the western does not usually amount to an unqualified endorsement of the virtues of the wilderness, however. The dominant figure of the western hero is a frontiersman who combines a feeling for the wilderness with some of the qualities of civilization. Not the 'superficial' niceties, maybe, but what is presented as the essence of civilization: a respect for the value of human life and liberty, perhaps. The frontiersman might have an understanding of the ways of Native American groups, an insight into some of their methods and customs, an ability to live on their terrain and to understand their languages. A clear distinction is usually made between this figure and the 'Indian', however, the latter often viewed in racist terms as a 'savage' entirely beyond the bounds of civilization. The frontier hero is often called upon to make a commitment to the 'civilized' township or community. This made, he tends to ride away into the sunset. Bets are hedged, in other words. The world of the frontier is privileged but the importance of civilization is acknowledged.

*From Dusk Till Dawn* could be read in terms of a version of the negotiation found in the ideal-type western. The preacher with family is the classic representative of 'civilization', travelling in the desert wilderness and across the 'frontier' into Mexico in a mobile home, a modern version of the covered wagon. The brothers, Seth and Ritchie Gecko, are the outlaws. Ritchie (Tarantino) is the one who has gone too far beyond the pale, his unacceptably 'savage' qualities indicated by the unmotivated sexual attack and murder of the innocent bank teller. Further beyond the boundaries of acceptability are the vampire hordes, the truly alien and savage others whose principal role is to be exterminated. Seth (Clooney) is the tough but ultimately decent outlaw put into a situation in which he is forced to make the classic frontiersman's commitment to the values of civilization. The preacher is the disillusioned representative of domesticated civilization who undergoes regeneration (followed, admittedly, by degeneration, undeath and death) through the exercise of violence.[6] The two opposites are brought together, initial contradictions to some extent resolved.

Such negotiations can be identified in other genre patterns. Science fiction often suggests that humanity is threatened by the products of science and technology. It does not usually advocate a total rejection of the latter, however, but a use of science and technology that is kept subordinate to human ends. The protagonists of horror films are often obliged to come to an acceptance of phenomena beyond the rational, but without necessarily abandoning all rationality. The musical and many comedies also work towards reconciliations of their competing dynamics.

What is the significance of this? A socially or culturally based theory of genre might suggest that what is involved is a process in which key issues in the wider society are being negotiated. The oppositions listed above can all be seen as real questions that confront the societies in which these genres have been prominent. Which should be favoured?

The virtues of settled civilization or those of the frontier? Human qualities such as emotion and empathy or the benefits brought by the application of science and technology? Rational thought or an openness to the irrational? Spontaneity and fun or careful organization? None of these questions are easy – if at all possible – to answer in reality. The oppositions are in many respects irreconcilable. Products of popular culture such as Hollywood genre films can be seen as *imaginary* ways of attempting to deal with such difficult issues. An imaginary reconciliation is sometimes offered, a way of appearing to resolve issues that cannot be resolved so easily in the real world. This is, essentially, a structuralist reading of genre, based originally on the work of the social anthropologist Claude Lévi-Strauss.[7]

The function of popular mythology, for Lévi-Strauss, is precisely to bring about such imaginary resolutions of real problems. Genre is seen here as a form of mythology, as one of the products through which a culture works out some of its difficulties through the construction of fictional narratives. This is another way of seeking to explain the pleasures of genre films, or any others that can be read in these terms. To work through and find solutions to difficult social issues is likely to be pleasurable, even when we are not consciously aware of the process. The viewer is given the luxury of 'having it both ways', of appearing to confront but ultimately avoiding some difficult and contentious issues. The pleasure this might produce offers a way of linking this social-cultural dimension to the industrial. The production of pleasure is clearly one of the aims of Hollywood, and this might entail a process of tapping in, at some level, to issues of concern in the broader cultural scene.

The fact that genre frameworks are repeated, sometimes over long periods of time, helps to justify this kind of analysis. It is based, usually, on more than just a few examples of any particular genre. It also suggests that any satisfaction obtained from an individual film might be short-lived and in need of constant reiteration. It is important to note, however, that not all films belonging to the genres cited in this context engage as clearly as others in this process. Large numbers of routine westerns pay little direct attention to the negotiation of oppositions between wilderness and civilization, as Douglas Pye suggests.[8] Culturally or mythologically inclined genre theorists tend to focus on films that fit clearly into particular patterns – often the more prestigious productions associated with 'name' directors such as John Ford, Howard Hawks and Sam Pekinpah – at the expense of others that might not. The relationship between genre patterns and broader social movements is a complex one, as is the relationship more generally between cinema and its social context.

What, then, of genre in the particular contexts of New Hollywood? Does it still perform these kinds of functions, at the industrial or at the social-cultural level? Or has it undergone the kind of mutation found in *From Dusk Till Dawn*? No single answer is readily available. Some major genres have undergone a good deal of change. Some, including the western and the musical in its traditional form, have come close to disappearance. Others have undergone a big-budget rebirth, most notably science fiction and the action film. Genre boundaries have been bent, blurred and deconstructed in some areas, but they have also been maintained elsewhere.

## Genre deconstruction

A prominent feature of some films of the Hollywood Renaissance is a deconstruction of traditional genres, especially the western. The western tradition was built to a large extent on a celebration of what is seen as a defining aspect of American history: the colonial and post-colonial movement of settlement across the continent from east to west. The landscape of successive western frontiers is seen as a key feature shaping the emergence of much that is distinctive in the American character. Hence the attraction of imagining a way of celebrating both sides of the equation: the virtues of both the frontier and of the kind of 'civilized' settlement that came to replace it. If this is a central American myth, it also serves ideological purposes. That is to say, myths of this kind have political implications, serving particular dominant interests, justifying a historical process of colonialism that has implications into the present. Hollywood films tend to buy into dominant myths of this kind, largely because they *are* dominant, widely accepted and so provide a familiar ground on which to build profitable production. The Hollywood

Renaissance witnessed some criticism of dominant myths, for reasons outlined in chapter 1. The western in particular came under assault.

Westerns that question some classical assumptions, such as the nobility of the 'white man' and the savagery of the 'Indian', date further back than the Renaissance period. They are found at least as early as the late 1940s and the 1950s in Hollywood.[9] The older literary figure of the 'noble savage' is found in a distinct Indian-western genre of the 1900s and 1910s.[10] The Renaissance period produced a number of more strident and openly ideological 'anti-westerns', however, films that radically deconstruct conventional formulae. *Little Big Man* (1970) is the quintessential example of irreverent and parodic revisionist genre production in the Hollywood Renaissance. Dominant ideological constructions are inverted. White 'civilization' is exposed as a mixture of hypocrisy, greed, trickery, arrogance, stupidity and murderous violence. Native Americans are presented as eccentric but essentially human, humane and in tune with their environment.

*Little Big Man* is very clearly a product of the Hollywood version of the counterculture, its lineage marked by the presence of Dustin Hoffman as star and Arthur Penn as director. Its vision of the past is marked strongly by the events of its time. Native American culture is valorized and viewed as an alternative to the destructive ways of white colonialism. A parallel is suggested between the indiscriminate killing of Indian women and children by the cavalry and the My Lai massacre in Vietnam, a feature also of *Soldier Blue* (1970). A number of other westerns of the late 1960s and 1970s continue this interrogation of the western, including *McCabe and Mrs Miller* (1971) and *Buffalo Bill and the Indians, or Sitting Bull's History Lesson* (1976), both directed by Robert Altman.

The assault on the western has been such that the genre struggles to exist today other than in a revisionist form that has become close to a new norm for the genre. Native American groups are celebrated or mourned as victims of colonialism in films such as *Dances With Wolves* (1990) and *The Last of the Mohicans* (1992), rather than being represented as alien others against which the 'white man' could be positioned. Many of the westerns made since the Renaissance period claim to provide more 'authentic' versions of the West than those of their predecessors, setting out to debunk earlier myths. *Unforgiven* (1992) exposes one gunfighter as a mean and cowardly figure, his fame the product of imaginative hack-written versions of his exploits.

These films continue to propagate myths of their own, however. In the case of *Unforgiven*, the deconstruction of one gunfighter is followed by the reassertion of the mythic qualities of another, as will be seen in the next chapter. The fate and nature of Native American cultures might be documented a little more accurately in New Hollywood westerns but the way they are represented continues to be a function of contemporary concerns. The Native Americans of *Little Big Man* are represented to a large extent in the image of the counterculture. Those of the 1990s reflect the willingness of some Hollywood players to buy into a degree of popular awareness of the importance of environmental issues. As ever, figures of the Native American are represented less in their own terms than those that reflect issues for the dominant culture.

Westerns continue to be made, but not as a major part of routine Hollywood output. A number of options are available. The western of the 'new sincerity', as it is termed by Jim Collins, makes its claim to worthiness and authenticity.[11] Stars associated with the western, such as Clint Eastwood, can still get westerns off the ground, as can some others: the brat-pack western in *Young Guns* (1988) or other western star vehicles such as Sharon Stone's *The Quick and the Dead* (1995). Or the western can mutate, working with the characteristics of other more commercially mainstream genres such as science fiction, as in *Back to the Future Part III* (1990) and *Wild Wild West* (1999), or the Hong Kong-style action movie in *Shanghai Noon* (2000).

*Little Big Man* offers an illustration of one form of genre deconstruction: that which has a serious political and ideological dimension. It also points towards another option: the genre parody. The familiarity of genre conventions can reach a point at which it is hard to continue to take them seriously. The longer a genre lasts, it seems, the more overtly visible its conventions are likely to become. An extreme might be reached in which the genre film makes direct reference to its own system of conventions, recent examples including the *Scream* series (from 1996 to 2000). Some writers have suggested that genres follow an evolutionary pattern of development along these lines. Genres are seen as going through a series of stages. The initial stage is where the basic conventions are established. This is followed by a 'classical' period, in which key conventions are sufficiently well established and familiar to be used with great expressive economy. The classical period is followed by phases variously described as offering refinement, baroque decadence and increased self-consciousness.[12]

Genres such as the western have often been located in the New Hollywood era in terms of the later, or 'post-classical', stages of this evolutionary process. There are problems with this account, however. Genres are not only shaped by internal processes of development. They owe many of their characteristics at any particular moment to broader social, cultural and industrial factors. It is also questionable that any simple linear development can be identified. Tag Gallagher takes issue with this variant of genre theory, especially as manifested in the influential work of Thomas Schatz.[13]

It is easy, from a distance and without close study, to oversimplify genre films from the past, as Gallagher suggests. We often assume earlier films to have been more straightforward and naïve than those of recent years. This can be an illusion, the product of a lack of detailed familiarity with more than a few examples from the history of a genre. The western is often assumed to have undergone a movement towards growing self-consciousness, uncertainty and ambiguity from the 1950s to the 1970s. But is this true? Gallagher identifies high levels of self-consciousness in westerns produced as far back as the decade before the first world war, the result of the very large numbers of westerns produced in that period.

A western such as *Stagecoach* (1939), often taken as an epitome of the 'classical', would have been received by audiences at the time as 'a virtual anthology of gags, motifs, conventions, scenes, situations, tricks, and characters drawn from past westerns'.[14] Another 'classic' western directed by John Ford, *My Darling Clementine* (1946), is filled with the kind of moral ambiguity taken by some critics to be a distinct product only of later generations.[15] Film history suggests that genres undergo various cycles rather than any linear process of evolution. More questioning or self-conscious versions of genre films can be associated with particular periods, but this is the result of particular contextual factors rather than any automatic or in-built dynamic.

How, then, might we explain the ultra-self-consciousness of the *Scream* films, in which the conventions of the 'slasher' horror film are a constant point of explicit reference? This is clearly not a form of deconstruction designed to unveil the political or ideological implications of the genre. The *Scream* films turn in on themselves, and on 'straight' predecessors such as *Halloween* (1978) and *Friday the 13th* (1980), but only in order to increase the pleasure offered to a youth audience similar to that attracted to the original slasher. New life is breathed into a tired but previously lucrative formula (*Halloween* having generated six sequels and *Friday the 13th* seven by the end of the 1990s, not to mention the number of imitations), which is sufficient explanation from an industrial perspective.

Self-aware films such as the *Scream* series might also be understood in social-cultural terms, as products designed to appeal to the audiences of a media-saturated world in which any point of non-media-literate 'innocence' is impossible to locate. Younger generation audiences of today, the argument goes, have been brought up in a world dominated so heavily by media representations that these have come to form the ground of reality itself, an account often based on the diagnosis of the existence of a distinctly 'postmodern' culture or society. It might not be surprising, in this context, for media conventions to become part of the subject matter of popular media.

The high level of genre self-consciousness does not evacuate all sense of reality in these films, however. It play into debates about the alleged 'effects' of products such as horror films. It can also be read, paradoxically, as an assertion of the 'reality' of the fictional world on-screen. The protagonists watch and talk about the same kinds of movies as the real-world audience. They are thus located more convincingly in the landscape of contemporary teen culture. The fact that the fictional world *includes* that of the slasher films makes it seem more real and complete than the world of the original sub-genre. The *Scream* films, as a series, also come to offer sub-genre pleasures of their own, with their own particular rules and conventions about the exploration of the rules and conventions of the broader slasher genre.

## Genre inflation and reconstruction

Some generic frameworks have been deconstructed in the New

Hollywood era, to varying degrees and some very different effects. Genres have also been reconstructed. The corporate blockbuster is founded to a large extent on genre films, often inflated to larger than previous-life proportions. Science fiction offers one of the clearest examples. Previously the preserve mostly of lower-budget B-movie or exploitation production in Hollywood, science fiction has become a major blockbuster genre, accounting for many of the most lavish and expensive productions of contemporary Hollywood. Action or action-adventure films have undergone a similar inflation of scale, although exotic action-adventure, usually with a historical setting, could also be a source of 'prestige' production in the studio era. These genres sometimes merge into one large and cumbersome category that might be termed science-fiction/action/adventure (usually with a dose of wise-cracking comedy added for good measure). Why should these genres have undergone such a revival? A number of explanations can be suggested.

Genres such as science fiction and action-adventure lend themselves very well to the kind of blockbuster production favoured by the Hollywood studios in recent decades. They provide ample opportunity for large scale spectacular entertainment. The Indiana Jones series (starting with *Raiders of the Lost Ark*, 1981) is a pumped-up version of old Saturday matinee action-adventure pictures. The *Star Wars* films are big-budget treatments of pulp science fiction adventures, modelled especially on *Buck Rogers* (1940). Science fiction as a genre lends itself especially well to the pre-sold characteristics of the blockbuster, many SF films being based on the recycling of existing properties from comic books, television and elsewhere. Particular genres are more suited to the demands of the corporate blockbuster than others.

Genre films as a whole can be appealing in the culture of pre-selling, the very fact of any reasonably clear genre location aiding the process of advance audience recognition that is so important to the economics of contemporary Hollywood. The relative commercial importance of identification by genre labels – in general, rather than for particularly favoured genres – may be reduced somewhat in the New Hollywood context, however. Genre-recognition itself might have been sufficient to help guarantee the moderate success achieved by large numbers of films in the classical era. It is less likely to be sufficient on its own to carry any individual title into the ranks of the fewer bigger hits around which Hollywood economics revolve today.[16]

Industrial factors go a long way to explain the proliferation of inflated versions of old B-movie traditions. These films can also be understood from a social, cultural and political perspective. If the western was to a large extent deconstructed by the end of the Hollywood Renaissance period, it could be argued that B-movie genre-based blockbusters re-established some of its mythic or ideological patterns. Science fiction films can in many cases be read as reinscriptions of key elements of the western in space, 'the final frontier'. Science fiction offers a different set of semantic elements. Spaceships replace men on horseback or railroads. Aliens stand in for 'Indians'. But some of the syntactic relationships, the patterns into which these elements are woven, remain much the same. Space, like the terrestrial frontier, offers a place of action, freedom and escape. The 'exotic' action–adventure sub-genre, including the Indiana Jones films and their numerous clones, provides what might be seen as another surrogate frontier domain: foreign lands filled with distinctly racist portrayals of a range of 'alien' others and a suitable terrain for the heroic adventures of the 'white' man.

Some revealing genre links and connections can be traced across what might first appear to be very different films. One thread with significant ideological implications runs from *The Searchers* (1956) to *Taxi Driver* and *Star Wars*. *The Searchers*, directed by John Ford, has the reputation of a 'classic' western, or more properly a late-classic entry, with its story of the efforts of the obsessive frontiersman Ethan Edwards (John Wayne) to track down a niece kidnapped by Indians. The status of the hero is deeply ambiguous. His aim throughout the film is to find his niece in order to kill her, because she has been 'tainted' by prolonged contact with the Indian. The film obliges the viewer to question a key aspect of the western tradition: the virtue of the frontier hero. Ethan Edwards is, without doubt, a figure of heroic stature, dwarfing all others and displaying a profound knowledge of the ways of the frontier. But he is also an implacable racist.

*Taxi Driver* owes a clear debt to *The Searchers*, a film that can be added to the already lengthy list of influences considered in chapter 1.

The plot of *Taxi Driver* eventually turns into an attempt to rescue a young woman from apparent distress. Iris is to some extent a captive of her pimp, Sport (Harvey Keitel). Explicit acknowledgement of the connection with *The Searchers* is made through Sport's Native American style long hair and headband.[17] Both films play on a longer American literary and mythical tradition, that of the 'captivity narrative', which dates back to purportedly true accounts of the capture of white women by Native Americans in the early colonial period.[18] *Taxi Driver* also follows *The Searchers* in its ambiguous characterization of Travis Bickle.

*Star Wars* also plays into this inheritance, although with a significant difference. The captivity narrative is repeated, this time in the capture of Princess Leia (Carrie Fisher) by the evil forces of the galactic Empire. The main events of the film are set in train by the rescue mission of the young hero Luke Skywalker (Mark Hamill). A link with *The Searchers* is again established quite explicitly. Luke's mind is made up when he returns to find his guardians killed and the family homestead smouldering – images almost identical to the pivotal moment in *The Searchers* in which Ethan confronts the aftermath of the Indian attack that led to the abduction of his niece.

So, what is the relevance of all this? To some extent it is typical of the movie-conscious referencing often found in the films of directors such as Scorsese and Lucas. John Ford, like Hitchcock, is frequently cited and admired by the 'movie brat' generation of film-school educated directors. The implications of the references are very different, however. *Taxi Driver*, as a product of the Hollywood Renaissance, follows closely the spirit of moral ambiguity found in *The Searchers*. *Star Wars* does not. Quite emphatically. Luke Skywalker is no Ethan Edwards or Travis Bickle. He is the stuff of straightforward, innocent and fresh-faced heroics. Even when his precocity leads him into an engagement with his own 'dark side' in *The Empire Strikes Back* (1980), no real doubts are harboured about his essentially clean-cut heroic nature.

This difference makes the *Star Wars* films far more affirmative and celebratory of dominant American myths and ideologies than *The Searchers* or *Taxi Driver*. The values of the frontiersman are questioned in *The Searchers*. *Taxi Driver*, like earlier examples of film noir, presents a world in which even the possibility of a frontier opening – whatever its merits might prove to be – has disappeared from view. Iris talks about moving to a commune in Vermont, a prospect entirely alien to Bickle and not achieved by Iris, who ends up returned to the family from whom she had sought escape. In *Star Wars*, though, there is a 'high' frontier onto which Luke Skywalker can move. It offers the escape for which he yearns from the quotidian life of a farmer; the possibility of action, heroics, triumph and romance. And all this was offered by George Lucas, apparently, with some conscious intention of delivering a renewed sense of optimistic mythology in the wake of darker products such as his own *THX 1138*. The B-movie genre-based blockbusters of the mid-1970s onwards are generally more conservative in their political implications than the genre deconstructions associated with the Hollywood Renaissance. This is a function partly of the industrial requirement for feel-good affirmation if huge audiences are to be attracted. It can also be understood in terms of the more general shift to the right in the dominant American culture and politics from the later 1970s.

## Genre bending, blending, blurring

A high-school romance. A teen coming-of-age movie. A science fiction special effects spectacular. Distinct elements of graphic horror. Combat movie conventions. Satire. And the obligatory slice of relocated western. All this in just one film, *Starship Troopers* (1997). No wonder genre boundaries are sometimes said to have come undone in the New Hollywood era. The bending, blending and blurring of genre is another feature that can be explained from more than one perspective. Industrial factors, as ever, play an important part. Different genres tend to appeal – or are assumed to appeal – to different sections of the audience. Science fiction, action, horror and war films are usually assumed to appeal primarily to male viewers. Romance, melodrama and costume pictures tend to appeal to women. These are not absolutes, of course. Plenty of women enjoy science fiction, horror or war films. Some males like romance, melodrama or costume films. On the whole, though, these assumptions appear to have some grounding in the preferences of

7. Coming at you from every generic direction: horror, sci-fi, combat movie and defending the 'western' fort in *Starship Troopers*, © Touchstone Pictures and TriStar Pictures, 1997. Ronald Grant archive

real viewers. Even if this is not the case, they are assumptions made by the industry that go a long way to shape the kinds of films that get made.

Likes and dislikes also vary within gender boundaries. So, if science fiction, horror and war movies are considered more likely to appeal to men than women, some males might prefer one to the others. A mixture of genre conventions is a way of trying to appeal to range of potential audience constituencies, a key requirement of contemporary blockbuster production. Gender is a major element but not the only one. The makeup of *Starship Troopers* can be understood in these terms. Male-oriented genre components (science fiction, horror, war) are combined with more female-oriented elements (romance, coming-of-age melo-dramatic tensions). There is also plenty of room for different sub-groups to find different elements of appeal within and across these categories. Some might be attracted to and enjoy the film on the basis of the pleasures of large-scale action adventure and spectacle. Others might prefer the satirical edge, or the combination of the two. The genre mixture found in *From Dusk Till Dawn* does not cross conventional assumptions about genre-gender boundaries. It remains within two areas likely to be of primary appeal to male viewers not averse to large quantities of violence, more and less 'realistic'.

Studio strategies in seeking to attract audiences in these ways have undergone significant change in the New Hollywood period. The dominant genres of the contemporary blockbuster tend to be strongly male-oriented. This is rather different from earlier phases of Hollywood production, in which women appeared to be much better served. A general assumption of the classical Hollywood era was that women played an equal if not dominant role in the choices of films seen by viewers. Films targeted at women enjoyed considerable prominence as a result. As late as the 1960s, blockbuster production was targeted to a large extent at women. Remember the list of some of the most attended films of all time cited in chapter 2? First and third places are held by *Gone with the Wind* and *The Sound of Music*: distinctly women-oriented productions.

Hollywood's assumptions have altered. Since the late 1960s male audiences have been targeted far more heavily, especially relatively young males, in their teens and twenties.[19] The audience for Hollywood films became distinctly younger as a result of the post-war baby boom and competition for more mature audiences from domestic and other leisure pursuits. Male viewers have been assumed to have greater dominance in this younger age bracket. The development of the ratings system, and industrial strategies based partly on exploiting the ability of the cinema to depict sex and violence unavailable in domestic media, is another factor that has worked against the interests of women. Numerous industry surveys have shown women to dislike high levels of sex and violence.[20] Whatever the reasons, the more male-oriented genres have flourished in recent decades. This provides another explanation for the prominence of science fiction and the action film in the contemporary blockbuster economy.

Films that mix genre components do not always do so very equally. *Starship Troopers* introduces 'women-oriented' elements but remains dominated by the conventions of science fiction, horror and the combat movie, even if women are also given prominent roles in these dimensions. *Titanic* is a notable exception. Its component of traditional

Hollywood romance more than holds its own against a wealth of special-effects spectacle. The film's appeal to women was credited with much of its enormous box-office success, especially through repeat visits by younger women enthusiasts. Signs of a shift in blockbuster production towards a more women-friendly approach were subsequently identified by some industry commentators, although the extent to which this is likely to be taken remains uncertain.

The bending, blending or blurring of genre conventions can also be approached from the perspective of social-cultural background. It might be seen to reflect the same social context as the playfully self-conscious version of genre deconstruction considered earlier in this chapter. A similar argument would apply: contemporary audiences are media-literate, highly aware of genre conventions and as a result receptive to a playful crossing of genre boundaries. The mixing of genre elements in Hollywood can be understood in terms of a 'postmodern' tendency to blur boundaries between different genres as part of a broader process of deconstructing older and more rigid cultural forms. Some caution is needed here, however. Accounts of the 'postmodern' character of contemporary western societies remain subject to much critical debate. The extent to which they can be applied to Hollywood films is far from clear.[21]

Complications arise even in the specific case of genre. It is easy to get carried away by the notion that previously solid genre frameworks have come apart and/or been recombined in all sorts of weird and wonderful ways in a postmodern New Hollywood era. Particular changes have occurred, for particular reasons. But two major qualifications need to be made if over-simplification is to be avoided. Many films still fit quite clearly into reasonably straightforward and long-standing genre frameworks. And if genres have been mixed up and recombined in some cases, a broader historical perspective suggests that this is far from new.

## Genre continuities and complexities

The 'ordinary' genre film, if we can call it that, still plays a significant role in New Hollywood, even if it is lost from sight on occasion. It may be one victim of the way this book is organized, initially, around two contrasting versions of New Hollywood. The most striking changes in the use of genre frameworks have occurred under the auspices of those two versions: the Hollywood Renaissance, with its element of radical critique and formal experimentation, and the corporate blockbuster, with its hyperbolic inflation of some genres and audience-maximizing mixture of others. The ordinary genre film, like the modest and run-of-the-mill Hollywood movie more generally, can become lost between the two extremes. This is partly what has happened in Hollywood itself. Fewer medium sized films are made and/or given significant distribution as a result of the industrial changes documented in chapters 1 and 2. Hollywood often appears somewhat polarized, between the ultra-high-budget blockbuster and lower-budget and more off-beat independent or semi-independent production. There is still a middle, however, and it is to a large extent occupied by solid genre productions, along (and often overlapping) with the solid middle-ranking star vehicle, a subject to be considered in the next chapter.

A glance through the lists of Hollywood films on offer week by week will reveal plenty of films of this kind. Romantic comedy is one example of a genre that continues to thrive relatively unchanged from the classical era, despite over-hasty predictions of its imminent demise during the 1970s.[22] A film such as *You've Got Mail* (1998) deploys much the same conventions as the film of which it is a remake, *The Shop Around the Corner* (1940), and many other romantic comedies of the classical era. Two characters of apparently opposite and hostile credentials eventually come together. The distinct qualities for which each stands are magically reconciled and wished away in the process. Textbook genre stuff; expectations entirely fulfilled. Romantic comedies of this kind continue to thrive in the New Hollywood climate. They offer familiar genre pleasures for audiences, relatively stable sources of profit for the studios and more than enough scope for readings of their social and ideological implications (in the case of *You've Got Mail*, the establishment of an opposition between the needs of small and large scale business that is entirely evaded in the climactic reunion: a classic case of the magical reconciliation of real and largely irreconcilable political-economic issues). Some contemporary romantic comedies position themselves as more 'knowing' than those of the 1930s or 1940s, seeking to distance themselves to some extent from the central myth of romantic love, often through self-conscious gestures towards its absurdity. The format is not usually subverted however; the process is one that allows a gesture towards greater cultural verisimilitude while enabling the principal fantasy to be maintained.[23]

If some genre frameworks remain relatively stable in New Hollywood, others prove to have been a good deal less so in the classical era than they might appear today. Discussions of genre destabilization in New Hollywood easily fall prey to the failing we encountered earlier in this chapter: a myopic view that misses the complexities of earlier generations of genre production. Genre hybridity is sometimes viewed as a distinct characteristic of New Hollywood. But it is not. Many of what are later recognized as single, stable genres go through a process of what appears initially to be quite complex genre combination. As Rick Altman suggests: 'This process is typically forgotten for genres created in the past, leaving us with what seems like an uncomplicated genre identified by a single name.'[24] What at one point appears to be a multi-genre brew might at some later date crystallize into a distinct new genre of its own. Genre hybridity was just as common in the 1930s as in the 1980s, Steve Neale concludes from an examination of the terms in which a substantial number of films were reviewed in *Variety* from 1934 and 1984.[25]

To demonstrate that genre identity and stability has never been guaranteed is not to reduce Hollywood's use of genre to a single unchanging phenomenon. Blendings and blurrings of generic elements today can be explained with reference to particular characteristics of the industrial and social contexts of the New Hollywood period. It is important to identify these, to understand what is specific to the workings of New Hollywood. The point is to avoid oversimplification. Some aspects of genre in New Hollywood can be related to relatively recent phenomena. Others need to be understood in a longer context that includes important continuities with the way genre has always operated in Hollywood. A broader view shows genre to be a complex phenomenon.

The closer we look at individual genres and their histories, the less straightforward they become. They are not self-defining, according to the mere existence of a body of 'similar' films, as was suggested in the 'simple' definition given at the start of this chapter. Genre definitions and boundaries are moveable, depending to a large extent on the perspective of those doing the defining. Genres can also be defined in a range of different ways, according to different kinds of criteria. Some are defined according to subject matter: the western, science fiction, the biopic. Others are defined according to the response they are intended to provoke: horror, comedy, the weepie. There is no single essence of what constitutes a genre. Genre labels are flags of convenience more than markers of entirely distinct territories. Hollywood films as a whole draw upon and recombine a variety of narrative components, devices and modes of presentation that range across a number of generic territories. Basic building blocks such as melodrama, action, spectacle, romance and comedy are assembled and reassembled to create structures that may not best be defined primarily in terms of distinct genre boundaries.

Many now-familiar genre frameworks have been the creation of critics and theorists more than the industry or viewers. Film noir is a frequently cited case, a genre initially defined in retrospect by French critics confronted in the immediate post-war years by a group of Hollywood films that might not otherwise have been lumped together.[26] Genres defined in such arbitrary ways can gain a life of their own, however, as the basis of future production and/or subsequent classification, as in the revival of elements of film noir in the 1970s or the creation of the science-fiction sub-genre 'tech-noir' in the 1980s and 1990s. The Hollywood studios themselves 'generally avoid identifying a film with a single unadulterated generic label', Altman suggests, because they do not want to limit its potential appeal.[27] They have always tended to sell a mixture of generic elements designed to attract different components of the potential audience.

A blend of romance and adventure has been offered as a cross-gender mixture throughout the history of Hollywood, from *Casablanca* (1942) to *Titanic*. Hollywood production follows a pattern of recombining various elements of recent successes, a process that often does not follow clearly marked genre lines.[28] Critics, theorists and publishers of film books have a much greater vested interest than the industry in the process of explicit genre labelling and boundary demarcation. Different groups of viewers are also liable to categorize films differently, according to varying aspects that might be of most immediate relevance to the viewers involved. Localized genres can be recognized, and hence constituted, by the activities of fan-groups, an example cited by Altman being the 'railroad genre' sustained by specialist magazines and model railway clubs.[29]

The genre location of particular films is often less clear cut at the time than it seems with the benefit of hindsight. Take, for example, *Deep Impact* and *Armageddon*, two films from the summer of 1998. What genre do these films belong to? Both are about asteroids or comets threatening earthly destruction. They might constitute a brief cycle of their own, especially if we add two other films along the same lines that were being planned at the same time but never came to fruition. From a broader perspective, they could be seen as disaster movies, part of a pre-millennial cycle in the 1990s including the volcano films *Dante's Peak* (1997) and *Volcano* (1997), the monster movie *Godzilla* (1998), the science fiction blockbuster *Independence Day* (1996) and a number of others.[30] But each of these 'disaster' movies is also subject to the gravitational pull of other genre and sub-genre identities: asteroid movie, volcano movie, monster movie, alien-threat science fiction. *Deep Impact* and *Armageddon* contain elements of science fiction and the disaster movie. They are both 'summer blockbuster' type films and have in common other characteristics of the big, glossy 'Hollywood movie'. They have much in common. But they can also be separated, again, on other lines of genre or mode of presentation. *Armageddon* is a noisy action movie. *Deep Impact* puts the emphasis on emotional and tear-jerking melodrama. How these films will be labelled in the future remains to be seen. What they illustrate is the way Hollywood films often possess multiple and overlapping identities rather than fitting neatly into single and unambiguous categories.

Major studios might also avoid an encouragement of identification on the basis of genre, Altman suggests, because genres are too freely available to be claimed as distinctive and controllable properties. What is often emphasized instead is 'the particular surplus that the studio brings to the genre.'[31] Each studio has its own exclusive or semi-exclusive access to particular stars, major directors, franchises and proprietary characters. 'By stressing these restricted qualities in the publicity for each film, a studio automatically develops a pre-sold audience for the next film featuring the same in-house star, character or look... Following this logic, Hollywood regularly eschews genre logic for production and publicity decisions, in favour of series, cycles, remakes and sequels.'[32] Individual studios often prefer to highlight the presence of their own legally restricted brand-name or franchise products. Genres can be created or reinforced, Altman argues, as competitors seek to cash in on the success of such products, translating them into broader generic terms to which no one has rights of ownership.

Complications and qualifications such as these have implications for socio-cultural theories of genre. As Steve Neale suggests, genres are not the 'closed and continuous' categories identified by Thomas Schatz, a major proponent of the genre-as-mythology approach.[33] This does not mean genres cannot have significant mythological or ideological dimensions, just that these are likely to be complex, multifaceted and far from easy to pin down with any certainty.[34] Individual films or cycles might be read in terms of a number of overlapping social issues. Engagements with particular issues might also be found across a range of films with different genre backgrounds.[35] Social theories of genre are usually justified on the grounds of the longevity and popularity of particular genres. Many genres, sub-genres or cycles are more temporary, however. The equation between popularity and social meaning also requires qualification. Film types are popular for many different reasons. The extent to which they play into major social issues is one factor, but not the only one.[36] Understood in these ways, genre remains an important but often rather hazy feature of the way films work at the levels of both production and consumption. It is significant, but only as one of a number of competing and sometimes overlapping dimensions of Hollywood cinema.

This chapter started with an exploration of the genre identity of *From Dusk Till Dawn*, a film that might just as readily have been approached from an auteurist perspective. Yes, the first half of the film can be seen as a manifestation of a particular brand of nineties thriller. It took a number of different formulations to pin down its characteristics in genre terms, however. Asked to supply a label for this sub-genre, many viewers – both fans and critics – might come up with a notion of the 'Tarantino-esque'. The film not only features Quentin Tarantino in the cast, but is from a Tarantino script and very much in keeping with the style and mood of the cult status Tarantino-written and directed hits *Reservoir Dogs* (1992, a commercial success primarily on video rather than in the cinema) and *Pulp Fiction* (1994), in each of which Tarantino also appears.

What starts as the signature of an individual filmmaker can easily spread out into something closer to cyclical, quasi-generic or sub-genre status. There are Hitchcock films, for example, and many more that might be described as 'Hitchcockian' thrillers. The same is true of Tarantino, if in a shorter time-span. Commercially successful 'auteurist' formulas are as liable to repetition as any others. The web of the 'Tarantino-esque' is also spread by the fact that Tarantino has himself been involved in screenplays for films he has not directed, including *True Romance* (1993) and *Natural Born Killers* (1994), films that vary in the extent to which they are said to carry the 'Tarantino' mark (Tarantino sought to disassociate himself from the latter). Tarantino did not direct *From Dusk Till Dawn*, however. Another chain of associations can be established through the presence of the director, Robert Rodriguez, a noted creator of explosive low-budget south-of-the-border action films. If the first half of *From Dusk Till Dawn* is a manifestation of the world of Tarantino, the fetishistically extended shoot-out scenes of the remainder carry the distinctive mark of Rodriguez, including more than one direct reference to his previous film, *Desperado* (1995).

Hollywood movies frequently offer multiple points of identification and expectation, to increase their potential appeal and the grounds on which they can be sold to audiences. Genre associations are often more widespread than those of the 'auteur', largely because they are more easily sustained in most cases in the highly industrialized context of Hollywood. It was for this reason that genre theory developed from the mid-1960s to the mid-1970s, as a challenge to the previously dominant theoretical focus on auteurism. Genres and cycles can spread out from the individual filmmaker, all the better to exploit short or longer-term trends. *From Dusk Till Dawn* might also be read – and sold

– from another perspective. It could be seen as a George Clooney vehicle, an opportunity to cash in on the matinee-idol looks of one of the then stars of the hit television series *ER*. Stardom is another competing but also potentially complementary basis on which to sell such a film, establishing its own industrial parameters and sets of expectations and associations.

# 5

# Star Power

A star's participation in a project can induce otherwise ambivalent executives to green-light it. With a superstar in tow, they are willing to tackle risky projects, feeling invincible in their company. Until that illusion crumbles under repeated flops, the superstar remains a highly desired commodity.

Mark Litwak[1]

Beliefs or concepts of identity are intangible things. Stars are significant for how they make such elusive and metaphysical notions into a visible show.

Paul McDonald[2]

Why might we have faith in the character played by George Clooney in *From Dusk Till Dawn*? Partly a matter of script and convention. Seth Gecko is mean and threatening, not mincing his words with potential victims. But the film is quick to establish an opposition between Seth and his utterly crazed trigger–happy brother Ricky (Quentin Tarantino). The broadest of Hollywood conventions provide insurance against the likelihood of being presented with *two* entirely unstable central figures. Both are desperadoes, but the qualities of one brother go some way towards balancing those of the other. Our expectations of Seth are also shaped very powerfully from another dimension: the fact that he *is* played by Clooney.

George Clooney is a star who brings particular associations of his own to the part. These are played against to a significant extent, just as the film plays around with expectations on the level of genre. Clooney's star image at the time was rooted in his television role as Dr Ross in *ER* (from 1994): a sometimes prickly, awkward, rebellious, womanizing but essentially decent and caring paediatrician; a figure prepared to break the rules in his commitment to the treatment of children.[3] Seth Gecko is very different. Not as dangerous as his brother, but a nasty piece of work all the same. His threats are cold and menacing, especially near the start. This verges on a breach of the character-balancing convention suggested above. *From Dusk Till Dawn* can get away with this partly because its own sub-genre or auteurist associations allow for a harsher edge than is usual in Hollywood. But also because of the reassuring presence of Clooney.

Clooney plays against type to a large extent in *From Dusk Till Dawn*, but this cuts both ways. Some Clooney fans might be upset by his portrayal of so unpleasant-seeming a figure. For the performer such a role might be appealing precisely as a way to escape typecast assumptions. These images are not easily eroded, however. More familiar Clooney associations continue to resonate beneath the surface of Seth Gecko. The film invites us to question the degree to which he can be trusted when, for example, he tells kidnap victims they will not be harmed if they cooperate. Exactly how individual members of the audience process such material is not easy, if at all possible, to quantify. Star-image associations are a major factor in the equation, however, in this case likely to contribute to the extent to which Seth might be given the benefit of the doubt. The genre shift discussed in the previous chapter also plays an important part in confirming the more positive qualities of the character. It enables Seth to be established as a force for good rather than evil, his worldly crimes being put into perspective, and his violent capabilities proving useful, in the larger battle between light and dark. A breach of genre conventions is meliorated in this case by a movement towards the restoration, to some extent, of more familiar star-image associations. *From Dusk Till Dawn* provides an illustration of the complex interactions that sometimes occur between dimensions such as genre and stardom.

Clooney is not the only star figure whose presence impacts on the way the film is likely to be read, especially in terms of the expectations encouraged during the opening scenes. The fact that the preacher Jacob

Fuller is played by Harvey Keitel brings its own associations. Genre and star expectations combine here as well. Generic expectations, and those of Hollywood movies more generally, might encourage us to expect something more than the glum pacifist to whom we are initially introduced. Clash-of-opposites films usually result in opposed figures coming closer together, the associations of 'Harvey Keitel' including a history of tough and implacable figures of the kind Jacob Fuller is destined to become. The same might be said of the character played by Juliet Lewis, Fuller's daughter Kate. A fresh-faced and innocent teenager, yes, but with Lewis bringing associations such as her gun-toting role in *Natural Born Killers* (1994).

A series of likely trajectories-of-expectation are plotted by the presence of these recognizable star figures. Various possibilities are created for the filmmaker. Expectations can be met or frustrated, depending on the effect desired. Hollywood movies generally tend to meet more expectations that they frustrate, for commercial reasons. The confirmation of pre-existing assumptions is probably a more reliable source of the kind of pleasure likely to generate mass-market profits at the box office; or, at the very least, it is likely to be seen that way by the studios. Tensions can occur between the wishes of stars to experiment with roles different from those with which they are most strongly associated and the desires of studios to continue to mobilize existing expectations. The commercial failure of some star vehicles has been blamed on audience rejection of attempts by stars to broaden their range (the movement of Sylvester Stallone or Bruce Willis into comedy, for example), a process perceived as a disappointment of expectations. *From Dusk Till Dawn* plays most of the characters in the direction of likely dominant expectations, a necessary hedge, perhaps, against its disruption of genre.

To complicate matters further, auteurism also comes into this star-image equation. Both Keitel and Lewis can be fitted into associations from the distinctive world of Quentin Tarantino (Keitel as a result of his role as the super-cool and dependable fixer in *Pulp Fiction*, Lewis from *Natural Born Killers*). And then there is Ritchie, played by Tarantino himself, a literal embodiment of aspects of the 'Tarantino-esque', in his attire (black suit, white shirt, tie), his quirky-crazy outlook on life and his predilection for sudden outbursts of under-motivated violence. Complex webs of associations can build up in this manner, ranging across and mixing elements of authorship, genre and stardom.

## Star persona

Stars, almost by definition, exceed the boundaries of the fictional characters they play. To be a star is to be recognized within and beyond any specific role. George Clooney remains George Clooney, whether he is also Seth Gecko, Jack Foley (*Out of Sight*, 1998), Archie Gates (*Three Kings*, 1999) or even Batman (*Batman and Robin*, 1997). Clint Eastwood is *always* Clint, whether playing according to type in numerous western and police-thriller roles, or playing against in light comedy (*Every Which Way But Loose*, 1978) or romance (*The Bridges of Madison County*, 1995). The way star images are created, and consumed, can be understood through the distinction made by Barry King between forms of performance based on 'impersonation' and 'personification'.[4]

Impersonation is used by King to suggest qualities that some might term 'proper acting'. Impersonation involves the disappearance of the 'real' personality of the performer into the part. 'Proper' actors, especially those brought up in the traditions of legitimate theatre, are taught largely to efface themselves, to take on the characteristics of the part to be played, even if this might include drawing on personal emotional experience. Personification is the opposite. It involves the cultivation of the persona of the performer. Distinct individual traits are not masked or subordinated to the requirements of the individual part but played up, recognizably, from one performance to another. The star persona is the product of a number of performances, but also cultivated off-screen, in press and publicity materials, interviews and other appearances. The persona is not necessarily any closer to the 'real' individual than any other acts of impersonation. It might be just as much a fiction and performance. Through repetition, though, it comes to be associated with the individual rather than just a series of separate roles.

Personification tends to be looked down upon, or seen simply as 'poor acting'. Oscars for best performances usually go to those deemed

capable of impersonation. Prominent names associated with impersonation in New Hollywood include Robert DeNiro and Meryl Streep,
performers who have demonstrated an ability to transform themselves
to fit their parts. DeNiro, most famously, altered his entire body shape
and musculature to take on the roles of both championship-shape boxer
and corpulent has-been in *Raging Bull* (1980). Streep has been lauded
for capturing the 'realistic' texture of prickly real-life characters such as
Karen Silkwood (*Silkwood*, 1983) and Lindy Chamberlain (*A Cry in the
Dark*, 1988). DeNiro and Streep are also stars, however, and it is not
clear that the distinction between impersonation and personification
always stands up entirely. Stars such as these are famous precisely for
their ability to give virtuoso performances that amount to something
close to 'doing a DeNiro' or a 'Streep' routine. The very act of such
impersonation can become a spectacle in its own right, associated as
much with the image of the star-as-impersonator/performer as with
the character-role. Christine Geraghty suggests a useful additional
distinction between stars-as-performers, in cases such as this, stars-as-
celebrities (famous for 'being themselves', off-screen as much as or more
than on) and stars-as-professionals (known for acting 'as themselves', a
variety of personification rooted primarily in the on-screen performance).[5]

Most major stars rely heavily on personification of one kind or
another. For good reasons. Most probably do not have the acting skills
of a DeNiro or a Streep. It also makes strategic sense for the individual
performer. Actors are heavily oversupplied in Hollywood, more so
than any other part of the labour force. The vast majority are usually
out of work. Of those in work, the top names receive vastly larger
payments.[6] In this environment, as King suggests, it is in the performer's
interest to seek to emphasize unique individual qualities. Any number
of performers can 'act', in the sense of giving an acceptable impersonation of one character or another. Competition is intense and there is
no guarantee that successful impersonation in one role will lead to
another. The development of a persona has two major advantages. It is
repeatable, if successful: the whole point is to do something very like
the same thing more than once. It is also the distinct property of the
performer, based on his or her own particular image and/or actual

physical or personal characteristics. Personification is a way for stars to turn themselves into profitable commodities with unique selling points, individual brand images.

The cultivation of branded images also makes sense for a studio or the industry as a whole. The principal outlines of star-images become known and familiar to viewers. They offer sets of expectations upon which films often play, in a manner that resembles the working of genre and auteur associations. Star images often perform a more important part than any other single factor in the selling of Hollywood movies. Their particular significance in the industrial regime of the New Hollywood era will be considered in the next section of this chapter. As far as the moment-by-moment experience of films is concerned, star and star-associations are often likely to be to the fore in the process of expectation and interpretation. The extent to which star-associations are in operation in any individual case (like those of genre or auteur) is liable to vary from one viewer to another. Some will be highly attuned, aware of both the general outline of a star persona and of various nuances and departures from one role to another. Others might have little or no familiarity. Most are likely to be situated somewhere in between. The presence of George Clooney is an important ingredient in the star-genre-auteur mixture of *From Dusk Till Dawn*. How strongly it figures in the overall equation depends on a number of factors, including familiarity with Clooney, Tarantino, Rodriguez and the relevant genre conventions.

If the Clooney persona offers additional guarantees of 'decency' at the heart of the violent and genre-transgressive *From Dusk Till Dawn*, it offers a number of related assurances in his other films. A 'softer' and 'safer' version is found in *Out of Sight*. Clooney's character, Jack Foley, is a serial bank-robber who escapes from prison and embarks on an interrupted romance with federal Marshall Karen Sisco (Jennifer Lopez). The relationship starts with Foley kidnapping Sisco after a jailbreak. He forces her to join him in the boot of her car. Ostensibly, she is under threat, the prisoner of an armed convict. Star associations assure the viewer this is not really the case. *From Dusk Till Dawn* might have generated a harsher component in the Clooney image; Seth Gecko is also an escaped bank robber, we might recall; and a hostage locked in the boot of a car meets a dire fate in that film, even if not at the hands of Seth himself. Even for the viewer coming to *Out of Sight* from *From Dusk Till Dawn*, however, it is unlikely that such factors will override the dominant Clooney associations, especially given the extent to which they are still mobilized in the latter.

The opening scene of *Out of Sight* establishes Foley very clearly as a witty and charming crook, his style of robbery relying on bluff and guile rather than any real menace. Very much the territory of the Clooney persona established in *ER*. That Foley immediately attempts to woo his prisoner comes as no surprise at all. It might not be what we are encouraged to expect in an escaped-prisoner thriller, but it is precisely in accordance with the Clooney associations around which the character has already been worked. Star and genre associations operate in tandem again, as in *From Dusk Till Dawn*, although in this case in a more straightforward process of mutual reinforcement.

*Out of Sight* is billed as a romantic comedy-thriller. The tagline 'Opposites Attract' establishes the central dynamic, a familiar recon- ciliatory trope of romantic comedy. This alone is sufficient to assure us of Sisco's safety. How the scenario of Foley and Sisco in the boot of the car is likely to turn out is overdetermined in a manner typical of Hollywood narrative: conventions of both star-image and genre combine to establish a fairly clear trajectory of expectation. The plot of *Out of Sight* is predicated on an 'unlikely' romance and one that is subject to constant interruption: the couple meet only occasionally throughout the film. The fact that the male lead is played by a performer heavily associated with romance – in terms of both the persona's public history, primarily as Dr Ross, and the presumed yearning of many female fans – joins with the conventions of romantic comedy to underwrite the expectation that the romance will be sustained.

The film plays both with and against these expectations, ending with a recaptured Foley being driven by Sisco from Detroit back to prison in Florida: an ending that leaves open the possibility that 'something' further might yet happen on the way. The fundamental premise of the film, without which it makes little sense, is that George Clooney (more than Jack Foley) is irresistible to women. That Sisco must fall for Clooney's character, even if in a relatively complex manner, seem structurally inevitable, her position being rooted in assumptions about the likely response of many potential women viewers.

Towards the end of *Out of Sight*, Clooney's Jack Foley, along with his partner Buddy (Ving Rhames), is in a position to escape with the loot around which the main crime plots revolves: a multi-million dollar haul of uncut diamonds. In *Three Kings*, Clooney's character, Archie Gates, is presented with a similar cornucopia. He and three fellow post-Gulf War American soldiers can get away with a fortune in Kuwaiti gold bullion liberated from the Iraqis. Both times, the Clooney character turns his back on riches. Instead, both times, he does the 'decent' thing. In *Out of Sight*, he goes back inside the mansion from which the diamonds have been taken to prevent the likely rape-murder of a maid and the murder of the owner. Foley, like Seth Gecko, is a crook with morals: he knows where to draw the line. In *Three Kings*, Gates turns over the gold to the American authorities in order to allow a group of Iraqi dissidents and their families to escape across the border. Seth Gecko also does the 'decent' thing at the end of *From Dusk Till Dawn*, spurning the opportunity to take with him the rather too young Kate Fuller ('I may be a bastard but I'm not a fucking bastard'): the eminently decent, if sometimes hot-headed persona associated with the paediatrician from *ER* could hardly do otherwise.

It might be argued that *any* leading Hollywood male would be similarly constrained. Hollywood heroes are rarely compromised, fundamentally, at the level of morals: that is about as firm a convention of mainstream Hollywood narrative as any. As we have seen in other respects, however, the expectations we are encouraged to bring to Hollywood movies are often overdetermined. Most Hollywood heroes are morally clean-cut, ultimately, however much they might flirt with darker sides on the way. Particular star associations can work to reinforce this. They might be especially effective in films that otherwise risk some departure from the norm. Thus, the value of Clooney's presence as an insurance policy for the initially menacing Seth Gecko.

In *Three Kings*, Clooney's presence might help to anchor another potentially unsettling set of generic and stylistic ingredients. *Three Kings* is an action-adventure romp, a caper film and a war (or post-war) movie. It is also strongly melodramatic at times, especially when invoking the suffering of Iraqi dissident families. This, in turn, leads it in the direction of political controversy, an indictment of Bush-era policy in the region. The film also changes its look more than once, switching between different stocks. Much is shot in grainy textures unusual in the commercial mainstream. Wide angle lenses are also used, in disorienting combination with highly mobile camera-work.

On various levels, *Three Kings* shifts tone quite radically, and potentially uncomfortably, for the viewer. This is a risky strategy in Hollywood terms. *Three Kings* mixes mood and elements of genre without the ultimately consistent 'it's-all-comic-book-fun-anyway' escape clause available to *From Dusk Till Dawn*. The Clooney persona provides a relatively stable set of associations at the heart of this cocktail. It is, perhaps, inevitable anyway that the film will have a soft-hearted conclusion, enabling the emotional release provided by the escaping refugees largely to predominate at the end over the more disturbing issues confronted by the film. The presence of Clooney makes such an outcome seem more likely, however, and the bulk of the film less potentially discomforting than might otherwise be the case. His performance is somewhat blank. A disadvantage in some respects, evidence perhaps of limited range, especially when considered in terms of impersonation. In this case, though, a degree of blankness serves quite effectively. Clooney does not seem to 'do' very much with the performance, merely to 'be': and just 'being' Clooney might be sufficient in this context.

Star images and associations are key elements in the range of devices and mechanisms with which we negotiate a way through Hollywood films. They tell us, very often, what to expect from characters. They anticipate narrative developments, effectively becoming part of the narrative infrastructure. Seth Gecko never quite 'becomes' the fully-realized 'George Clooney, the nice-but-unconventional doctor from *ER*'. But he is never entirely separate from that figure, either, except in the experience of viewers who have never seen or heard of that dominant character-association. It is not unusual for characters played by stars to become 'more like' the star persona as a film unfolds. This is the case with a number of films starring Jane Fonda in the decade from 1970 (including *A Doll's House*, 1973, *Julia*, 1977, *Coming Home*, 1978,

*The China Syndrome*, 1979, *The Electric Horseman*, 1979, and *Nine to Five*, 1980): 'In the course of the film the character usually changes and moves closer to the Jane Fonda star-image of an enlightened, independent, radical women.'[7] The 'narrative satisfactions' offered by these films, as Tessa Perkins puts it, 'are bound up with the character becoming more like "Jane Fonda"; being radicalised.'[8] One major source of pleasure, in popular entertainment, is generated through the development and satisfaction of expectations. Another example of this process is found in the Clint Eastwood western *Unforgiven* (1992).

William Munny. Face down in pig manure. A farmer, who does not appear very competent even at this 'lowly' occupation. A widower with two children to look after. A past, we are told, as a feared gunman. Invited to a bounty hunt with an arrogant youngster. Preparations. Out with his pistol. But he cannot shoot straight. Tries to mount his horse, but is thrown. Humiliation all round. But it will not last. His fortune will change, and we know it. We know it absolutely for certain. Why? Because, of course, William Munny is played by Clint Eastwood, a star who comes with very strong associations and expectations. Eastwood's William Munny at the start of *Unforgiven* is not simply a figure incompetent in the key skills of the western hero: marksmanship and horsemanship. He is a quivering bundle of latency. The viewer familiar with the Eastwood persona – shaped, principally, by his performances in spaghetti westerns, the Dirty Harry series and subsequent westerns and crime-thrillers – is strongly conditioned to expect a reversion to type.

Much of the dramatic tension structured into *Unforgiven* is invested in this expectation (broader Hollywood narrative expectations about the fate of the central character are also in play, of course, but so strong are the Eastwood associations that they are likely to carry the greatest weight, or at least to be most explicitly in play). Munny suffers a number of reverses, beaten almost to death at one point. The distance the character can be allowed to fall from the action-heroic ideal is measured by the strength of the star-image-related assumption that he will, must, eventually prevail. And so he does, in a climactic shoot-out (or massacre) in which Munny achieves the kind of mythic embittered 'superman' qualities with which Eastwood is often associated. The power of this

8. Latent star potential: Clint Eastwood as William Munny, in the mire, at the start of *Unforgiven*, © Warner Bros., 1992. Ronald Grant archive

finale comes to a large extent from delayed realization of prior expectations.

A very different film could be imagined without Eastwood in the lead role.⁹ *Unforgiven* might have been a film throughout which we would *really* doubt the capabilities of the hero. Real questions could be raised about his ability to win the day. The heroic myth surrounding Munny could have been subjected to critical examination, as are some others in the film. The presence of Eastwood changes all this. It would still be possible to play against expectations, to deny the cathartic ending. The expectations would still dominate the bulk of the film, however, and it would be a bold move to undermine so central a feature of the emotional investment and pleasure offered by the film. Stars help to shape our experiences as viewers. They are also crucial from an industrial perspective.

## Marquee value

How does a film like *Three Kings* come to be financed, made, given mainstream distribution? A number of factors come into play. The genre-type associations are positive: the promise of action and adventure, with a twist of both politics and comedy, plus the novelty of a setting in post-war Iraq. An interesting, relatively new screenwriter/director, David O. Russell, who established a reputation for the commercial-offbeat in *Spanking the Monkey* (1994) and *Flirting with Disaster* (1996). A substantial but not excessive budget of $48 million. Casting, though, is crucial. The *Three Kings* package includes three figures with 'cool' associations from the world of contemporary music: the singer Mark Wahlberg (aka Marky Mark) and the rap artist Ice Cube, plus Spike Jonze, a noted director of music videos and of the contemporaneous critical hit *Being John Malkovich*. And then there is the major-league star: Clooney. It is a safe bet to assume that the presence of Clooney alone was a significant factor.

*Three Kings* has its 'risky', edgy elements, in terms of both form and content. If the figure of Clooney offers a point of stabilization for the viewer, as I have suggested, it is arguably even more important in achieving the same function at an industrial-commercial level. Major stars can, quite simply, get films made and seen. A few directors have this power, as we saw in chapter 3. Generally, however, stars loom larger in the industrial equation. A big enough star is sufficient to get most projects off the ground, especially if they might otherwise be seen as 'difficult' or potentially less commercial. If this was the case with Clooney in *Three Kings*, the same could be said of his appearance in *The Thin Red Line* (1998), an 'arty' and philosophical war epic directed by Terrence Malick: Clooney figures quite high in a long list of stars, helping to sell the movie to the general audience despite the fact that his character appears for only a very few minutes. Hollywood, generally, assumes star names to be among the best guarantors of box-office success.

Stardom has always played a crucial role in Hollywood's industrial strategy, as far back as the nineteen-teens.[10] 'Glamorous' or attractive star images are among the most familiar terms in which Hollywood films have been sold. If movies have been designed according to genre categories or blends, they have also been made as vehicles for particular stars. A classical-era studio might have decided to make so many gangster films, musicals or emotional melodramas in any given year. It is equally or more likely, however, to have carved up its slate largely in terms of suitable material for its stable of stars, properties over which it had more exclusive rights: vehicles for James Cagney, Fred Astaire or Bette Davis.

Stars have, if anything, become even more important in the New Hollywood era. Films have to stand on their own, to a greater extent than before, in the era of one-off production. This has heightened Hollywood's need to contrive something as close as possible to in-built guarantees of success. Directors, genres and pre-sold or recycled materials all play their part. Stars, however, are generally seen as the most consistently reliable indicators of box-office potential. They are often at the centre of the film-packaging process. The importance of television as a launch-pad for Hollywood stardom, for the likes of Clooney, has also increased in recent years. Television stars, once generally looked down upon by Hollywood, are seen as particularly valuable attractions in the important overseas market, in an era in which American television shows are beamed to an ever-wider global audience.[11]

The presence of Clooney, along with Arnold Schwarzenegger and Uma Thurman, might not have been the most important selling point of *Batman and Robin*, for example. Component number one, in this case, is the Batman franchise, a lucrative commercial property in its own right (although this particular instalment performed disappointingly). But the franchise itself has been sold partly on the basis of the scope it offers for a shifting set of star performers, both in the title role and in the repertoire of larger-than-life enemies featured in each episode. The presence of a major star or stars is generally a key ingredient in Hollywood, likely to attract funding – by convincing potential backers of the ability of a film to open successfully in both the domestic and overseas markets – and other creative personnel.

There is no absolute guarantee that the presence of major stars will lead to success. There are plenty of examples of features led by stars that have disappeared at the box office, one of the most notorious of recent years being the failure of the apparently sure-fire self-conscious Schwarzenegger star vehicle, *The Last Action Hero* (1993).[12] Not all of the biggest successes are built around the presence of the biggest stars. Neither the *Star Wars* nor *Jurassic Park* franchises, among other recent mega-hits, depend greatly on human star performers to draw audiences. Across the board, however, stardom is generally considered the single most important factor in the commercial viability of many films. The appeal of major stars tends to be relatively long-lasting, usually surviving the occasional box-office disaster, especially in the overseas market.[13] The major- or middle-ranking star vehicle remains a central feature of the Hollywood landscape. Stars offer that one ingredient deemed so important by Hollywood today: the audience recognition factor, the ability to 'open' a film, to give it a presence in the marketplace on the opening weekend, all neatly packaged into the body of the individual performer.

Stars have certainly gained more power in the New Hollywood context. However important their role in the studio era, and however high some salaries might have been, most stars were tightly constrained. The standard deal was a seven-year contract, according to which the star had little scope for choice of parts or creative freedom. In the New Hollywood industrial arena stars are able to exert great control over their work. They are not usually cemented inflexibly into lengthy contractual arrangements with the studios. Instead, they act largely as free agents. The top flight are much sought-after, and so able to dictate their own terms. Press reports abound of stars making excessive demands or throwing their weight around, to considerable effect. Much was made, for example, of the ability of Mel Gibson effectively to dismiss the first-time director Brian Helgeland from the production of *Payback* (1999) when he refused to make changes demanded by the star.

Stars often become producers of their own pictures, as was the case with Gibson and *Payback*. They have the clout to insist on being director as well, in some cases, a feature of many of Clint Eastwood's films, including *Unforgiven*. Many stars have established their own companies. Mel Gibson has Icon. Eastwood's company, Malpaso, was formed in 1968. As with the companies created by some directors, these often exist primarily for tax reasons. Malpaso, however, is an example of an actor-based company fully involved in the development and production of vehicles for the star.

Major stars have carved out much freedom. The big studios are keen to tie them down, as far as possible, to establish exclusive or ongoing working relationships with such bankable commodities. The result is that many stars have special deals with individual studios. Star-led production companies, like all others, need access to the distribution and marketing resources of the studios. Malpaso worked initially with Universal, switching allegiances to Warner Bros. from 1975. Icon also has an arrangement with Warner. Stars sometimes negotiate multi-picture deals with studios, on generous terms, which provide them with offices and resources on the studio lot. After establishing his reputation and image in *ER*, produced by Warner television, George Clooney says, the studio sought to 'invest' in his future prospects, signing him to a four-picture deal.[14] Agents often secure 'pay or play' deals, according to which a star is brought into a project while it is still in development and gets paid whether or not the film actually gets made. This is expensive but has its uses. It keeps the star component committed while other elements in a package are assembled. For the major studios as a whole, deals such as these have the advantage of making it difficult for anyone else to gain access to the biggest stars. Small operators cannot afford to compete at this level, unless they offer sufficiently 'challenging' or 'artistic' projects to attract big names to lower their usual rates.

Stardom as an institution helps the majors to maintain their dominance of the industry. Emphasis is put on the particular image or persona of the star rather than on aspects of impersonation that are 'generalizable to the craft'[15] of acting and hence potentially available at lower cost to outside competitors. Other performers might attempt to impersonate the star, but, as Barry King suggests, 'attempts at impersonation only reinforce the "uniqueness" of the star.'[16] The institution of stardom puts the focus on the personal characteristics of a finite number of stars to whom access is limited by cost: 'the ideology of stardom, with its associated individualism, protects the studio from the risk of their property becoming public domain.'[17]

Stars are not so easily tied to individual studios in the New Hollywood era although they remain for the most part within the orbit of a small number of dominant studio companies: a system that can be of mutual benefit to each. Studio executives frequently complain about the level of star salaries, which tend to increase well above the rate of inflation. On one level, their complaints are very real. Star costs often account for disproportionately large percentages of budgets, upwards of $20 million a film for the highest earners. The escalation of star salaries has been one of the major factors driving up the cost of production in recent decades; at the same time, the negotiation of lucrative gross revenue participation deals can eat deeply into studio receipts (to the tune of some $40 million in the case of *Lethal Weapon IV*, 1998, according to some reports). The three leading talent agencies – William Morris, Creative Artists Agency and International Creative Management – gained the entrenched power of a cartel from the 1970s and 1980s, as Stephen Prince suggests, primarily through their control of access to star talent (and in their influence as developers and packagers of entire projects).[18] This is a significant gap in studio control of the business. In the longer term, however, and taking a broader view of the industry, the high cost of stars is another way effectively of raising the 'barriers to entry' that prevent anyone else from competing in serious or sustained fashion with the dominant players. Stars are at the heart of many of Hollywood's commercial calculations. They can also play a role in the business of corporate synergy discussed in chapter 2, a good example being provided by the recent career of Will Smith.

## Cross-over appeals.

Will Smith, as movie star, has a distinct persona. Its development can be traced from his early career in pop music to the latest blockbuster film role. The established Will Smith persona is charming, witty, stylish in a goofy kind of way, cheeky, sexy though clean-cut, sometimes mock-outraged and, like that of George Clooney, essentially very safe. Will Smith as the Fresh Prince, half of a rap/hip-hop act with DJ 'Jazzy Jeff' Townes, achieved millionaire success in the music industry of the late 1980s. The persona of the Fresh Prince was translated intact onto screen in the television series *The Fresh Prince of Bel Air* (1990–96), a popular sitcom in which Smith, with no acting experience, played a character named none other than 'Will Smith', a 'streetwise' teenager (although not a rapper) from Philadelphia (Smith's home city), sent to live with relatives in the rich Los Angeles suburb. The image was one of charm, wit and style, although at this stage with an emphasis on the gawkiness and prominent ears more than the sex appeal developed in his film career. As both musician and television star, Smith was considered a perfect racial 'cross-over' artist. His music is rap made safe for black and white middle-class teenagers and their parents, devoid of the controversy often associated with the form. The same goes for the TV show, which was designed for a general and mass audience, like *The Cosby Show*, rather than for a specifically black constituency.

Smith made the transition from small screen to big screen blockbusters via a number of less prominent film roles, billed usually in press interview/profiles and popular biographies as part of an effort to improve his ability to act 'properly', rather than merely to rehearse an existing persona. To develop at least some status as impersonator, not just personification, in other words. He began with a small part in *Where The Day Takes You* (1992) and was cast partly against type (although playing on his reputation for 'charm') for his first substantial role, as the gay con man interloper in *Six Degrees of Separation* (1993). The performances that turned Smith into a major star play to a large extent on developments from and around the original persona. In *Bad Boys* (1995), *Independence Day* (1996), *Men in Black* (1997) and *Wild Wild West* (1999) Smith plays, in various combinations, the charming, stylish, 'cool' and capable but also youthfully exuberant and somewhat goofy half of central partnership roles. The same persona is largely to the fore in the more 'serious' thriller, *Enemy of the State* (1998).

The trick, it seems, is to retain a central core of persona traits, while allowing the space for some variation, if only of the deployment of familiar components.[19] *Enemy of the State* was seen as taking Smith into a more substantial realm of performance, improving by degree his credentials as a 'serious' actor. Shifts such as this involve an element of risk, of alienating existing fans or disappointing expectations. Smith hinted in one interview at the time of release that he was concerned that the film would make him appear too serious.[20] A careful process of image-negotiation is involved. As the director of the film, Tony Scott, puts it in a magazine cover-story also tied to the release of the film: 'It's not as if people won't recognize him... He plays an affable guy with a sense of humor. But they'll also see him playing some tough, strong, emotional moments – doing things that, as an actor, he's never been asked to do before.'[21] A further move in the direction of more 'serious' impersonation was marked by Smith's starring role in *Ali* (2001); but here, again, a blend is offered, of characteristics associated with a real historical individual, to be impersonated (including an extensive regime of boxing training, as part of the film's commitment to 'realism', and those rooted in the star's own fast-talking persona.

Smith's appeal to the industry appears to be based partly on assumptions about his ability to attract audiences across racial boundaries, even if he has usually been partnered with white performers (the exception being *Bad Boys*).[22] The qualities of the persona are central to this, Smith's image being essentially unthreatening. Smith's market value as a cross-over artist works in other ways as well, straddling media as well as racial divides. His music career was largely abandoned in 1993 as a result of disappointing sales and an increased commitment to *The Fresh Prince* (he became co-producer) and Hollywood. It has since been strongly revived, however, and closely integrated with some of his film appearances.

Will Smith's music comeback was launched with the title song to *Men in Black*, a hit that earned large revenues and provided a potent source of marketing for the film. This is a perfect example of internal corporate synergy. Both film and music appeared under the corporate umbrella of Columbia/Sony (the film was produced by Steven Spielberg's Amblin Entertainment but distributed by Columbia). Both earned substantial sums of money. The single, as the 'B-side' to 'Gettin' Jiggy With It', was a chart success, as was the soundtrack album containing another Will Smith track. The film earned some $570 million worldwide. Each was able to promote the other. Hit records are an ideal form of marketing for films. Radio play and record sales in advance of the release of the film provide what is effectively hours of advertising that is not only free, but for which the company gets paid. Associations with a major blockbuster film and film star, in return, help to sell the music. The sum total is likely to be greater than the parts.

The hit records associated with *Men in Black* and *Wild Wild West* are particularly blatant forms of cross-promotion, their lyrics revolving primarily around constant repetition of the titles of the films, creating strong advance recognition. The refrains 'here come the men in black' or simply 'wild wild west' plant the film titles into the public imagination, or at least that of the pop-music-radio-listening or record-buying audience. This is likely to overlap with potential or target audiences for the films, increasing the effectiveness of this form of promotion. Music videos represent an especially privileged marketing location, designed to sell the music but also foregrounding the films through the use of images and extracts that turn them into hybrids between the world of MTV and the traditional movie trailer. A second round of film-music synergy, with even higher potential earnings, is found in the coordinated release of the films on video and single-artist Will Smith albums containing the movie themes ('Big Willie Style' with *Men in Black* and 'Willennium' with *Wild Wild West*).

If the Will Smith of *Men in Black* represented the ideal synergistic commercial property for Columbia/Sony, the star's subsequent allegiances demonstrate the difficulty the studios have in gaining exclusive control of such profitable talents. For a moment, Columbia achieved the perfect combination of mutually reinforcing in-house properties.

It did not last. Smith's next film, *Enemy of the State*, was made under the aegis of Disney's Touchstone imprint. It was followed by the heavily music and music-video promoted *Wild Wild West*, which was a Warner Bros. picture. Warner, however, did not capture the full commercial benefit of any cross-media synergies. The film performed disappointingly at the box office, despite a blockbuster-worthy opening weekend take of $49 million (it earned $113 in the domestic market and in the region of $104 overseas, a total of $217 million that was well beneath studio expectations and the sum amassed by *Men in Black*; video rentals and sales were also lower, while *Wild Wild West* was sold to television for a mere $6 million, compared with the $70 million earned by its predecessor).

The music did not fare so badly, however. The single sold 500,000 copies and the soundtrack 2 million, respectable comparisons with *Men in Black* (500,000 for the main theme as B-side to a free-standing single and 3 million for the soundtrack). Will Smith's distinct appeal as a rap artist appears to have been largely insulated from the negative buzz that accompanied the film, offering the kind of insurance policy that might explain the appeal of cross-media synergies, where available, to the studios. The solidity of the performance of Smith-as-musician helped to offset the relative failure of the film. Unlike Columbia with *Men in Black*, however, Warner Bros. was not in a position to reap the benefits. The single and 'Willennium' were on Columbia Records, to which Smith's music career has maintained its primary loyalty. The soundtrack was released on Overbrook Records, part of Overbrook Entertainment, a film, television and music operation run by Will Smith and his partner, James Lassiter.

Overbrook Entertainment has a first-look film deal with Universal Pictures, while the record division is associated with Interscope, one of the numerous labels in the Universal Music Group. In the case of *Wild Wild West*, this new set of allegiances enabled Universal to gain access to one of the more successful parts of the revenue stream attached to the product of a rival studio. Universal has not succeeded very far, however, in its attempt to establish a privileged relationship with Will Smith as movie star. Since its formulation in 1997, Overbrook's deal with Universal has not led to the production of any projects in which Smith has starred for the studio. Numerous titles have been reported in the trade press and elsewhere but, at the time of writing, Overbrook

Entertainment said no projects were at a stage at which any details could be discussed. A spokesman for Universal said: 'While they have projects they are developing, there is nothing currently in production or pre-production for Universal Pictures.'

Arrangements such as that between Smith and Universal are often described as 'vanity deals', designed to indulge the dabblings of stars in areas such as production and direction in order to secure access to the on-screen services that are really in demand. They can be expensive investments, the rewards of which are variable. The studios are caught between contradictory desires. On the one hand, they are prepared to lavish millions on the costs of various semi-independent in-house commitments, in an attempt to secure privileged longer term access to potentially lucrative producer, director and star talent; deals such as these are also important to the studios, or to particular executives, as manifestations of their own prestige, a factor of no little importance in the far from entirely 'rational' or economically-based culture of Hollywood. On the other hand, they face more immediate demands to cut overhead costs. Spending on these kinds of arrangements alternates with bouts of cost-cutting. Annual surveys by *Variety* over the four years to 2000 show an overall trend towards a reduction and tightening of in-house production deals in the second half of the 1990s, including those involving actors who produce (but not including deals with actors or directors who do not also produce).[23] Casualties during 2000 included Nicholas Cage's Saturn Films at Walt Disney and deals involving Sigourney Weaver and Denzel Washington at Twentieth Century Fox.

Stars play a major role in the economics of Hollywood. Many films are built around the presence of particular stars or get made as a result of the attachment of star names. The way audiences read films is shaped by the associations brought by star personas, as we have seen. Star power also reaches into the wider social-cultural domain.

## Embodiments of culture

What is the 'meaning' of Will Smith? Particular sets of expectations or associations are attached to his presence in a Hollywood film. Such expectations are one factor in guiding us through the narrative, at the level of our individual experience of the text. They also have social, cultural and ideological implications. A star persona is in effect a coalescence of identity traits. These are never neutral. To ascribe particular qualities to a character is, inevitably, to enter into the arena of social and cultural meanings. These, in turn, are rarely free from political or ideological resonance. How might this work in the case of Will Smith, a figure who has usually distanced himself from much in the way of explicit political controversy? Race is one of the most obvious dimensions in which to consider this question. One 'trait' of Will Smith, of course, is that he is black. In this context, other traits take on a particular significance.

That the Will Smith persona is 'nice', charming and unthreatening has already been seen as a major factor in his ability to be seen as a performer appealing to white and/or middle class audiences. This has ideological-political undertones: only by appearing 'safe', or by appearing to mask the existence of racial divisions, can a black performer become a major Hollywood star. Why? Because of the very real and pointed racial divisions and inequalities in American society. A more 'dangerously' angry, assertive or openly political black persona might bring such divisions to the fore. This is something Hollywood would want to avoid, largely for commercial reasons: racial controversy is likely to alienate particular audiences and to deny the feel-good reconciliatory dynamic at the heart of much of Hollywood's appeal. The effective denial or masking of real and deep-rooted social inequalities is an expression of an ideology beneficial to those who profit, wilfully or otherwise, from the existing distribution of power and wealth.

Two potentially opposed components of the Will Smith persona are reconciled, we could say: 'blackness' (tending to signify a threat of some kind, in racist-inflected dominant American ideologies) and 'niceness/charm/unthreatening'. The same might be said of other aspects of the persona mobilized, in varying degrees, across screen roles and constructions of the 'real' Will Smith. One set of characteristics revolves around an opposition between relatively 'plain' home-centred domesticity and more outgoing and cavalier hipness, sexiness and adventure. The Will Smith of the interview pages and fan biographies is depicted as a clean-cut figure of strong family and domestic ties, despite his workaholic tendencies, living outside Hollywood in a neighbourhood of 'ordinary' rich people.[24] But he is also very much the sexy and charismatic movie and music star. Contradictory elements are held in tension in some of the characteristics already attributed to Smith in this chapter. He is, by turns, both 'cool'/hip and a goofy clown.

In *Independence Day*, *Men in Black* and *Enemy of the State*, the Smith character is forcibly separated from the domestic scene: to carry out the (supposedly) suicidal mission after hasty marriage to his girlfriend in *Independence Day*, permanently to surrender the connections of normal life in *Men in Black* and as a result of a conspiracy to destroy his credibility in *Enemy of the State*. It is in the non-domestic arena that the Smith character is able to put his distinctive qualities to wider use: saving the world or at least protecting it from 'alien' intrusions of a federal-surveillance variety. This is balanced against the commitment of star-as-character or the star-as-real-person to family life: a very firm commitment in *Enemy of the State* and in Smith's comments about his own life; a being-established commitment in *Independence Day* (and in *Bad Boys*, in which Smith's independently wealthy and womanizing playboy-detective gains unexpected satisfaction after being forced by plot contrivance to move in with his partner's wife and children); and one that is manifested in *Men in Black* by a long dissolve-to-night sequence, suggesting that James Edwards ponders long and hard before deciding to join the elite force, and by the fact that his mentor Kay is able, eventually, to retire to the domestic hearth. This issue – the pull between the worlds of domesticity/family and those of action/adventure/heroics – can be found in various forms in many Hollywood films.[25] The resonance attached to a particular star performer can play a part in way such issues are negotiated, particularly for the viewer who also consumes star interviews, biographies or fansites.

The exuberant, comic and unconventional qualities of some of Smith's major characters (Lowrey in *Bad Boys*, Captain Hillier in *Independence Day*, James Edwards/Jay in *Men in Black*, James West in *Wild Wild West*) are also balanced by their location within institutionalized authority roles as, respectively, detective, USAF pilot, newly recruited elite federal agent and US Marshall. Contrasts such as these can be seen as inconsistencies, undermining the concept of coherent image. But the Will Smith persona might also be viewed as a construction within which some of these tensions can be resolved, or at least held in parallel. It is not hard to see the potential appeal of this. Bridges can be built, flatteringly, between the worlds of the cool, sexy movie star and that of the 'ordinary' domesticated filmgoer. Ideological implications also come into play. Smith's persona in *Bad Boys*, *Independence Day*, *Men in Black* and *Wild Wild West* gives a cosy and appealing face to policing and military institutions that might, in other circumstances, be seen as part of the oppressive apparatuses of the state.

This latter effect is particularly noticeable and explicit in *Men in Black*, which begins by establishing an opposition between Smith's not-so-plain clothes detective James Edwards and the mysterious federal agency. In the early stages of the film Edwards appears in three different sets of 'loud' and funky 'street' clothes: baggy orange pants, big sporty white t-shirt and trainers; lurid scarlet/orange jacket, jeans and desert boots; yellow and black pants and matching yellow/black/white shirt. Gear that might be at home on a primary-colours rap singer such as Will Smith. This stands in obvious contrast to the black-suit/white-collar/black-tie conformity of the Men in Black. Other potential recruits against whom Edwards competes for a place in the agency are stiff and formal in both mannerisms and assorted military uniforms. Edwards is the sassy non-conformist. The distinction is not made to rest on racial characteristics. The first of the rivals to be supplied with any lines is also black: an implicit disavowal, it seems, of any suggestion that the looser 'hipness' of Edwards is merely a familiar racist stereotype. He has 'a real problem with authority', we are told. This is precisely his appeal, both to his mentor Kay (Tommy Lee Jones) and, presumably, the viewer. Selected to join the elite force, Edwards is transformed into Jay (for the letter 'J') and is obliged to shed all signs of his previous identity. His finger-prints and computer records are wiped and he dons the suit.

The signifiers of 'Will Smith-ness' remain, however. 'I make this look good,' the character declares, and his swagger does, indeed, make the uniform appear 'cool' (the shades help). Jay retains the street-smarts, the wit and the element of goofiness that characterizes his previous

9. 'I make this look good!' Will Smith as Jay, retaining his 'cool' in the anonymous federal garb in *Men in Black*, © Columbia Pictures, 1997. Ronald Grant archive

identity (he is also shown, just for good measure, to be extremely quick, mentally and physically). These characteristics are translated into what amounts also to a more 'human' and caring approach to his work. Jay is not jaded. He is fresh and alive, not a 'seen-it-all-before' cynic like

Kay and his colleagues. Such qualities seem significant to a film that, seriously or not, presents the anonymous forces of the secret state – icons of a number of American paranoias – in a positive light. The presence of Will Smith, in the agency and the uniform but still recognizably the endearing Will Smith persona, offers what might been seen as a reconciliation of seemingly contradictory characteristics.

This is another respect in which stardom has been understood in terms similar to those used by some theorists of genre. The appeal of some stars, suggests Richard Dyer, one of the most influential theorists of stardom, can be to offer magical reconciliation of opposites. If American society has demanded that women be sexy but also pure and ordinary, for example, 'one can see Lana Turner's combination of sexiness and ordinariness, or Marilyn Monroe's combination of sexiness and innocence, as effecting a magical synthesis of these opposites.'[26] Star personae, like some genre products, can offer the best of all worlds. Stars are particularly effective mechanisms for such processes, Dyer suggests, because of the overlap between the persona on-screen and off: 'the value embodied by a star is as it were harder to reject as "impossible" or "false", because the star's existence guarantees the existence of the value he or she embodies.'[27] Both the apparent 'ordinariness' and 'sexiness' of the 'real' Will Smith, just like the 'blackness' and the 'unthreateningness', help to ground the fictional projections of these qualities in his film performances.

Stars can come to embody particular social issues, quite literally. The physical body itself can become a signifier. In the case of Will Smith, the prominent ears have always been one of the signifiers of a comic and somewhat goofy persona. In the move from gawky teenage Fresh Prince to blockbuster action-adventure-comedy movie star, Smith's body was made more robust and muscular; the ears remain, however. Much has been written about the 'excessive' musculature of male star bodies in the Hollywood action cinema of the 1980s and 1990s, in relation to stars such as Sylvester Stallone and Arnold Schwarzenegger. What exactly these bodies signify remains open to debate. For some, they are embodiments of 'traditional' masculinity. For others, their excess is such that they open this version of masculinity to ridicule or reveal its status as no more than a social construct or masquerade.[28]

The persona of the star does not necessarily 'express' issues such as these, but it can become a vehicle around which a range of cultural meanings condense, coalesce or compete. Stars, like Hollywood films more generally, do not simply reflect their social context. But they are prominent features in the cultural landscape, onto which a variety of meanings might be projected. Stars sometimes become icons, viewed not just in themselves but in terms of what they appear to symbolize. The figure of Clint Eastwood has attained this status: an icon of a particular construction of implacable masculinity. There is more to this than just a passive and unchanging image, however: again, we can find a process of negotiation. The Eastwood persona fits into some classic stereotypes of masculinity in our culture. The image forged in the early stages of his career was one of strength and resilience: tough and taciturn, a man of action rather than of words. Attempts have also been made to make some of his screen characters more sensitive and emotional, as in *Play Misty for Me* (1971), or to include aspects of a feminist critique of Eastwood's brand of masculinity, in *Tightrope* (1984), in which discomforting parallels are established between the detective played by the star and a misogynist killer.[29]

A negotiation of social and political issues around the Eastwood character is also found in the Dirty Harry series, launched with *Dirty Harry* (1972). Eastwood's incarnation as the detective Harry Callaghan is presented as a maverick figure, violent-but-effective, cutting through bureaucratic inertia to get results. Repeatedly, during the series, Callaghan is seen striding into some ongoing criminal activity and solving it through sheer audacity and direct action, in defiance of what are defined as 'petty' rules and procedure. It is not hard to read this in terms of the political and ideological background of the early 1970s. Eastwood's character has often been understood as part of a broader authoritarian and right-wing backlash against the supposed 'liberalism' and 'permissiveness' of the 1960s.[30] He has been seen as an advocate of vigilante action, a critic, for example, of new rights given to suspects to guard against police abuses of power. This is, almost certainly, part of the appeal of the character. It is qualified, however, in *Magnum Force* (1973), the second film in the series.

Here, again, we get the same Eastwood character/persona, set in opposition to the bureaucratic hierarchy of the police force. In this case another element is introduced into the equation. A group of 'real' vigilantes is depicted within the ranks of the force: an assassination squad of young officers that murders a number of prominent criminals who have escaped conventional justice. This time, there is a distinct negotiation of the issue of the use of vigilante force. On one side is the bureaucratic rule-book. On the other is out-and-out vigilante action. Eastwood's Callaghan is located, strategically, in the middle, mediating between the two. He offers the appealing prospect of direct action – shown to be extremely effective – but a version that is made to seem reasonable and acceptable in contrast to the death squad.

Negotiations such as these can be understood through a combination of social–cultural and industrial perspectives. Star images do, without doubt, attract encrustations of cultural meaning. In some cases these might be courted by the stars themselves. Eastwood, for example, entered the political arena himself and is not shy in expressing his own rightward leanings. Will Smith definitely 'is' or plays the clean–cut charming wit in the presence of journalists.[31] In other respects, these meanings might accrue regardless of the intentions of filmmakers or the individual star. Stars have a cultural prominence that makes them irresistible targets for criticism or adoption as role models. Where star images can be read in terms of the negotiation or reconciliation of issues, this can also be understood in terms of Hollywood's familiar commercial logic: offering, again, the best of both worlds, a source of potential pleasure for the viewer and a way of trying to limit the offence given to any substantial constituency of potential filmgoers.

## Identifications?

Hollywood stars tend to be appealing figures. They are usually attractive, strong in various ways, seductive. Their power, both as sources of orientation and as means of negotiating social issues, is often understood in terms of their ability to offer a point of identification for the viewer. Hollywood narratives are usually structured around the experiences of a central figure or figures acting as our guide through the events. Dominant editing and point-of-view regimes do not place us in the exact subjective position of the protagonists. They usually offer a combination of perspectives *close to* the subjective – shots from just behind or alongside the central characters, for example – and a variety of more distant or 'objective' perspectives. Entirely subjective camera-work, shot from the point-of-view of the major protagonists, is used but only to a limited extent. This is partly to avoid disorientation, but also to enable us to *see* the character: the pleasure of watching the star performance being, of course, a major appeal of mainstream cinema.

Viewer desires associated with stardom might be divided into two main categories. On one hand, there is the desire *for* the star, as an appealing (often sexual) object of the gaze or (ideally, in fantasy) to possess. Think, for example, of the yearnings of the many teenage-girl fans of Leonardo DiCaprio[32] or the assumption that female stars are defined to a large extent by their ability to appeal physically to the sexual fantasies of males. On the other, is the desire *to be* the star, or something closer to the star-image, or at least to play around with such fantasies. Young males might want to be as hip and charming as 'Will Smith' or as tough and assured as 'Clint Eastwood'.

The shot-sequences and other formal strategies used in Hollywood invite us to identify with the main protagonists to some extent. That these figures are played by attractive stars is usually assumed to aid this process: we might be very happy to align ourselves with such desirable personae, thus increasing any power they might have to shape our expectations or to serve ideological purposes. This remains an area of much debate. Exactly how we might identify with star-personae-characters, and to what effect, is a contentious theoretical issue. Much has been speculated, for example, on the basis of psychoanalytical theories.[33]

Stars, it is sometimes suggested, offer attractive images that can compensate for our own psychological inadequacy; an aura of plenitude and coherence to make up for our incoherence, for example. This might be one way of understanding the attraction towards a Will Smith or a Clint Eastwood: their ability to some extent to hold together or reconcile what might otherwise appear to be divisive and contradictory traits. This approach can be put in psychoanalytical terms, deriving especially from the work of Jacques Lacan. It can also be grounded socially or politically. Dominant western culture tends to privilege notions of coherent individual identity and agency. Notions such as these, enshrined in the gleaming persona of the star, can have ideological implications, denying as they often do the role of multifarious cultural factors in the shaping and control of our lives. Identification with star-images might be seen, from this perspective, as a bulwark of individualist and/or capitalist ideology.[34]

Approaches such as these are open to question, however, or at least a good deal of qualification. They tend to imply that viewers are in thrall to stars (along with other aspects of films), that they are somehow deceived or 'taken in', one way or another, by the power and aura of the star. The reality is more complex and nuanced. As Murray Smith suggests, we might be *aligned* with the perspective of a character, through optical point-of-view and related structures, without necessarily being in a position of *allegiance*; the latter suggests some kind of structure of sympathy, but one that might remain well short of what is often implied by the term 'identification'.[35] We might admire and take pleasure in the star-presence in different ways, none of them very easy to access or to quantify. The pleasures of star-consumption, even at their most intense, do not necessarily involve a 'loss' of self or self-awareness. They might entail exactly the opposite. Or a range of negotiations between delight in the constructed persona and knowledge that it is a construct; between desire to be 'like' the star and awareness of, and pleasure in, the fantastical nature of both the star-construct and the imaginary notion of self-transformation.

'Identification' with stars takes many forms, as Jackie Stacey shows in a study of the responses of British women viewers to Hollywood stars in the 1940s and 1950s.[36] Different kinds and degrees of identification are traced both in the cinema, during the viewing process, and outside, in forms ranging from games of pretence to efforts to copy aspects of star appearance such as hairstyles and clothing. Different aspects of the star image might also be the source of appeal for different viewers. The image of Will Smith in *Enemy of the State*, for example, might be read in terms of a reconciliation of oppositions. But some viewers might take their pleasure more from one part of the equation than others: from the 'domestic' or the 'action-adventure' components, for example, or their combination with differing degrees of emphasis.

Aspects of Hollywood films such as authorship, genre and stardom can be separated out for purposes of analysis, but they often operate simultaneously across the space of any individual film and from one film or group of films to another. The ways we are invited or encouraged to read films are multiple. They also operate in different directions. On the one hand, there is the internal dynamic of the individual film, unwinding in sequence across the running time. Plot dynamics pull us towards a linear focus, forward moving. One the other hand, there are numerous factors that interrupt or shape this dynamic from other directions. Considerations of authorship, of genre and of stardom can all have this effect. They operate *across* a range of texts and performances. They are inherently *intertextual*, their dynamics not limited to the boundaries of the individual film.

Hollywood films are not seamless narratives. It is not so much that the narrative is undermined by these external influences. Narrative comprehension is to a significant extent *shaped* – variously, depending on both individual text and viewer – by the dynamics of authorship, genre and stardom; by the various pre-existing sets of expectations brought to bear on the text (schemas, as they would be termed from the perspective of cognitive psychology[37]). This has always been the case, especially in terms of genre and stardom. The assumption that Hollywood narrative was once somehow more coherent or free-standing is largely responsible for an argument to be explored in the next chapter: the claim that New Hollywood cinema, especially that of the corporate blockbuster, is characterized by a surrender of narrative to the dimension of spectacle.

6

# Narrative vs. Spectacle in the Contemporary Blockbuster

Spectacle is needed, as are variety and strong emotions. How can these be obtained in a form that precludes overt episodicity? With no difficulty. Decide which spectacles are needed, then make it seem that they are there for internally motivated reasons.

Rick Altman[1]

Dinosaurs. Sinking ships. Fantastic cities. Spaceships. Alien landscapes. Explosions (lots of explosions). War. Disasters. Even a return to the traditional epic, Rome and gladiatorial combat. Hollywood blockbusters trade to a large extent on the appeal of big spectacular audio–visual effects: scale and impact. This, as we saw in chapter 2, was an important aspect of Hollywood's response to the destabilizing events of the 1950s. Spectacular imagery, often utilizing the latest in special effects and other technologies, has remained a key ingredient of the big-budget attractions around which the fortunes of the studios revolve.

The release of *Gladiator* (2000), a throwback to an historical epic tradition that gained its greatest prominence in the 1950s and 1960s, is a reminder of the extent to which little has changed, in this respect, in nearly a half century of New Hollywood production. Spectacle is a quality offered by Hollywood in its attempt to maintain the distinctive appeal of cinema, of the big-screen event that is so important to its broader commercial interests. Spectacular imagery, of various kinds, sells. It is an intrinsic part of many of the properties on which the studios draw for their big franchise products. It sells particularly well abroad, in markets where nuances of plot and dialogue might be lost in translation. It also plays an important role in the aesthetics of spin-off products such as computer games and theme-park rides.

Some suggest that spectacle has become the dominant tendency of contemporary blockbuster production. Narrative is usually identified as the victim. The narrative coherence of the blockbuster is often said to have been undermined by an emphasis on the provision of over-powering spectacle. This is one way in which it has been argued that the New Hollywood defined by the corporate blockbuster can be distin-guished at the formal level, in terms of the development of a distinct or 'post-classical' film style. A similar claim is often made about the impact of merchandising and product placement on the aesthetics of contem-porary Hollywood. Films are designed to showcase commercial pro-ducts; narrative, again, is said to suffer, to be interrupted, broken up or made secondary to other concerns.

The same kind of dynamic is identified in both cases. Two dimensions of the film-viewing experience compete. Narrative is understood primarily in terms of the telling of a coherent and carefully developed character-based story throughout the course of the film. Spectacle is seen as a source of distraction or interruption. Our focus on narrative development is halted while we sit back to contemplate with amaze-ment/pleasure/horror (or whatever particular reaction) the sheer sensory richness of the audio-visual experience: the special effects dinosaurs of the *Jurassic Park* films, the sinking Titanic, the transformations of alien beings, explosive action or quasi-apocalyptic destruction on earth. Or, in the case of merchandising or product placement, narrative is interrupted by the intrusive presence of the commodity-form insuf-ficiently integrated into the fictional world, a mere advertisement forced arbitrarily onto the screen.

Spectacle is, undoubtedly, important to the contemporary block-buster. It is mobilized in ways that might differ, in some respects, from the traditions associated with the 'classical' era. There are a number of problems with the suggestion that spectacle has displaced narrative, however, either the big-screen spectacular audio-visual experience in general or the particular effect of merchandising, product placement and other marketing strategies. Such claims are often based on an exaggerated assumption of the extent to which Hollywood movies were ever *dominated* by a commitment to classical narrative forms. The principal source of this assumption is the contribution of David Bordwell to the influential volume *The Classical Hollywood Cinema: Film Style and Mode of Production to 1960* (1985), co-authored by Bordwell, Janet Staiger and Kristen Thompson.

A particular form of narrative, for Bordwell, is the dominant component of classical Hollywood cinema: a form based on clear and unambiguous patterns of cause-and-effect in which events are justified and motivated (rather than arbitrary or coincidental) and organized around the actions of goal-driven characters seeking to overcome a variety of obstacles.[2] The narrative structures of classical Hollywood films are often characterized by tightly organized and carefully honed plots, in which most if not all events are clearly explained to the viewer. But this is far from always the case. Narrative drive and coherence may be part of the appeal of these films. Particular pleasures are offered by plots structured around mysteries or enigmas to be solved or around obstacles to be overcome. Much of the pleasure of classical Hollywood-style narrative comes from the working through of a combination of anxiety/uncertainty and the knowledge that all will, ultimately, be revealed or resolved. Such dynamics are usually heightened emotionally by the interweaving of such structures with heterosexual romantic subplots. Narrative is important. But it is only one among a number of factors.

The overriding aim of the studio system was not to produce 'classically' balanced and harmonious compositions, but to make money. The industry was, and remains, governed by what Richard Maltby terms a 'commercial aesthetic, essentially opportunistic in its economic motivation',[3] in which a variety of ingredients are used to increase the potential profitability of a film. It was for commercial reasons that the story-film became the dominant form of American production, by the

1910s at the latest, as part of a move to attract a middle-class audience that could afford higher ticket prices and gain a more respectable reputation for the embattled film business.[4] From this period onwards, however, a concern with narrative development might be combined at any moment with other pleasures: those of action or motion (the chase, for example, whether on foot, horseback, cars, trains or space-ships); performance (the musical number, elaborate stunt, comic routine or star presence); spectacular vistas (the landscape of Monument Valley, the musical set, exotic overseas locations, special effects); emotional intensity (fear, horror or 'tearjerking' devices such as terminal illness). And so on. Spectacle has always been an important part of the equation in Hollywood, including the spectacle of formal innovation or of violence and bloodshed in the films of the Hollywood Renaissance.

The presence of stars is an example of a routine 'disruption' of a certain form of internal narrative coherence. The star-as-persona is, by definition, a disruptive presence, not entirely integrated into the fictional world of character-driven narrative. The star might be consumed as a form of spectacle: an audio-visual presence to be enjoyed in its own right. Films featuring favourite stars might be experienced in terms of the star presence as much as their place within, and helping to shape, a developing narrative. The point, as Maltby suggests, is that viewers can pick and choose among different elements as the principal sources of pleasure. Seamless narrative might be more important to some viewers than to others. It might figure more centrally in some types of films, such as mystery or suspense, in which the complexity or resolution of plot elements is heavily foregrounded. Elsewhere, or for other viewers, the quality of narrative might be of less importance, subordinated to or combined with the display of star presence, action, locations, or what-ever.

Maltby is one of a number of commentators who have questioned Bordwell's assertion of the dominant role of 'classical' narrative con-ventions, a perspective that assumes a hierarchy in the relationships between different components of Hollywood films. Classical narrative is only one aspect of classical Hollywood. Non-narrative aspects are also important, including elements of sensation and spectacle. Even at the level of narrative, Elizabeth Cowie suggests, 'classical Hollywood included forms of storytelling which lack the "well-made" qualities associated with classical narrative form.'[5] Hollywood narratives of the studio era utilize many devices that owe more to stage melodrama than to 'classical' works of literature.[6] These include strategies such as a dependence on coincidence, on events that are motivated only minimally and on heavily typecast star performers. 'At the same time non-linear, episodic narrative, in which a series of narrative scenes are presented which are causally self-contained or only weakly causally connected, remained acceptable in Hollywood.'[7] Classical narrative devices play an important part in the films of the studio era, but they are often combined with these various non-classical or extra-narrative dimensions: a non-hierarchical system of 'multiple logics', as Rick Altman puts it, rather than one in which a particular brand of narrative is dominant.

Bordwell does allow for influences other than the classical. The role of melodrama, as one of the antecedents of Hollywood, is acknowledged in his account of the classical style. Departures from classical narrative are accorded an essentially secondary status, however; they are said to be 'motivated' by other factors. Melodramatic films often flout causal logic 'and rely shamelessly upon coincidence',[8] suggests Bordwell, but this is motivated generically: the fact that they *are* melodramas allows for, justifies and explains what is viewed as a departure from the norm, rather than challenging the norm itself. Displays of spectacle or of technical virtuosity are said to be motivated 'artistically', as a way of calling attention to the artistry or 'showmanship' of Hollywood.[9] Bordwell thus seeks to contain elements that depart from the norms of 'classical' narrative, to compartmentalize them rather than allowing for the possibility that they might be just as much a part of the essential fabric of classical-era Hollywood as the classical form of narrative structure.

Very many Hollywood films are in fact 'melodramatic', beyond the confines of those usually ascribed to a single melodrama genre. The term was used within the industry from the 1900s to the 1960s to describe a wide range of mainstream Hollywood films, including westerns and other action-adventures, rather than just the product of a single or atypical genre.[10] It is only in more recent decades that 'melodrama' has come to be used more narrowly, in reference to particular groups of films focused on 'overblown' or 'excessive' emotional relationships. The dominant use of the term changed when it was taken up by a number of academic commentators, especially feminist critics revisiting and seeking to re-value classical Hollywood films targeted at women.

Characteristics generally associated with 'melodrama' remain applicable to many Hollywood products, old and new: oversimplified moral conflicts between good and evil central characters, formulaic action and strong doses of emotion heightened by the use of music and other expressive devices (reminding us of the literal definition of the term: 'melo-drama' being 'music-drama', originally a theatrical form in which music was used to underpin the events). As Neale suggests: 'Instances of "melodrama" run the gamut from horror films to thrillers and westerns, from women's films to war films to action-adventure in general.'[11] Viewed this way, melodrama escapes from the generic straitjacket suggested by Bordwell and poses a more substantial challenge to the notion of a Hollywood style dominated by classical narrative conventions.

One tendency in debates about the relationship between narrative and spectacle in the contemporary blockbuster has been to exaggerate the importance of classical narrative in the studio era, at the expense of other appeals. Another has been to *under*estimate the importance of narrative – 'classical' and otherwise – today. Narrative construction remains an important ingredient in the mix offered by even the most spectacular and special-effects-laden blockbuster productions.

The term 'narrative' can be used here in two senses. The first, as above, refers to 'plot' or 'story': the on-going events of a film, both as depicted on screen and as the viewer is invited to recreate them. The second refers to thematic structures such as the patterns of oppositions, negotiations and in some cases imaginary reconciliations that can be found in – or read into – Hollywood narrative structures. The corporate blockbuster is very often a noisy, action-packed and spectacular affair. Much of its investment goes into these dimensions. It is not a format noted for the finer nuances of narrative structure. True. But it is easy to get carried away, or so it seems for some commentators. The pleasures of narrative might not always be the main or most obvious appeal of such films. Narrative structures remain important, however, in terms of both story/plot and thematic issues, often working in combination with the delivery of spectacle.

In some cases, narrative structures might be found to have changed from those employed in many Hollywood films. It is misleading to put this in terms of a simple shift from 'classical' to 'New' Hollywood or 'post-classical' eras, however. Too many products of the studio era veer away from an exclusive reliance on what are described as 'classical' norms. And too many blockbuster products of recent decades have a continued investment in quite carefully honed narrative structure, including elements consistent with Bordwell's version of 'classical' narrative. Elements of spectacle and narrative co-exist across the history of Hollywood cinema, in varying combinations. Narrative is subjected to institutionalized disruption in some forms, especially the musical and some types of comedy. The context of the corporate blockbuster helps to account for the particular configuration that dominates some big-budget production today. This needs to be examined, in all its specificity, without the exercise of sweeping and over-stated general-izations.

The remainder of this chapter will begin with an examination of changes that have been identified in the way spectacular sequences are mobilized within the structure of the contemporary blockbuster. The term 'spectacle' will be used here primarily to refer to sequences that employ a heightened degree of spectacle or spectacular action: the 'big' chase sequence, the 'big' explosion or the 'big' outburst of special effects, for example. There is a continuum between these and relatively smaller moments of spectacle and/or action, including phenomena such as star presence that might operate throughout the length of a film and that complicate the picture. A number of possible explanations will be considered, at both industrial and social-cultural levels. Evidence will also be supplied for the continued importance of many narrative devices familiar from the studio era. Consideration will then be given to the presence of 'underlying' thematic structures. The last part of the chapter will move on to examine the impact of merchandising and other com-mercial strategies.

## From rising curve to roller-coaster

A gradual development of narrative events, building slowly and inexorably across the length of a film towards a climax, often spectacular in nature. Or a pounding and incessant piling up of spectacular action from start to finish? A disciplined structure based on restraint and the careful building of tension released only (or primarily) at the end. Or a virtually non-stop roller-coaster 'thrill-ride'?

It is in these terms that Fred Pfeil establishes an opposition between the cinema of classical Hollywood and that of the contemporary action spectacular. Classical narrative style offers 'an accumulation of unspent dramatic or suspenseful elements throughout the narrative's so-called "rising action" into a force that is discharged most completely at the story's climax'.[12] A simplified version of this structure might be represented graphically, as in figure 1. The development of the action depicts a curve, rising gradually, the rate at which it rises accelerating in the latter stages as the film moves towards a climax. An example of a film from the studio era that follows this model to a significant extent is *San Francisco* (1936), a drama of personal relationships that climaxes in the spectacular depiction of an earthquake. This is, of course, an oversimplification. The model might be complicated by the addition of one or more peaks along the way, as in figure 2: a moderate peak, say, approximately mid-way through the film, after which it builds again towards the higher peak at the end, a structure probably more typical of the studio era than that suggested by Pfeil.

Many of the blockbuster productions of the corporate era produce a rather different graphic profile. Pfeil's principal example is *Die Hard with a Vengeance* (1995), the third in the Die Hard series, which 'offers us an altogether different economy of pleasure, in which the giddying blur of the high-speed chase and/or the gratifyingly spectacular release of aggressive impulse occurs at regularly recurring intervals throughout the film.'[13] This kind of narrative/spectacle relationship is represented in figure 3, a series of peaks and troughs resembling the roller-coaster structure with which such films are often compared. Another example of a recent blockbuster that fits this kind of profile is *Armageddon* (1998), a film that opens with a series of spectacular bursts that are maintained,

Figure 1

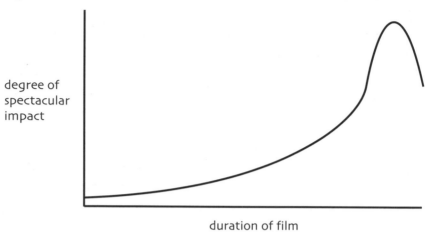

duration of film

Figure 2

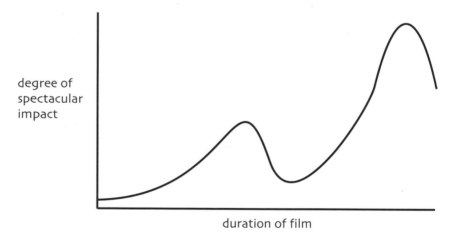

duration of film

with only relatively brief pauses for breath, across almost its entire length.[14] It would be possible to draw up approximate profiles of the kinds used in figures 1 to 3 for individual films, plotting their moments of spectacle/action and repose minute-by-minute across the running time.

Another way of indicating the relationship between spectacle and narrative is suggested in figures 4 and 5. Figure 4 is offered as a model of what is said to be the more 'classical' type of construction, the line

Figure 3

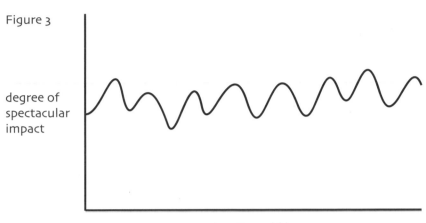

degree of
spectacular
impact

duration of film

representing the linear progression of the narrative and the explosion symbols representing moments of spectacular display or action. The classical version is one in which the narrative component is supposed to be largely dominant, sustained through periodic moments when the emphasis shifts towards spectacle/action that are not overwhelming, before building perhaps towards a more sustained spectacular climax. Figure 5 shows the relationship implied in some accounts of the contemporary blockbuster. Spectacular moments here are both larger and more frequent, fragmenting the narrative. Narrative, in this model, becomes attenuated, its short segments cut off from one another and serving as little more than the glue that holds together a series of spectacular displays.

How adequate are models such as these? They might be useful, up to a point, as approximate indicators of some of the spectacle/narrative dimensions of contemporary Hollywood. They are rather subjective – how exactly is the degree of spectacular impact to be measured, for example – but might give a sense at least of the *relative* differences between one film or another; or, potentially, the films of one period and another. The problem of how to 'measure' degrees of spectacularity opens up more substantial limitations, however, particularly when 'spectacle' is defined in broader terms than those of 'big' action or other set-pieces. The models suggested above tend to distract attention from the ways spectacle and narrative often interpenetrate. Many

Figure 4

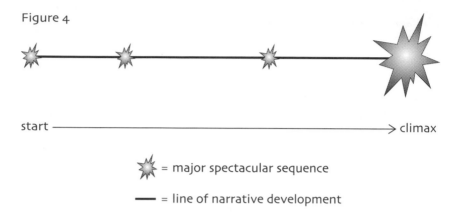

start ————————————————————————————————> climax

Figure 5

contemporary action, action–adventure, action–adventure–science-fiction and other blockbusters present a pattern of peaks and troughs of action/spectacle akin to that suggested in figures 3 and 5. But they also offer dimensions not easily conveyed by such models. We might start with a closer look at Pfeil's own example, *Die Hard with a Vengeance*. How, firstly, does it deploy its moments of greatest spectacle or spectacular action?

*Die Hard with a Vengeance* starts with a bang, literally, an explosion being provided just over one minute into the running time as a bomb blows out the ground floor of a department store. The next major action sequence begins approximately at the 26-minute mark: a high-speed chase down Manhattan from Harlem to Wall Street. On the way one of the two main protagonists, John McClane (Bruce Willis), exits the car to leap onto a speeding subway train on which a bomb has been planted. The whole more or less non-stop action sequence comes to a climax after 10 minutes when the train explodes and is sent flying across the Wall Street station platform.

The film maintains a steady supply of smaller action/tension sequences for the next 45 minutes. Another higher-point comes at the 81-minute mark, when McClane attempts to outrun a wall of water in a truck driving through a pipeline; he climbs onto the roof of the moving vehicle, grabs an overhead hatch and is ejected into the air by a water-spout. A brief moment of repose is followed by gunfire and a lengthy sequence cutting between: McClane and his partner Zeus (Samuel L. Jackson) being chased and fired upon by bad guys; the hunt for a bomb in a school and plans to evacuate children; and the two heroes eventually spinning their car around to face the enemy, shooting at them and crashing. This takes us to just under 90 minutes.

A brief moment of relative quiet is followed by a shift into another sequence of improbable spectacular action, as McClane and Zeus slide down a cable from a bridge to reach the ship on which the bad guys are escaping. A series of incidents on the ship, intercut again with events at the school, culminate in a huge explosion that destroys the ship (McClane and Zeus escaping by a hair's breadth) at about 106 minutes. A few minutes of transition are followed by a final conflict, a shoot-out involving helicopters, that culminates in the fireball explosion of the enemy chopper at 115 minutes, a minute or so before the start of the final credits.

Major sequences of action and spectacle are distributed throughout much of *Die Hard with a Vengeance*, more or less as Pfeil suggests. The single biggest sequence is the ten minute chase-leading-to-explosion located approximately a quarter of the way into the film, rather than being saved for the end. Large fireball-explosions, one of the key signatures of the contemporary action cinema, are provided at the start, after about 36 minutes, 106 minutes and 115 minutes. Two in each half, in other words: one to get us started, another to keep us going once the film is in its stride, and two more to bring the film towards its climax. Plenty more action, sometimes spectacular, sometimes more intimate, is provided in between. More needs to be said about the way these spectacular sequences are related to the narrative structure of the film, as we will see below. For the moment we can consider some other examples. *Die Hard with a Vengeance* maintains a high level of action, spectacle and excitement for some extended sequences. The ultimate in this type of delivery is provided by *Speed* (1994), an almost literally 'non-stop' action spectacular.

*Speed* opens with a 22-minute prologue, plunging the audience directly into a 'high-tension' drama revolving around an attempt to rescue a group of passengers from an elevator to which a bomb has been attached. The successful operation is followed by sequence lasting about three minutes in which the protagonists, Jack Traven (Keanu Reeves) and his partner Harry (Jeff Daniels) receive awards and celebrate in a bar afterwards. Another minute or so is taken up with the establishment of a scene the following morning in which Traven visits a café. A huge fireball then destroys a bus. A nearby telephone rings, the thwarted 'psychopath' responsible for the elevator incident, Howard Payne (Dennis Hopper), informing Traven that a bomb has been placed on another bus. It will be detonated if a ransom of $3.7 million is not paid; the bomb will be armed once the bus reaches 50 mph and will explode the moment it drops below that speed. Within just under three minutes of the previous explosion, Traven is in hot pursuit of the bus. Nine minutes later, after a series of action-adventures, he is on board. *Speed* then sustains a rhythm of almost unbroken action and tension until the bus eventually explodes, empty, just under 87 minutes into the film. Only brief and fleeting interludes of repose are provided during this entire episode.

A graphic profile of the main central portion of *Speed* would depict a line remaining high in the action-spectacle range and showing a rapid sequences of sub-peaks as a large number of minor crises follow closely upon one another. The destruction of the bus is followed by some moments of repose and a fresh movement in the plot involving Payne's escape with the ransom money. This, a chase and some shooting is followed from the 96-minute mark by a spectacular finale in which Traven leaps McClane-like into a speeding subway train, duels with Payne on the roof and eventually deliberately derails the train, which crashes through an underground construction site onto the surface, a sequence that lasts about eight minutes. Again, this structure of regular or constant peaks of high-octane action and spectacle seems to fit the kind of spectacular profile suggested by Pfeil.

Another example of a film that offers a high ratio of noisy action-spectacle is *Deep Blue Sea* (1999), a tale of genetically modified sharks terrorizing the occupants of a underwater research station. *Deep Blue Sea* opens with a prologue in which an escaped shark menaces a party of teenagers on a catamaran. Many points of heightened action, accompanied by an urgent score, occur during the film, especially in the last hour (out of a running time of approximately 98 minutes to the start of the closing credits). A notable feature of the film is the level of impact produced in the spectacular destruction of the surface portion of the research station that occurs just over 39 minutes from the start. This follows nearly seven minutes of noisy action starting from the moment a scientist loses an arm to one of the sharks. The injured man is being airlifted by helicopter, amid a heavy storm. The helicopter eventually crashes into the superstructure of the station, setting off a series of thunderous fireball explosions.

The remainder of the film is comprised mainly of an incessant series of tense shark-awaiting suspense, death, destruction and loud chase and action sequences, with only a few relatively brief moments of quiet and/or comic relief. None of this ever reaches the pitch of the minute's worth of explosive cacophony that follows the helicopter crash, however. A graphic profile would, again, depart from the 'classical' rising action: this time with an enormous peak before the half-way mark, followed by a series of high, but not *as* high, peaks running consistently to the end. The climax is a tense sequence, in which only three are left alive and one of the principals dies, but it offers no greater peak of spectacular excitement than many of those found in the preceding hour.

The noisiest and most spectacular outbursts of the contemporary action-oriented blockbuster are deployed in a variety of ways. Some still reserve the biggest showpieces for the end, a good example being *Mission: Impossible* (1996), which includes numerous sequences of high-tension and/or explosive action but climaxes with an outlandish set-piece involving a helicopter chasing a train into the Channel Tunnel. *Face/Off* (1997) was generally regarded as superior to the general run of action films, providing much excitement along the way, but ending with what was criticized by some as a excessively prolonged spectacular chase.

How do these films compare with action-adventures or other spectaculars of the classical period? Whether or not a measurable trend towards the roller-coaster type of profile can be identified in the New Hollywood era – or any particular part of that era, or in any specific genres or sub-genres – is a question that can only really be answered through close analysis of a large and representative sample of texts from this and the studio period, a task beyond the scope of this chapter. Some provisional suggestions can be made, however.

Musicals of the studio era provide one source of comparison, offering a variety of strategies. Some reserve the biggest 'showstoppers' for the latter stages; others offer a more consistent supply throughout their running time.[15] Most action-adventure films tend to build towards a spectacular climax but they also deliver substantial scenes of action and other forms of spectacle along the way. *The Charge of the Light Brigade* (1936), for example, is clearly structured around the expectation of a climactic spectacle – the infamous 'charge' at Balaklava. The narrative builds inexorably towards that end. Plenty of other spectacle and action is provided along the way, however. The film opens, like many recent examples, with a prologue sequence that supplies an immediate dose of spectacle in the form of a sumptuous mountain palace in Suristan, an 'exotic' leopard hunt and a dramatic incident in which the hero Geoffrey Vickers (Errol Flynn) saves the life of the local chief.

A number of other incidents of heightened excitement are supplied well in advance of the climactic charge, including a lengthy battle and a massacre that forms the emotional fulcrum of the narrative ('explaining' and rendering 'heroic' the charge itself). The profile of the film might be located somewhere between the extremes suggested by Pfeil. The precise balance varies from one film to another, as it does today. Two more Errol Flynn adventures from the period offer further variations of the mix. *Captain Blood* (1935) offers a brief moment of action at its opening (a figure galloping, dramatically, on horseback). The next real 'action' is delayed until the 45-minute mark and followed by several skirmishes that culminate in the major spectacular sequences of the film: a six-minute climactic sea battle. *The Adventures of Robin Hood* (1938) offers a big fight sequence after approximately 14 minutes and another, on a larger scale, at the end; each lasting some four minutes. A steady supply of smaller action and adventure sequences are supplied in between, to a greater extent than is found in *Captain Blood*.

Separating out the elements of spectacle and narrative is not as easy as sketches such as these might suggest. More generally 'spectacular' qualities are offered throughout these films: qualities such as 'exotic' locations, costume and spectacular displays of emotion. Take the all-time hit *Gone with the Wind* (1939). Sequences of grand spectacular action are included, most notably the scenes of devastation and chaos (c.60 minutes into the running time of 222 minutes) that culminate in the fiery and explosive destruction of Atlanta (c.81 minutes). It is far from just these sequences that constitute the spectacular attraction of a film that offers a constant supply of 'larger than life' costume, production design, passion and lurid use of colour and other elements of *mise-en-scène*.

What is the difference between these films and the contemporary blockbuster? The latter often seems to be louder and more insistent in its more frequent deployment of physical action and excitement, although it would be hard to be a great deal more insistent at the level of emotional melodrama than *Gone with the Wind*. Is there a qualitative difference, broadly, between the films of the two periods? Perhaps there is, but it is easily overstated. One way to explore this issue further is to examine some of the ways it might be possible to account for the existence of the high-peaking, roller-coaster format in the particular context of contemporary Hollywood – as an increased tendency or in a particular form, even if not as something entirely new. A number of different explanations might be attempted, ranging from broad social-cultural factors to those more specific to the industrial realm.

## Economic/psychic context: from Fordist/Oedipal to post-Fordist/pre-Oedipal

Fred Pfeil offers a bold and sweeping analysis, locating these formal tendencies within large-scale changes in the economic and psychic configurations of western society. Heady stuff. Classical narrative structure is associated by Pfeil with both a particular kind of economy and a particular psychic regime. Economically, it is associated with a

Fordist version of capitalism (the version based on processes of mass production and mass consumption). Psychically, it is associated with a version of patriarchy and male sexuality rooted in Freud's notion of the Oedipus complex. The two, according to this account – a blend of Marxist and psychoanalytic theory – are closely linked. What relevance do these have to the formal characteristics of Hollywood films, in the dimensions of narrative and spectacle? There is, Pfeil argues, 'a deeply rooted and organic affiliation' between the 'accumulation of unspent dramatic or suspenseful elements' throughout the rising curve of action – eventually 'discharged most completely at the story's climax' – 'and the preferred rhythms of saving and spending, of repression and release, inscribed into the operations of Oedipal masculinity.'[16] Both involve a dynamic of containment and restraint, a gradual building up of tensions that are only eventually granted release.

This pattern of discipline and containment has been undermined, Pfeil suggests. Changes at the economic level have created a more fragmented and unstable environment. A post-Fordist landscape is one in which older mass-production industries have often been undermined, especially in high-labour-cost areas such as the United States. A Fordist economy was the bulwark of a particular form of male dominance. It encouraged the construction of a form of masculinity constructed within the confines of the gender positions claimed by Freud to be the outcome of the Oedipal triangle (the male child, basically, coming to take up a position of identity with the father). A post-Fordist environment, in Pfeil's account, undermines this structure. Post-Oedipal constructions of masculinity are replaced, to some extent at least, by the uncertainty and fluidity of the pre-Oedipal situation, before clear-cut gender roles have been allocated. The pre-Oedipal tends to be seen as a realm lacking the structure and discipline of the Oedipal. It is characterized not by 'rhythms of saving and spending, of repression and release' but by urges for constant gratification. Hence, in Pfeil's analysis, the appeal of the roller-coaster experience, with its constant provision of the spectacular and/or aggressive moments of gratification. None of that Puritanical deferral: let's have it all *now*, and *again* and *again*.

Pfeil concedes that developments in the real world do not fit so easily into schemes such as this. His argument is interesting and provocative, but also subject to a number of qualifications. On both the economic and psychic levels, the propositions summarized above invite a large number of questions. Neither the notion of a shift from Fordism to post-Fordism nor the Oedipal/pre-Oedipal opposition are uncontroversial. If these frameworks are themselves subject to debate, their mobilization here to explain the characteristics of Hollywood films is also problematic. Many questions remain, not the least being those related to the specific processes that might link the economic and/or psychic domains to those of Hollywood production and consumption. How, in addition, might an account such as this explain the extent to which some films of the classical era deviate from any rigid economy of 'saving and spending'? Such problems are often encountered, as we have seen, even in more modest attempts to draw direct connections between the qualities of films and the social-cultural context in which they appear.

This does not mean Pfeil's explanation need entirely be rejected. It does appear to make some sense. The over-insistent rhetoric of action/adventure/excitement/heroics/spectacle/noise found in many contemporary blockbusters does suggest an excessive compensation for what might be understood as a loss of prior 'certainties' about the ideal construction of masculinity. They might be an expression *of* a particular variety of the 'masculine'. But, like the excessively 'built' bodies of some males stars, they might equally betray an underlying lack of grounding for such constructions. This might be linked, at least speculatively, to changes in dominant patterns of work in the western economies of the late twentieth century/early twenty-first (although we should beware of assuming too readily that any of these structures were so firmly grounded at any earlier point).

Spectacular blockbusters usually offer plenty of scope for socio-cultural analysis in terms of gender-role construction, both in their themes and in the seemingly testosterone-driven dynamic of the roller-coaster aesthetic. This remains, ultimately, an arena for speculative interpretation rather than any great certainty. Industrial factors also intrude: another dimension that, as ever, requires a qualification of any explanations based exclusively on broader social context.

## Industrial context I: from blockbuster opening to theme park

The provision of an incessant supply of pounding spectacular action in contemporary Hollywood can be explained in terms of the blockbuster strategy examined in chapter 2. The aim of the corporate blockbuster is to make a big splash, to create impact both in pre-publicity and during the crucial opening weekend. A big, noisy, no-holds-barred spectacular offering might be assumed to do this most effectively. Audiences might be thought more likely to flood in droves to films described in these terms. Such films are more easily sold in the hyperbolic rhetoric used by Hollywood in an attempt to give blockbuster productions the coveted 'must-see' quality.

Films celebrated for their nuanced narratives and more selective deployment of spectacle might be less likely to flourish in an environment in which the norm is for wide openings and saturation advertising. The method of selling can shape the product itself.[17] If the film needs to start with a bang in terms of its early box-office returns, perhaps it makes sense sometimes for it to start, literally, with a loud bang, a huge fireball conflagration of audio-visual impact in the cinema. Gradual development and more nuanced structure might be fitted better to a release pattern that is also gradually developed and nuanced. This is not an absolute distinction, of course. Not all films given wide releases are of the spectacular blockbuster variety and not all blockbusters deploy their resources of spectacle and narrative in the same way.

The roller-coaster variety of spectacular entertainment also lends itself particularly well to some of the secondary markets that have become important sources of revenue for Hollywood in the era of multi-media corporations. Spectacular films might, indeed, become roller-coasters, or other attractions, in theme parks. *Jurassic Park*, *Terminator 2*, *Back to the Future* and *Men in Black* are among the principal attractions at the Universal Studios park in Los Angeles. The Indiana Jones series provides one of the newer rides at Disneyland.[18] Commentators such as Scott Bukatman suggest that blockbuster productions have become more like rides in a context in which the cinematic and extra-cinematic experience merge.[19] Similar claims about an erosion of distinctions, usually at the expense of classical forms of narrative, have been made about the relationship between Hollywood films and computer games. Both rides and games based on films are often structured around the frequent and regular delivery of spectacle–impact thrills. Which comes first is not always easy to say.

Much was made of the placement of the pod-race sequence in *Star Wars: Episode One – The Phantom Menace* (1999), a sequence that not only looked like a computer game but that was extracted from the film as the *Racer* game released by LucasArts.[20] Whether the sequence was designed primarily to be extractable in this way, or whether that was merely an afterthought, is perhaps less important than acknowledgement of the mutually reinforcing influences of the two media, particularly when combined in a single corporation. Films that in some respects resemble games are a source of exploitable games material. This relationship can run both ways, however. Spectacular films might also play on the appeal of games, incorporating some of their features. Such a development would hardly be surprising, given the growing popularity and revenues of games and the fact that Hollywood and the games industry target similar market groups.

## Industrial context II: audiences

A heavy emphasis on the non–stop spectacular dimension might also be explained to some extent in terms of the principal target audiences of the Hollywood blockbuster, on grounds ranging from age to gender and social class. Films that display the characteristics of the roller-coaster may be targeted particularly at relatively young, male and lower-class audiences.

Fast-moving and/or noisy spectacle is seen by Hollywood as attractive to younger audiences, from teenage to twenties and thirties (sections that constitute a large proportion of the audience: from 65 to 70 per cent of those admitted to the cinema from 1995 to 1999 were aged between 12 and 39, according to industry figures[21]). There might not be any scientific basis for this assumption, but it seems prevalent in our culture. Older or more mature audiences are thought more likely to appreciate works that are quieter, more subtle and take their time, building gradually to a climax. Relatively young males have become the principal target audience for Hollywood blockbusters: hence the number of films that offer what they are expected to find attractive. Women are assumed, according to the dominant gender roles of patriarchal societies, to prefer products focused more closely on sustained character-development and emotional relationships that tend not to be in the foreground of the noisiest and most spectacular blockbusters.

What about class? The instant and repeated gratification offered by the roller-coaster aesthetic fits with prevalent notions of the kinds of products deemed likely to appeal to those from lower-class backgrounds. The appreciation of more subtly graded works is associated with those of middle or upper-class background. Taste, as Pierre Bourdieu argues, is a socially defined product.[22] What we 'like' is a matter less of individual choice than of social background. A 'taste' for subtlety does not spring from nowhere. It is the product of a particular kind of education, an accumulation of what Bourdieu defines as 'cultural capital': a learned ability to appreciate certain types of products. 'Subtlety' is appreciated as a quality that enables the consumer to make full use of, and display, his or her accumulation of cultural capital. An important component of this process is Bourdieu's central notion of 'distinction'. The ability to appreciate certain forms has value largely through establishing a distinction from those who lack such ability, such cultural capital, or, ultimately, such a social class position.

In expressing a taste for subtlety, viewers who dislike the everything-but-the-kitchen-sink style of spectacular blockbuster are marking themselves out from those who do, but in a manner that is expressed as a difference of natural or individual 'taste' rather than of class or cultural background. 'Instant gratification' might be rejected by some as a way of defining themselves, implicitly, in particular terms of social class. For others, the appeal of instant gratification might be understood in social terms. Audiences from less privileged backgrounds may lack the time or money to defer their gratification; either to accumulate the cultural capital necessary to enjoy products based on deferral of gratification, or to have much reason for putting faith in the likelihood that the sacrifice of short-term pleasure will be met by future reward. Material grounds can begin to be suggested for the appeal of this kind of entertainment to particular sections of the population defined broadly by social class. This remains a complex business, however, and fraught with difficulties, like all sweeping attempts to understand the appeal of popular cultural products such as Hollywood films in social-cultural terms. In reality, many shadings and overlappings of tastes, and many idiosyncrasies, are likely to intrude on analysis of so broad-brush a variety, some of which may be picked up by closer analysis of particular audience groups.

None of the above is to suggest that spectacle-heavy blockbuster entertainment is the exclusive preserve of young lower-class males. Even the most over-insistent Hollywood spectacle is designed to attract a broader audience than this, and industry surveys have shown a higher than average proportion of college-educated individuals – with the likely social background and cultural capital that implies – among regular cinemagoers. Certain tendencies may exist, at certain levels, but distinctions need to be made between the assumptions and targeting expectations of Hollywood and actual patterns of filmgoing that are always likely to be more complex.

Distinctions also need to be made between one type of spectacle and another. Many young women were drawn to *Titanic* by its romantic narrative more than by the spectacular effects. But a major attraction was also the spectacle constituted by the presence of Leonardo DiCaprio. The spectacular deployment of the ship-effects is also used at key moments to heighten the emotions of romance. Differences are found between one spectacular blockbuster and another. The balance between spectacular and narrative or non-spectacular material is variable, some mixture of the two being characteristic of all mainstream Hollywood production. In some cases it might be possible to explain this at least partly in terms of the target audiences for which Hollywood studios appear to have aimed.

*Armageddon* appears to be targeted primarily at a male audience. It also contains a dimension of emotional family melodrama, however, designed to offer something for women (along with the male-star appeal of the likes of Bruce Willis). One trailer opens with a focus on the romance between two of the younger principals, a conscious effort to target women as well as male viewers. *Deep Impact*, a similar-themed earth-threatened-by-space-rock production released in the summer 1998 blockbuster season, reverses the emphasis. The principal focus is on a network of emotional relationships and sacrifices among its ensemble cast. Major spectacular impact is reserved for the climax. How exactly this is put depends on how we choose to limit our definition of 'spectacular', however: *Deep Impact* offers plenty of 'spectacle' in the form of emotional impact, particularly in a series of 'sacrifices for children' sequences, the number and intensity of which build towards a climax that goes beyond the immediate requirements of the narrative. *Titanic* (1997) offers a carefully balanced equation: highly spectacular special effects sequences and a dramatic disaster scenario, combined in equal proportions with melodrama and romance. The huge success of *Titanic* prompted industry speculation that a lesson might be learned: that future blockbusters might be designed to appeal more explicitly to a female audience.[23]

*Titanic* appealed to a youthful audience, especially an audience of teenage girls attracted by the presence of Leonardo DiCaprio. But it also attracted a considerably older audience, on the basis perhaps of its claims to the status of classic 'old fashioned' Hollywood epic (*Titanic* was certainly reviewed in these terms by some critics[24]), as did *Deep Impact*.[25] The same was true of *Gladiator*. Demographic changes have led to an increase in the proportion of the cinema audience constituted by older viewers. In 1984, only 15 per cent of the audience was aged more than 40. This increased to 24 per cent by 1990.[26] From 1995 to 1999 approximately a third fell into the 40-plus age category, according to the Motion Picture Association.[27] The shift towards an older demographic has been more rapid in parts of the international market, a particularly important arena for the spectacular blockbuster: attendance by those aged more than 45 in the United Kingdom was shown by one study in 2000 to have increased by 450 per cent in a decade.[28] This is a significant, if not dominant, sector of the market, and another factor to enter into industrial calculations. Large scale box-office success is unlikely to be based on this audience alone, however. A combination of appeals is necessary.

*Gladiator* starts with a bang – a spectacular battle, the highest point on its overall spectacle/narrative profile – and offers a number of spectacular combat sequences, aiming at the audience for the contemporary style of action-spectacle and perhaps those familiar with gladiatorial-style engagements from the world of 'beat–em–up' videogames. If this is a source of appeal primarily for younger males, *Gladiator* also offers personal intrigue and domestic/family reference points aimed at women (along with the display of male gladiatorial bodies). Charted along the graphic lines suggested earlier in this chapter, *Gladiator* would produce a profile in which spectacular sequences are more than balanced by those devoted to the development of character and narrative progression. Television advertising was designed separately to capture male and female audiences. Fight scenes were used in TV spots in male-oriented programmes, such as sports, while sequences highlighting qualities of drama and romance were placed in more female-oriented programmes such as *Ally McBeal*. Other advertisements played on 'a rather undefinable and yet undeniable epic quality that could attract the hard to reach older group who often only go to the cinema once a year.'[29] *Gladiator* successfully attracted the wide-ranging audience it targeted, achieving box office revenues of $186.6 million in the US and $258.2 million overseas. Its domestic audience was measured as 65 per cent male on the opening day but shifted subsequently to an equal male/female split, a fact that may have contributed to its ability to sustain its performance.[30]

## The persistence of 'classical' narrative forms

The balance between spectacular and narrative elements varies among contemporary Hollywood blockbusters. Spectacle is important, sometimes dominant. In no cases, however, do we find a complete abandonment of narrative components familiar from the studio or 'classical' era. A ratcheting–up of the intensity or frequency of spectacular display in recent years might be explained by specific aspects of cultural or industrial context; or, more generally, by a perceived need to up the ante to combat audience over-familiarity and to maintain a sense of producing something 'newer', 'bigger' and 'more sensational' to compete with the proliferation of rival media attractions. Even the loudest, most non-stop action spectaculars rely on narrative constructs to a considerable extent however. The narrative dimension might not be drawn to our attention as much as the spectacular display, for good reasons. Traditional Hollywood narrative devices are designed usually to make a film flow effortlessly, rather than to claim attention in their own right.

At its most limited, narrative is seen by some as little more than a device to take the viewer from one spectacular treat to another. Martin Barker and Kate Brooks offer a literal version of the roller-coaster metaphor. For those wishing to enjoy the thrill of sheer spectacle, 'narrative is like a carrier-wave, similar to the role that rails play on a big dipper – necessary to carry you along, but in themselves not the point of the exercise.'[31] Narrative is only worth mentioning by audiences if badly designed. Even here, however, the narrative role remains important. If the principal business is the delivery of spectacle, this still has to be done effectively. Many spectacular blockbusters display carefully honed narrative structures designed not just unceremoniously to unload a series of great dollops of action-spectacle but to engage viewers and to increase the impact of the action and spectacle by locating it in relation to character and plot.

Take *Die Hard with a Vengeance*. The film delivers a regular supply of action-spectacular thrills, but these are integrated into a carefully developed narrative line that employs many of the conventions associated with classical narrative. This is true of the three main examples of high-peak action-spectacular discussed previously in this chapter. *Die Hard with a Vengeance*, *Speed* and *Deep Blue Sea* focus on pairs or small groups of individual characters, one of the strongest conventions of Hollywood narrative. Each presents a narrative structured around the goals and actions of these characters. One event leads to another in a chain of causes and effects, another major convention of classical narrative. Elements of narrative and spectacle are closely integrated, down to the fine moment-by-moment detail. The opening moves of *Die Hard with a Vengeance* provide a good illustration.

There is a large explosion in the opening minutes, but this is not all. A series of narrative dynamics is also established, with considerable precision and economy. The bomb goes off; cut to scenes of activity at police headquarters. A woman seeks the attention of the man in charge (later revealed as Inspector Arthur Cobb), calling him to the telephone. 'I think you'd better take this', she says (indicating that something important is to come from the call). The caller (the bomber, later revealed as Simon Krieg, played by Jeremy Irons) tells Cobb (Larry Bryggman) the initial explosion 'was just to make sure I had your attention' (a self-conscious nod, perhaps, to the viewer familiar with action movie conventions such as the opening jolt). He asks for 'a detective named McClane' (who many viewers will know to be the distinctive Bruce Willis character from the previous two Die Hard films). McClane is on suspension, Cobb informs him (calling up recollections of, or helping to establish, McClane's character as a nonconformist). Not now, he's not, replies the caller (confirming our expectation that McClane is soon going to be back in action).

The caller says he will tell McClane what to do. Non-compliance will mean a penalty: 'another big bang in a very public place' (setting up two rival dynamics: our anticipation of another fireball, as enjoyable spectacle, combined with a suspense narrative devoted to the desperate attempt to prevent it; we can enjoy it either way). McClane is to be despatched to Harlem (we do not know exactly why, or why the caller is picking on McClane: narrative enigmas are established, provoking our curiosity, although those familiar with the franchise might not be entirely surprised that McClane's past actions have provoked such rancour).

Just three minutes have elapsed at this point. A big spectacle has been provided, and more have been promised, but so has a quantity of narrative matter. The call goes out to find McClane. Next thing, he is on the screen, hung over and worse for wear (confirming his unconventional, on-the-edge-cop status). As an aside, Walter asks a colleague about events they had been discussing before the bomber's call. The answer includes reference to the theft of 14 dump trucks, followed by banter about lottery tickets and the fact that cops tend to play their badge numbers. Each of these seemingly marginal details is carefully planted in order to play a significant role later in the narrative, another classical strategy: the dump trucks are used by Krieg's gang in a theft of gold bullion; a detective's badge number will help McClane to twig what is going on.

All this is established in under five minutes. A better example of 'classical' narrative economy would be hard to find. The viewer is offered a number of hooks and points of reference, ranging from the central narrative enigma to expectations of further action/spectacle and nuances of character. Details to be built upon later have been planted. Space is even found for a touch of 'postmodern' reflexivity.

*Die Hard with a Vengeance* might offer a regular succession of action sequences but it is misleading to suggest that it holds nothing back. Spectacle is interwoven with a developing series of narrative questions, partial answers and further questions designed to keep the viewer guessing. What is the bomber up to? The first suggestion is that he is a megalomaniac with a grudge against McClane. Fair enough. The psychiatrist who makes this diagnosis is not far wrong, but his verdict sounds a little formulaic and routine: we might expect something more distinctive. Nothing further is forthcoming until after the Wall Street subway explosion, when we learn that the bomber is the brother of the arch-criminal killed by McClane at the end of *Die Hard* (1988). Now, it seems, we have an answer: a character with plenty of motive. But we are only 41 minutes in. A Hollywood action movie could go on from here to offer little more in the way of plot development: merely the series of action-spectacular sequences implied by some critics.

This is not the case with *Die Hard with a Vengeance*. More twists are to follow. Some four minutes later we are given privileged access – signified by an omniscient overhead shot – to the fact that the bombs are cover for something else: 'they bought it', Krieg gloats, but we still do not know exactly what he is up to. A few hints follow, as Krieg enters a massive Wall Street edifice that we learn is a bank, before his target is fully revealed when the camera homes in on a shoulder badge informing us that it is the Federal Reserve Bank. We now know more than McClane, who has a moment of enlightenment close to the 60-minute mark, confirmed nearly eight minutes later ('this is a heist!'). The shift in the relative knowledge of audience and character creates a change of gear in the narrative dynamic: a movement from enigma (what is really going on?) to one of character-centred suspense (when will McClane find out what we already know?).

The separation of the knowledge-basis of McClane and the viewer also helps the film to supply another quintessential Hollywood narrative quality: redundancy. Repetition is used to ensure maximum comprehensibility of significant plot detail. We might work out that bank robbery is in store before it is made entirely obvious; if we fail to pay attention to this, it is made plain in the shot of the shoulder badge. Exactly what is at stake is spelled out further in exchanges between Krieg and a colleague. This knowledge is reinforced, and the moment of revelation re-enacted, through McClane's discovery. Further reinforcement is provided in the belated understanding conveyed to Arthur Cobb.

The bad guys appear to be escaping with the gold on board the ship, but we get a hint that something is amiss. One of Krieg's henchmen is suspicious. Krieg subsequently proclaims that the gold is to be destroyed as part of a radical political intervention against the global capitalist economy. The viewer is informed otherwise, by McClane: the political rhetoric is merely a gloss to cover theft. Twists and developments in the underlying plot are dispersed through the film, in a manner similar to, and often integrated with, the provision of action-spectacle. Narrative devices operate across the length of the film, and also in its smaller units. Another classical convention utilized constantly in *Die Hard with a Vengeance* is a temporal structure built around a series of deadlines. McClane and Zeus are set a number of puzzles and tasks, all to be completed within pressing time limits, culminating in the threatened bombing of a school by 3pm.

Moments of intensified spectacular action in *Die Hard with a Vengeance* are located within a carefully constructed narrative frame. The same goes for *Speed* and *Deep Blue Sea*, each of which takes time amid the mayhem to sketch a range of distinct characters, relationships and motivations. The narrative format of these films has something in common with the episodic structure of the B-movie adventure stories of the 1930s and 1940s, moving at times from one deadline-jeopardy situation to another. The structure of the B-movie and adventure serial has been seen, more generally, as an influence on the contemporary blockbuster format, other examples in which it has been cited including the *Star Wars* and Indiana Jones series.

Warren Buckland examines *Raiders of the Lost Ark*, the first of the Indiana Jones films, as a series of six distinct episodes, often involving the kind of unlikely escapades and last-second escapes found in *Die Hard with a Vengeance*, *Speed* and *Deep Blue Sea*. The sequences in *Raiders* are not entirely separate, however; they generate an overarching pattern that reaches a resolution in the final episode: 'The point to make here is that this pattern transcends individual episodes, and it is dependent for its very existence on the presence of a feature-length story.'[32] *Die Hard with a Vengeance* is less episodic than *Raiders of the Lost Ark*. Its narrative structure is quite tightly organized, although it has its share of coincidences. *Speed* and *Deep Blue Sea* also have strong overall narrative dynamics that run through the various individual crises, clearly focused around the efforts to save the bus passengers or escape from the underwater labyrinth of the research station.

Even at its most episodic, the contemporary Hollywood blockbuster does not represent a clear break from the studio era. It is still strongly driven by the dynamics of the feature-length narrative, numerous developments occurring across and between any divisions between distinct episodes. And, as suggested by Cowie, episodic structure – in which narrative events are sometimes displaced by set-pieces and not always given clear causal explanation – is found in plenty of products of the 'classical' period.[33] This is the case at the levels of both 'prestige' and B-movie production; the latter, in which action, thrills and pace were typically favoured over narrative coherence and characterization, was a crucial factor in the stabilization of production at the height of the studio period.[34]

For Thomas Schatz, the distinguishing characteristic of some New Hollywood blockbusters is not an absence of narrative drive but precisely the kind of 'hell-bent' and careening form of narrative found in the films discussed above. The principal example chosen by Schatz is *Star Wars*, in which he suggests an 'emphasis on plot over character marks a significant departure from classical Hollywood films, including *The Godfather* and even *Jaws*, wherein plot tended to emerge more organically as a function of the drives, desires, motivations, and goals of the central characters.'[35] *Star Wars*, in this account, remains 'a masterwork of narrative technique'.[36] The precise balance between factors such as plot and character does vary from one film to another. It remains questionable, again, whether this should be seen as 'a significant departure' from the films of the classical era, given the scope for variety that appears to be available in both the studio and post-studio eras.

The spectacular action sequences of *Die Hard with a Vengeance* are narrative events in their own right, even if they offer sensational pleasures that go beyond the requirements of moving forward the plot. The big chase sequence in *Die Hard with a Vengeance* is spectacular but also an integral part of the narrative dynamic. It is tied in to a deadline structure. It is also used to develop the relationship between the two main protagonists. The fact that it is more spectacular than necessary to achieve these ends does not mean these narrative dynamics are not also in play. The 'excessive' quota of spectacle is a source of pleasure in its own right, and one that merits attention as a distinct component in this kind of film. It is rare, however, for spectacular audio-visual display to be unleashed more than fleetingly in Hollywood without bearing some relation to narrative dynamics.

Narrative processes often continue during and through sequences of spectacle, a fact easily concealed by graphic sketches such as those suggested in figures 4 and 5, which separate out dimensions of narrative and spectacle that often work in tandem. They create a rather one-dimensional picture, failing to account for less overt aspects of spectacle – elements such as star presence or smaller-scale instances of action, scenery or costume – that are liable to operate throughout the length of a film. A more complex model would need to take all of these factors into account. It would also need to be less hermetic, focusing not just on the individual text but also on a range of intertextual forces that are brought to bear at any particular moment. Whether it would be possible to capture such complex and sometimes fleeting relationships in a manner subject to any objective measurement is doubtful.

Spectacle and narrative often work closely together and interpenetrate across the length of Hollywood films from both the classical and New Hollywood periods. As Maltby puts it: 'In the experience of its audience, a movie is the emotional equivalent of a roller-coaster ride at least as much as it is a thematically significant story: borrowing a term, we might call the combination a "story-ride".'[37] The term 'story-ride' captures nicely the spectacle/narrative dynamic found in many Hollywood products. It does this not as a way of condemning the shortcomings of the contemporary blockbuster, as the comparison with theme-park rides is usually used by critics; or in marking a qualitative shift from 'classical' linear plotting to 'post-classical' episodic roller-coaster. What the term more usefully suggests is the variable mixture in which the two dimensions are found in Hollywood; particular explanations being available to account for particular configurations at any specific historical/industrial moment. If spectacle and narrative often work together at the level of the development of linear story, a similar argument can be made in terms of the thematic issues and structures with which Hollywood blockbusters engage.

## Narrative themes

A white cop with a reluctantly recruited black civilian partner. An antagonistic relationship – including accusations of racism on both parts – that develops into an exercise in teamwork. A bi-racial opposites-brought-together 'buddy' partnership lies at the heart of *Die Hard with a Vengeance*, a narrative framework that lends itself to a reading in terms of the negotiation or reconciliation of social-cultural or ideological issues. A combination of the skills and qualities of both McClane and Zeus is necessary for the success of their mission. McClane appears to offer the unlikely action-heroics (driving crazily through Central Park, leaping onto a moving subway train); Zeus the brains (solving the first of the riddles set by Krieg). Each exhibits some of the qualities of his rival/ partner, however. It is Zeus who suggests the hazardous attempt to board the ship from a bridge, while McClane works out the solution of the riddle involving the use of two jugs of water to measure an exact quantity of liquid required to disarm a bomb planted in Tompkins Square Park. Racial differences and divisions are highlighted in a number of testy exchanges between the two. The impression offered, however, is that such differences can be overcome through teamwork.

A good example can be found in the sequence involving the water jugs. The first riddle encountered in the park is solved by Zeus. The pair argue when tackling the puzzle of the jugs. Zeus accuses McClane of being about to call him a 'nigger'; McClane accuses Zeus of being a racist himself. Each denies the accusation, defining their hostility in non-racial terms: McClane was just going to call Zeus an 'asshole'; the dislike of Zeus for McClane is not because he is white, as McClane claims, but because 'you're going to get me killed'. Under the growing

10. Arguing, deflecting accusations of racism and eventually combining to save the day: McClane (Bruce Willis) and Zeus (Samuel L. Jackson) in *Die Hard with a Vengeance*, © Cinergi Pictures Entertainment Inc, Cinergi Productions N.V. Inc. and Twentieth Century Fox Film Corporation, 1995. Ronald Grant archive

pressure of a countdown deadline, McClane reaches a last-second solution to the riddle and the two cooperate to complete the task. The negotiation of racial tension is inserted into a series of exchanges focused on the ability of the two to work together, to combine their forces, to overcome what the film tends to present as 'petty' or inessential differences or misunderstandings in pursuit of what is seen as a larger and common objective: the prevention of mass destruction.

These devices are typical of the way Hollywood tends to handle potentially contentious ideological-political issues: projecting differences onto individuals; reconciling the individuals, thus evading while appearing to reconcile the issues themselves. This is all carefully structured narrative material, a significant part of the fabric of the film. The ability of films to seem to take on board such issues, to avoid any real confrontation and to offer a kind of 'magical' reconciliation, might be part of their appeal; a source of pleasure understandable in social-cultural terms. It is also related to, rather than separated from, the dimension of spectacular action. It is in the heat of the action, to a large extent, that the relationship between McClane and Zeus is forged: a environment of heightened intensity presented as one in which 'petty' prejudices can be cast aside.

*Deep Blue Sea* plays into oppositions between the Frankensteinian meddling of scientists with the forces of nature (given a contemporary twist in the theme of genetic modification) and the respect for nature personified by the hands-on shark 'wrangler' Blake Carter (Thomas Jane), a figure of western 'frontier' credentials. Even *Speed*, which might appear to be a limit-case in its focus on almost incessant action, implies thematically an opposition similar to one found in the *Die Hard* films and *Deep Blue Sea*.

Jack Traven, like John McClane, is a representative of no-nonsense direct action. The *Die Hard* films establish an opposition between McClane and impotent police bureaucracy, especially in the first two instalments. This kind of framework is traceable in the background of *Speed*: the bomber Payne is a former bomb-disposal officer with a grudge resulting from the cursory treatment he received on being retired after an injury incurred in the line of duty (an early reference suggests that Traven's efforts will eventually receive similarly meagre reward). Much more space could be devoted to these issues than is possible here.[38] The point is that the Hollywood blockbuster has a considerable commitment to these dimensions of narrative, with all their considerable ideological implications. It is rare, if ever, that an example can be found that is not open to such readings, a factor generally ignored by commentators who argue the case for the supplanting of narrative by spectacle.

## Toy stories

The camera turns and pans across shelves of merchandise. Dinosaur figures, branded sweat shirts, lunch boxes, drink bottles, a 'making of' book. A strange and much-cited moment in *Jurassic Park* (1993), a fulcrum around which we can go in either of two directions. One is inwards, towards the fictional events of the film: the products are on sale at the fictional venue, the imaginary dinosaur theme park. The other movement is outward, away from the fiction and into the real space of the corporate Hollywood blockbuster: the merchandise on display clearly mirrors the products sold on the back of the real *Jurassic Park*, in its day the top-grossing film of all time and for which some 1,000 products were officially licensed.[39]

A number of commentators have drawn attention to the inclusion of this gesture in the film. It might be seen as an amusing touch of self-reference. For some, however, it has been seen as an undue and potentially fatal intrusion of the commercial realities of blockbuster production into the fabric of the film, a blatant and explicit extra-textual 'plug' for *Jurassic Park* merchandising. This is only a brief and passing moment, however, hardly capable of destabilizing a fast-paced action thriller. A similar gesture, on the subject of competition between rival summer blockbusters, is found in *Armageddon*, in the shape of an inflatable Godzilla toy attacked by a dog belonging to a minor character.

Examples such as these appear marginal, quaint even, compared with the extent to which merchandising invades *Toy Story 2* (1999). Here we have a central character, the cowboy toy figure Woody, who clearly exists in large part as advertisement for the Woody toy available in the shops – along with many others including the more popular 'space ranger' figure, Buzz Lightyear. Not only this. His role in the sequel to *Toy Story* (1995) is centred on his own status within the fiction *as* a merchandising spin-off. Woody is stolen/kidnapped because he turns out to be a rare surviving artefact produced as part of the merchandising associated with an ill-fated 1950s television show.

Merchandising is not only present, but a significant *theme* of the film. Some of the events of *Toy Story 2* take place in a large toy store. No brief pan along a shelf of merchandise here; instead, a lengthy highlighting of a range of toy-characters featured in the film. Shelves full of Buzz Lightyears. An aisle of Barbies. All lingered over and integrated into the events of the plot. The worlds of toy-merchandise and film characters are mutually implicated in a sustained fashion to a point at which they are impossible to separate. There is even a reference to the merchandising hiccup in which 'short-sighted retailers' failed to stock enough Lightyear figures to meet demand last time around.

11. Playing the game... *of* the movie *in* the movie: Woody and Buzz go commercially self-referential in *Toy Story 2*, © Walt Disney Co., 1999. Ronald Grant archive

The Buzz Lightyear figure was advertised in the commercials shown before the main feature in the cinema (in Britain, at least). It is then given a starring role in the film, the toyshop scenes foregrounding its availability for purchase. The adverts accompanying the film included a plug for the *Toy Story 2* PlayStation game, which is also featured prominently in the movie. The commercials appeared somewhat redundant, in fact, given the promotional power of the feature. The film appears to be designed as the perfect showcase for the merchandise. As such, it is the product of a partnership well placed to cash in on such qualities. The film was produced as part of a multi-picture agreement between the Pixar animation house and Walt Disney, a powerful cross-media operation with many other avenues in which to exploit the film, ranging from network television (ABC) and cable (the Disney Channel, home to Buzz Lightyear's television spin-off, *Star Command*, and ESPN) to its own video label, theme parks and retail stores.

What is the fate of the films themselves, in this corporate environment? To what extent are blockbusters, or other potential money-spinners, viewed as products in their own right? Or are they seen as little more than arbitrary means to earn profits in other forms and formats? Does it matter that the film divisions are often relatively small fish in the corporate pool? Sony Pictures, for example, the principal corporate example used in chapter 2, accounted for $4.6 billion in sales and operating revenue in the year ended 31 March 2000. A large sum, but only a small proportion of Sony's total of $63 billion. The film and television division is heavily outweighed by electronics ($41.4 billion). Music ($6.2 billion) and videogames ($5.9 billion) also account for larger revenues than pictures.[40] Does this increase the likelihood that film will be seen as less important in itself? Does the greater value of the games division make it more likely that films will be shaped to provide potential for game spin-offs? Probably not, in any direct or clearly measurable fashion, even if some kind of influence might sometimes be exerted.

Apart from anything else, it is easy to exaggerate the extent to which Hollywood operates in so 'rational' and calculating a manner, as merely a part of larger media empires. Yes, many ideas for films are exhaustively concept-tested and overseen by businessmen interested primarily in the extraction of profits. But Hollywood retains its own distinctive culture, practice and oddities. Decision-making remains often a haphazard and somewhat eccentric business, particularly in the crucial area of which of the many films in development at any time achieve the 'green light' to go into production.[41]

Some go as far as to announce, rhetorically, the 'death' of the film itself, as a distinct and free-standing medium of expression.[42] For James Schamus,

> the supposed 'identity' of the filmic text comes increasingly under the dissolving pressures of its various revenue streams. Do *Volcano* (1997), *Mission: Impossible* (1996) or *ID4* (1996) need 'classical Hollywood' narrative construction, when it is precisely the fragmentation of their narratives into soundtrack albums, somatic theme-park jolts, iconic emblems stuck on T-shirts, and continuous loops of home entertainment that are really what is being sold? I don't think so.[43]

Has the cinema of the blockbuster, at least, become little more than an adjunct to a multimedia and merchandising exploitation machine? It seems an inescapable conclusion that many blockbuster productions are designed with more than passing consideration of their potential beyond the confines of the movie frame. *Godzilla*,

*Batman* and the *Toy Story* films are among prominent candidates for such assumptions. Would they have existed if it were not for the particular industrial context that made them so attractive in terms of an array of spin-off products? It is hard to say; negative arguments are always difficult to prove himself.

It is likely that decisions about what films to produce are shaped by such factors, especially at the blockbuster end of the market. Should we be so surprised, or outraged – as seems to be the case with some critics – that this might be the case? It is more than a little naïve to expect Hollywood to put its faith in the more subtle, nuanced and self-contained features favoured by many commentators. The heavily merchandised blockbuster smacks too much of blatant commerce for the tastes of some. This, in itself, is understandable, as a value judgement. But it often seems to lead to a blunting of critical faculties. The fact that even the most heavy-handed blockbuster is seen as a potential cornucopia of profits beyond the box office does not necessarily undermine its status as a more-or-less coherent narrative text.

It is useful here to distinguish between different levels of exploitation. One line of additional revenue remains focused on the film as a distinct and bounded audio-visual text. A film shown on the small screen, in whatever format, might lack some of the qualities of theatrical exhibition. It might also be watched rather differently in a domestic environment. But it remains basically the same product. Exactly how New Hollywood films might have been shaped by the importance of showings on small-screen media such as videotape, cable, satellite or terrestrial television will be examined in the next chapter. The emphasis is still on the qualities, merits or shortcomings of the screen fiction itself. Other sources of revenue go beyond the boundaries of the text. This is especially true of merchandising products and promotional tie-ins. What is the impact of this on the coherence of the film itself? A number of commentators have argued that narrative coherence has suffered from the increased importance of merchandising and product placement strategies in New Hollywood cinema.

Product placement has become institutionalized in Hollywood since the 1980s. Many large corporations have divisions dedicated to paying to have their goods inserted strategically into movies, to gain access to what is seen as a glamorous medium with a relatively captive audience.

'Add the magic of movies to a promotion, and you can rise above the clutter to get people's attention,' as Mark Crispin Miller quotes one unnamed Disney executive.[44] The appearance of branded products, such as colas and beers among others, is 'anti-narrative', Miller argues, 'for the same movie-glow that exalts each product high above the "clutter" of the everyday also lifts it out of, and thereby makes it work against, the movie's story (if any).'[45]

Is this really the case? Or are critics such as Miller and Schamus guilty of rhetorical exaggeration? Miller provides numerous examples that do not seem to work against narrative. Many are designed to function at a subliminal level, as he suggests, used both to plug one set of products and to undermine rivals through negative associations. In one scene in *Missing* (1982), the sympathetic father-figure (Jack Lemmon) 'takes rare (and noticeable) solace in a bottle of Coke – whereas inside the nightmare stadium where the army does its torturing and murdering, there stands a mammoth Pepsi machine, towering within this underworld like a dark idol.'[46] The aim of such placements is not to disrupt narrative, however: their potential effect resides largely in the resonances provided by the narrative context. Another example to which I have referred elsewhere is found in *Twister* (1996). Wing-like attachments made from cut-up pieces of Pepsi cans are used as a final improvisation that makes effective a device used to monitor tornadoes, a development at the heart of one of the narrative structures of the film. Pepsi shines in the limelight, not disrupting narrative but gaining the full benefit of its plug through its location at a narrative crux.[47]

*Cast Away* (2000) is not far short of a feature-length advertisement for Federal Express, the company for which the hero Chuck Noland (Tom Hanks) works, a demonstration of the ability of Hollywood to product-place even on a desert island. But significant narrative events (the contents of packages washed up on shore after a FedEx plane crashes) and themes (principally involving time) are organized through the prominent placement of the FedEx logo on the screen. The principal secondary 'character' in much of the film is another example of blatant product placement that is also integrated strongly into the narrative domain. A volleyball christened 'Wilson' after its maker, and given a face painted in blood, becomes Noland's source of companionship on his island, an inanimate object the eventual loss of which we are encouraged to mourn almost as much as that of a real person; an extreme example of product placement through positive-vibe personification.

Justin Wyatt suggests that narrative coherence can be disrupted by strategies used to market both the individual film and a range of spin-off products. One argument concerns the impact of music videos related to films. The promotion of some features is helped by the use of videos featuring music from the film. In some cases sequences akin to music videos appear in the body of the text. The principal examples cited by Wyatt are *Flashdance* (1983), *Footloose* (1984), *Purple Rain* (1984), *Staying Alive* (1983) and *The Bodyguard* (1992). In these films, 'the excess created by the conjunction of music and image creates a module separate from the narrative, working against the sequential structuring of the film.'[48]

This, for Wyatt, is part of a post-classical 'high concept' cinema prevalent from the 1980s, a style of filmmaking based around simplified narrative concepts designed to fit into strategies led by marketing and merchandising. The existence of such a style is linked by Wyatt to some of the industrial development traced in this book, including the location of the film industry within the world of giant corporations and the development of new marketing and distribution strategies since the mid 1970s. Music sequences interrupt the narrative in many high concept films, Wyatt suggests, in much the same manner as the numbers of the classical musical of the studio era. Two differences are identified, however, marking the distinctive nature of the high concept version. Disruptions of narrative are familiar and institutionalized in the musical. But, Wyatt suggests, this style is found in some films that 'cannot appeal to the musical genre as an explanation for their excess.'[49] Examples include *Batman*, *Pretty Woman* (1990), *Risky Business* (1983), *Cocktail* (1988) and *Wayne's World* (1992). The fact that the disruption of narrative by high concept music-related sequences is said to go beyond the realm of the musical is significant because the musical is a form in which departures from narrative might not be seen as undermining 'classical' Hollywood style, because they are generically motivated, as a familiar exception to the rule.

Narrative is further destabilized, for Wyatt, by the separate existence of music videos, designed to promote both the music and the film. In some cases the music video includes re-workings of parts of the film narrative: characters engage in activities different from those depicted in the film, clips are shown out of order or in combinations that imply events that do not occur in the film: 'If the excess within the film seeks to destroy the unity of the filmic system, then this process is strengthened by the extra-diegetic promotion, such as the music video, which reshapes and even reconceives the narrative.[50] A further degree of 'rewriting' is found in albums that include music not featured within the film but 'inspired' by it, Wyatt suggests, prominent examples being the music by Prince and Madonna, accompanying *Batman* and *Dick Tracy* respectively.

Wyatt's arguments are more nuanced, and more grounded in the specific industrial context of New Hollywood, than those of Miller. It is far from clear, however, that the existence of extra-filmic elements such as music videos and soundtrack albums really constitutes any significant destabilization of narrative, even in a relatively small number of cases. Is there really a pluralization of narrative, a dispersal of the viewer's understanding of films, as a result of the presence of music videos or soundtrack albums which do not conform strictly to the material on screen? It is one thing to identify discrepancies between one form and another, and Wyatt provides numerous examples. But do these translate into a loss of the sense of the largely coherent film text at the centre of the marketing and merchandising enterprise? This seems doubtful.

Wyatt also suggests that a focus on the qualities of the high-gloss visual style of many high concept films tends to halt or 'freeze' the narrative, a style attributable both to the influence of film directors with a background in advertising and to the commercial imperative to create images that can themselves be raided for purposes of advertising and spin-off merchandising. This is accompanied, for Wyatt, by several other qualities: a lack of character development; a higher than usual reliance on star-persona and style-based character-typing; a dependence on familiarity with the icons of genre, often placed in altered contemporary contexts; and a self-conscious process of referring to other films and aspects of popular media culture:

> Perhaps the most striking result of the high concept style is a weakening
> of identification with character and narrative. The modularity of the

film's units, added to the one-dimensional quality of the characters, distances the viewer from the traditional task of reading the film's narrative. In place of this identification with narrative, the viewer becomes sewn into the "surface" of the film, contemplating the style of the narrative and the production.[51]

Wyatt offers some useful analysis of a format that became popular in Hollywood, especially in the 1980s. Style, design and 'lifestyle' images are foregrounded in the films Wyatt examines. Some of these might use rather compressed and shallow formulations of genre and character-type. It is debatable how different this is from the way genre or character have often been used throughout the history of Hollywood, however. Whether any of this adds up to a weakening of narrative or identification with character remains even more questionable.

Prominent examples of the high concept style, such as *Top Gun* and *Flashdance* (and most if not all of the others cited by Wyatt), still revolve closely around the aspirations and fate of their central characters; goal-driven figures existing within strongly cause/effect structured narratives and with whom we are encouraged to identify at some level. Music may have been extractable from *Top Gun*, as a source of promotion and of revenue in its own right, but the main theme also serves narrative purposes *within* the film. It plays an important part in foreshadowing the moment when the two principals first make love, for example. Broad Hollywood convention encourages a firm expectation that this will happen, but the music helps to orchestrate the specific manner in which the expectation is played upon and realized. The theme builds slowly and teasingly under scenes of the characters clashing-when-we-know-they're-really-going-to-make-it. The dynamic established by the music – anticipation of its movement towards eventual-but-delayed crescendo – becomes part of the narrative infrastructure, helping to establish as well as to confirm anticipation of the imminent sexual con-summation.

The narrative of *Flashdance* is interrupted by dance/music sequences, especially in its first half, in which narrative development is often delayed. But there is still a strong overarching narrative framework, very much along classical Hollywood lines (a typically linked dual-focus narrative of romance overcoming contrasting social backgrounds and of aspiring 'outsider' dancer achieving her goal of moving from bar-room performance to upmarket dance conservatory). Style and image is important to these films, and reflected in their glossy cinematography. But it is also a major aspect of the appeal of the characters. The way these films draw on elements such as genre and star-image seems, at most, to be an intensification of familiar Hollywood strategies.

Similar claims to those of Wyatt are made by Timothy Corrigan. Plot and character motivation have been attenuated, he suggests, since the mid 1970s. Complexities of character 'have been replaced these days … by the most solid and unflinching displays of untrammeled personality and pure image.'[52] Narrative structures and expectations 'are now dispersed rather than coherently motivated across the barest of stories and a most fragmented collection of incidents.'[53] Particular sources 'of this wasting and evacuation of contemporary narrative', for Corrigan, are the prevalence of the sequel, the series and the remake. These forms are certainly appealing to the Hollywood of the corporate era, as ways of creating franchise properties exclusive to particular studios and reducing risk through strong pre-selling and prior audience recognition. But, as Thomas Simonet has shown, the series, the sequel and the remake are not more common today than they were in the studio era, even if some examples, such as the *Star Wars* films, have gained disproportionate attention and box-office revenue.[54] Even given the industrial significance of these forms today, Corrigan overstates their impact on the narrative dimension. In all three, he suggests, 'an original plot becomes a minimal background for figures of technological or stylistic extravagance… These figures in effect detach themselves from the path of character psychology and plot incident and become located instead as an imagistic or technological performance, which then moves from the margins to the centre of the narrative logic.'[55]

Is this really what happens in the Hollywood sequel, series or remake? Particular narrative strategies might sometimes be adopted in such films. A long-running series can develop a shorthand of its own, based on assumptions of familiarity. This does not constitute an 'evacuation' of narrative, however, and is probably not qualitatively different from the intertextual operations of stardom, genre or auteurism. The sequel or series film does not usually take for granted too large a measure of audience foreknowledge. The opening of *Die Hard with a Vengeance* supplies some narrative cues that appeal to the prior knowledge of the viewer. It also sketches in enough detail to accommodate the viewer new to the franchise, however, and to satisfy general principles of narrative reinforcement and redundancy. Its status as the third part in a trilogy might create some particular effects, but these do not undermine the basic fabric of the narrative.

Much of the criticism aimed at contemporary blockbuster or 'high concept' production appears to derive from unfavourable comparison between these films and the more challenging minority of Hollywood films, such as those of the Hollywood Renaissance and its successors. This is understandable from a qualitative point of view, but it is not always put in the most appropriate terms. Qualities such as complexity of character, for example, are far from typical of the mainstream classical norm.

## Narrative does matter

The *Toy Story* films can be seen as quintessential products of the corporate version of New Hollywood, the world of massive promotional spending and prodigious merchandising. Films based around figures clearly recognizable as toys are among the most blatantly merchandised productions. A notable feature of both the original and the sequel, however, is the critical acclaim they received as narrative entertainments, as well as spectacular digital animations, in their own right. Both seemed to transcend their status as products implicated in the business of extra-cinematic merchandising. This suggests that certain agenda are becoming rather mixed-up in this area of debate.

*Godzilla* was slated by most critics and subjected to negative treatment generally in the press. This seems to have been encouraged by more than one factor. One was the perceived quality of the film itself. Most critics did not rate it very highly. This appears to have been over-shadowed to some extent, and mixed up with, a backlash against the noisy promotional hype attached to the film. It is hard to understand the *Toy Story* films as any less profit- and merchandising-driven than

*Godzilla.* They are part of a distinct Hollywood sub-genre of films targeted at children that seek to tap into one of the most potentially lucrative markets: the cross-over between film, other media and popular toys. The careful management of the licensing and exploitation of movie spin-off products aimed at children has long been a key part of Disney strategy, dating back as far as the 1930s. This strategy has been adopted more widely since the huge success of merchandising products associated with *Star Wars* and *E.T.*[56] The extent to which these operations are seen as a threat to the integrity of the films themselves appears in some cases to be a function of the perceived quality of any individual feature.

Two rather different issues risk being conflated here. Qualitative value judgements can become mixed up with conclusions about the broader fate of certain kinds of popular filmmaking in the corporate Hollywood era. Some films might be considered to be of higher quality than others. In some cases, a feature made primarily as a vehicle for selling products such as toys or to create a new franchise such as *Godzilla* might suffer as a result. This might be even more likely to be the case where the feature film is itself a spin-off rather than the original source of momentum for other products. The low-production-value *Pokémon: The First Movie* (1999), for example, distributed by Warner Bros., began life as a Nintendo hand-held computer game. It was translated into television, video, trading cards, toys and a range of other merchandised products before reaching a big screen incarnation generally deemed to lack the qualities of animation or script likely to have the cross-over appeal to adults of the *Toy Story* films. Earlier unsung toy-based feature spin-offs include *The Care Bears Movie* (1985), *The Care Bears Movie II* (1986) and *My Little Pony* (1986).

It is questionable that there is anything in the economy of merchandising, for toys or any other products, that is *inherently* threatening either to the coherence of a film at the level of narrative or its status as an entity capable of standing in its own right. All mainstream Hollywood films are assembled from a variety of components with commercial considerations in mind. A corporate environment in which large companies can increase revenue by designing particular kinds of products intended to supply in-house operations other than those directly involved in screen entertainment creates pressures in certain directions. It helps to dictate some of the kinds of films that get made. Especially favoured is the heavily promoted blockbuster that can make the splash that establishes momentum through the rest of the revenue chain. Preference might also be given sometimes to genres such as science fiction and fantasy that have plenty of scope for the design of distinctive figures that can be sold as figurines or used to adorn products ranging from clothing to lunch boxes.

The first link in this chain cannot be ignored, however. The film itself is not simply an incoherent and dispersible series of fragments. It has to hold its own, as a film-narrative, usually, if it is to be a reliable engine to drive the rest of the corporate machine. The contemporary blockbuster might be 'strategically "open" to multiple readings and multimedia reiteration'; it is far from clear that to achieve this it is also, as Thomas Schatz suggests, 'purposefully incoherent'.[57] The latter by no means follows automatically from the former.

*Godzilla* might have been swamped to some extent by marketing hype and excessive industrial expectations; it might not have been greatly liked or admired; much emphasis might have been put on the provision of spectacular special effects. It is still a solidly coherent narrative, however, displaying many standard features of the Hollywood narrative style. It combines the 'big' story of the mutant lizard with the 'small' and character-led story of a few individuals, including the obligatory restoration of a broken romance. Instances of noisy spectacle are interwoven with various developments in the character-centred plot. The hero (Matthew Broderick) is banished by officialdom, obliged to become the outsider-hero familiar from innumerable Hollywood productions. The narrative might not be rated very highly in terms of quality or originality but that is not same as lacking significant dimensions of coherent narrative at all.

*Godzilla* created early momentum but stalled somewhat after the starting line, at the US box office at least. The *Toy Story* films got off to flying starts and never looked back, at the box office and throughout the subsequent-media and merchandising chains. The lesson from these examples is a ringing endorsement of the importance for Hollywood itself of a film that is received well and sells in its own right, however much it might be assembled with a view to its potential elsewhere.

Merchandising and product-placement strategies might exert some influence on the shape of the New Hollywood blockbuster. If so, this is another aspect of the industry that is not entirely new. The glamour of Hollywood was recognized as a valuable marketing tool in the 1920s and 1930s. Products ranging from fashions and furnishings to cosmetics and cars were widely showcased in the films of the time. This appears to have influenced some production trends, sometimes encouraging the use of contemporary rather than historical settings in which such goods could be featured.[58] It is not usually suggested that this seriously undermined narrative coherence in the studio period.

The contemporary Hollywood blockbuster is the product of a different era, shaped by its own particular industrial demands. A premium is often placed on the provision of spectacle, or on the creation of film components that can be exploited in other forms and formats. The specific context and qualities of this kind of production need to be examined in detail. The expansion of the overseas market following the break-up of the Soviet bloc is one historical factor that might have helped further to encourage a tendency towards exaggerated spectacular display in the 1990s, as Kristen Thompson suggests. Another factor specific to the 1980s, 1990s and 2000s might be a generic cycle – rather than any epochal shift – that has favoured extravagant action and special effects productions.[59] Such a cycle, or some of its aspects, might be broken: the penchant for explosive destruction of office blocks or aircraft reduced in the aftermath of the attacks on the World Trade Centre and the Pentagon in September 2001, for example; although it is unclear how long-lasting or wide-ranging such fallout from specific historical events might prove to be, or what alternative forms of spectacular impact might be promoted in its place.

Spectacle and narrative are both important to Hollywood, generally and in these particular blockbuster manifestations. The two are now, and have always been, available to be deployed in a variety of different combinations. The spectacular productions of the corporate blockbuster have their own specific qualities. It is doubtful, however, that these amount to a clear break from a 'classical' to a 'post-classical' style. Differences are important, but so are a number of substantial continuities.

# From Big Screen to Small

Try wherever possible to fill the screen. This is something that you can get in no other medium.

Darryl Zanuck[1]

The motion picture experience is rapidly becoming, for many spectators, the video experience.

John Belton[2]

Lavish and spectacular sounds and visions, of various kinds, are important to the big-screen experiences of Hollywood cinema. Images are of high resolution and luminosity, even when not particularly large-scale, luxurious, spectacular or action-packed. Sound, including the important and often neglected role played by music, is rich, resonant and multi-layered. Most mainstream productions play on the audio-visual resources of the cinema, many of which have undergone improvement in recent decades. Yet...

Most acts of film-viewing occur somewhere else. On the small screen, via broadcast or video recording. The small screen, even in its latest digital widescreen or DVD incarnation, offers a rather different audio-visual experience, greatly diminished in scale and resolution. For large numbers this has become the principal – or only – arena in which Hollywood films are seen. The largest numbers of viewings, by a substantial margin, occur on free-to-view broadcast television. These contribute a relatively small share of Hollywood's profits (about 3 per cent from free-view television in the United States). Overall, however, the small screen has become more important than the cinema in terms of total revenues. Home video makes the largest contribution, sales and rentals accounting for nearly half of the global total (46 per cent, of which 30 per cent is from the domestic market and 16 per cent from overseas[3]). Pay-per-view and other premium television screenings in the United States account for 14 per cent, while the combined total for all types of international television income is 11 per cent. Cinema screenings account for 26 per cent (11 per cent domestic, 15 per cent overseas). In total, screenings on the small screen account for a whopping 74 per cent of global revenues. This is a significant distinction between the classical and New Hollywood eras.

What are the implications of this? Industrially, Hollywood is part of a broader media economy. The development of links between cinema and television will be outlined further in this chapter. What of the formal or stylistic qualities of Hollywood cinema in the age of television and video? How far do big and small screen media impose or encourage contradictory demands or tendencies? How do products designed to be projected onto screens up to 60ft wide and 30ft tall 'play' on those whose parameters are measured in inches?[4] To what extent might new aesthetic strategies have been developed to fit – or under the influence of – televisual media? If the 'New Hollywood' that began to take shape in some respects in the 1950s put the emphasis on wide and spectacular formats, in contrast to television, has that of more recent years been characterized by stylistic traits designed to fit the confines of the small screen? Or is this relationship more complex, given the continued importance of the big-screen showcase to the ability of Hollywood films to earn heavily in other media?

The main emphasis of this chapter will be on the formal dimension, although viewed in the context of industrial imperatives: that is to say, the extent to which formal qualities might be influenced by the principal sources of revenue. First, though, we need to look a little more closely at the changing industrial relationship between Hollywood and small screen media.

## Embracing the small screen

Hollywood cinema and television have often been assumed to be implacable enemies, the latter especially seen as a threat to the profits of the former. This assumption is based on the claim that the advent of television was one of the principal reasons for the decline in cinema-going from the 1950s. The full story is rather more complex, television being only one of a number of factors contributing to the problems of cinema, and not the first (attendances began to drop rapidly at the start of the decade, before television had spread to more than a minority of households). Television was seen as an enemy to some extent in the 1950s, an attitude reflected in some of the films of the period. In *All That Heaven Allows* (1955) the provision of a television set for the widow Cary Scott (Jane Wyman) is an index of the potential desolation of middle-class conformity and loneliness. Spectacular films of the 1950s and 1960s, and new formats such as widescreen and 3D, were designed to emphasize the scale and scope of the theatrical experience, particularly in relation to the limited fidelity of television.

But even at this stage the relationship was more complex than this familiar portrait suggests. The Hollywood studios, especially Paramount, had themselves experimented with various possibilities of television in the 1930s and 1940s. They aspired to gain a foothold of their own in the new medium. Paramount operated early television stations in the 1940s in Chicago and Los Angeles. Warner, Loew's and Fox applied for licenses to run stations during the war.[5] Hollywood's move into television was not prevented by hostility or a lack of interest but by the Federal Communications Commission, which delayed decisions on studio applications until after the resolution of the legal action against vertical integration, the result of which ended any prospect of expansion into broadcasting.[6]

Paramount also led the way in another abortive venture of the early 1950s: theatre television. Exclusive broadcasts were relayed onto cinema screens, with major sporting events the main attraction. Television has come to be associated predominantly with domestic consumption; film with the public arena of the cinema. These locations were not pre-given or inherent in the two media, however. A fluidity of possibilities existed as far back as the development of early film technologies in the late nineteenth century, a period in which the domestic market was sometimes seen as the likely destination of film along with predecessors such as the telephone and phonograph.[7] Theatre television was a precursor of today's big-screen cable or satellite broadcasts (also mostly involving sports events) in venues ranging from cinemas to bars. Another option explored by Paramount, ahead of its time, was subscription television, an attempt to broadcast films and sport to the home. The FCC blocked the possibility of successful expansion into television in any of these directions.[8]

Television, by the late 1950s, was as much a saviour of Hollywood as a threat. Much of what was retained of the 'plant' of the studios, the production facilities and salaried employees, was kept in business by work for television. Initial doubts were overcome by 1955, a year in which Hollywood produced ten times as much film for television as it did for cinema exhibition.[9] Almost all prime-time programming in the United States was broadcast live from New York in the early 1950s. By the end of the decade, something like 80 per cent was on film and came from Hollywood.[10] For the major studios, production for television was the flipside of the blockbuster syndrome, in which resources for films released in the cinema were concentrated into smaller numbers of bigger and more extravagant films. Lower-budget television production provided a valuable source of cash-flow and stability to balance the uncertainties of the blockbuster. Early studio-produced programmes were also used to promote features at their time of release in the cinema.[11] Production for television fulfilled much the same role as the B-movies and shorts produced during the studio era, for which there was no longer a theatrical market.

Television became an additional source of revenue when the studios sold their back catalogues for broadcast. This was initially resisted on two main grounds: the fact that television was seen as a competitor, especially by exhibitors, and that it could not yet afford to pay what the studios considered the market value of their products. Initially, only the minor studios or independent producers sold films to television. Sales by the majors started in 1955, when RKO sold its assets to a syndication company on withdrawing from production. It was followed in 1956 by Columbia, Warner, Universal and Twentieth Century-Fox. Paramount delayed until 1958, 'apparently to protect its pay-TV schemes.'[12] Within three years some 3,700 films were sold or leased to television for a total of more than $220 million.[13] The revenue came as a bonus source of income on properties that were generally expected already to have covered their costs (even if the first batches turned out to have been sold for far less than their potential value). The advent of television, and later home video, turned back catalogues into one of the most valuable assets of the studios, a key source of their attractiveness to corporate buyers and of their own future stability.

During the 1960s the status of income from television changed from being an extra to an integral part of the economic equation: 'Few new film projects were put into production without assessing their potential on TV, and a TV sale was used as collateral in obtaining financing.'[14] Moves into television production were a key element in the general process of diversification that led to the creation of the current form of media conglomerate Hollywood. Hollywood's relationship with television was characterized by initial uncertainty and suspicion, mixed with substantial forays of its own, difficulties, and eventual integration. Much the same goes for its position with later forms such as cable/satellite and home video in the 1970s and 1980s. Cable and video became major sources of revenue; both were treated, initially, with a mixture of disdain, hostility and attempted colonization.

Cable television was opposed by the exhibition end of the film business but largely ignored at first by the majors. Until, that is, Hollywood decided that it wanted its share of the success achieved by the pioneering Home Box Office (HBO) channel a few years after its launch by Time Inc. in 1975. The main issue was not one of principle, but who was to control and profit from what proved to be a valuable new outlet. The studios responded by creating their own cable channels (initially Warner with The Movie Channel, 1979, Nickelodeon, 1979, and MTV, 1981), by trying to take legal action against HBO and by withholding their films from the channel. A broader attempt to dominate the cable business was launched in 1980, when Twentieth Century Fox, Paramount and Columbia combined with Getty Oil to propose their own Premiere Channel, a venture halted after indications that it would be blocked on anti-monopoly grounds.[15]

Initial hostility towards home video took stronger form. In 1976 MCA/Universal and Disney took Sony to court on the grounds that the use of its Betamax system for home taping from television represented an infringement of copyright. The case was lost but won on appeal, prompting an acrimonious public debate; the Supreme Court eventually upheld the original decision against the two studios in 1983. By this point the studios were already in two minds about the merits of video, the hostility of some combined with the recognition that it offered a substantial source of profits – $400 million in the year of the Supreme Court ruling.[16]

The studios also opposed video rental at first, on the grounds that it represented a loss of direct control over revenues: why should a third party earn repeated rental fees after buying copies of Hollywood films? Rental took off, however, despite the efforts of the studios to prohibit it in sales contracts. A series of battles ensued between the studios and video dealers, including legal actions and the proposition of new legislation.[17] Hollywood eventually settled on a variable two-tier system which remains largely in force today. Most films are released initially for rental only. Copies go on general retail sale at much lower prices once the rental market is deemed to have been fully exploited, a strategy developed in the second half of the 1980s. Early clashes between Hollywood and the rental market disappeared, largely because both ends of the business became parts of the same media corporations. The giant rental and retail chain Blockbuster, for example, became allied with Paramount, both coming under the corporate umbrella of Viacom in 1994.

Sales of pre-recorded films on videotape increased astronomically between 1980 and 2000. Total sales to US dealers grew from 3 million to 701.7 million, an increase of 23,290 per cent according to MPPA figures.[18] The biggest proportional rise occurred during the 1980s: 40.9 million by 1985, 241.8 million in 1990. Half of American households had VCRs by 1986, the year in which revenue from cassette sales equalled box-office gross for the first time.[19] As Robert Allen puts it: 'Between 1987 and 1990 – in less time than it took the average undergraduate to accumulate enough hours to graduate with a film studies major – watching a feature film rented from the local video store at home supplanted going to a movie theatre as the most common mode of engagement with "the movies" for a large proportion of the population of North America.'[20] US video sales ($11.6 billion) and rentals ($8.3 billion) accounted for nearly three times the domestic box office ($7.5 billion) in 2000.[21]

Cable has also become an integral part of the corporate Hollywood economy, with the major cable channels located within the same conglomerates as the studios. The Time-Warner merger, for example, brought HBO into the corporate fold; a similar combination was achieved by the linking of Paramount with Viacom, one of the dominant forces in the cable industry. By 1984 the studios were estimated to receive pay-cable revenues of about $3 million for the average film (at a time when the average negative cost was $14.4 million), a total of some $600 million in that year.[22] The number of American households with basic cable provision grew from 17.6 million in 1980 to 68.5 million by 2000; pay cable subscriptions rose from 13.4 million in 1982 to 41.5 million in 1998.[23]

Cinema box-office takings accounted for 80 per cent of the domestic revenues of the studios as recently as 1980. The situation today, in which they account for less than a third of this figure, marks a huge shift in the relative economic importance of big and small screen arenas. The boom in video had an impact on the structure of Hollywood in the 1980s. Pre-sales to video distributors funded a generation of new independent producers, many of which went out of business as a result of over-production at the end of the decade.

The Hollywood studios remain major beneficiaries of outlets such as video and cable, which have not generally been used to increase the diversity of materials on offer to the viewer.[24] The same is likely to be the case with current or future developments in areas such as video-on-demand or distribution via the internet. Delivery systems such as video, cable/satellite and terrestrial broadcast television have effectively replaced the old studio-era system of subsequent runs in the cinema – with one important difference: they earn more than first-run exhibition, which, in the earlier system, remained the most important source of revenue.

What impact might this have on the formal dimension? Have the stylistic qualities of Hollywood films been affected by the growing importance of small screen media? An obvious place to begin is with the fate of one of the formal innovations deployed in the 1950s to emphasize the qualities of the big-screen experience: the widescreen format. Other possibilities to be examined in the rest of this chapter are that Hollywood has embraced aesthetics drawn from predominantly small-screen media such as advertising and MTV, and/or that techniques such as rapid editing or rapid camera-movement have been used to create forms of spectacular 'impact' that translate more effectively from big screen to small.

## From widescreen composition to 'safe action area'

A conversation between a nervy Benjamin Braddock and the 'sophisticated' Mrs Robinson. He thinks he is being seduced, but is not sure and all the more embarrassed for having suggested so. The two are framed at either extreme of the widescreen image; Benjamin's head and shoulders to screen left, Mrs Robinson's head to the right. Bookends, each in focus. Between is a blurry unfocused background expanse of house-plant foliage and soft furnishings. Composition draws our attention to the separation of the two figures, the shallowness of focus emphasizing the flat and wide plane of Panavision and the emotional as well as physical distance between the pair.

How does this early scene from *The Graduate* play on television? Not so well. The single shot is broken up into a series of abrupt cuts between separate shots of the two characters, each looking from one side of the frame across into empty space. The original dynamic is largely destroyed. Such is the fate of many films composed for the wide screen when viewed on conventional broadcast television or video.

Widescreen processes came into general use in Hollywood in the mid-1950s, partly in response to the threat posed by television, and as a marked contrast to the limited scale of the small screen.[25] It is hardly surprising that problems should be encountered in the movement of widescreen films from cinema to television set. Compositional strategies such the example from *The Graduate* were typical of those adopted at the start of the widescreen era. Darryl Zanuck, the head of production at Twentieth Century Fox, the studio that pioneered CinemaScope, the first widescreen process developed by one of the majors, 'repeatedly stressed that in order to take advantage of the new widescreen format directors should stage action to emphasize its width.'[26] The first CinemaScope release, *The Robe* (1953), duly obliged, as did many that followed: full of compositions in which characters interact across the width and spaces of the frame.

If films such as *The Robe* were at the forefront of what John Belton terms 'the widescreen revolution' of the 1950s, they were also intimately connected with the growing importance of Hollywood films to television. This created contradictory demands. Films did not achieve the status of the most prestigious prime-time programming on network television until the launch of 'NBC's Saturday Night at the Movies' in 1961. The release of films made after 1948 had been delayed during negotiations over royalties and rights between the studios and craft unions that ended with a settlement in 1960. NBC's series was launched with a screening of Fox's second CinemaScope feature, *How To Marry a Millionaire* (1953). As Belton puts it: '*Millionaire* ushered in not only the era of the prime-time network feature film but also that of the panned-and-scanned film.'[27]

*The Graduate* was to suffer the same treatment. Panning and scanning is the name given to the process in which films using the full scope of the wide screen are reconstructed to fit the small. To pan-and-scan *How To Marry a Millionaire* and other CinemaScope features, Fox developed an optical printer that could move across the width of the frame to follow the principal action during the process of transferring a film to video. 'The finder frame could be programmed to pan (at two different speeds) to the right or to the left or to cut from one position to another during the printing operation, permitting the technician in charge of the transfer to reframe during a shot or to edit from one side of the CinemaScope frame to the other.'[28]

The scene from *The Graduate* described above has been 'edited' in this way, cutting from one side of the original image to the other. The alternative would be to pan across the frame, from Braddock to Robinson. Pans of this kind are used in many cases to introduce the viewer to parts of the image that do not fit into the television frame. They might have been avoided in this case because the need for more than a single movement would make the process even more overt than the imposition of the secondary-level editing.

In some cases the television viewer has been provided with more of the image than shown in the cinema. Many early 'widescreen' effects were created on the cheap, cashing in on the success of processes such as CinemaScope and Panavision by cropping or masking the top and bottom of the standard frame, changing the traditional 1.33:1 ratio to 1.66:1 or 1.85:1. Such films were usually shot using the full 1.33:1 frame. This meant they fitted more easily onto the television screen, 'providing viewers with more image at the top and the bottom than had been intended.'[29] The result could be unfortunate, the extra dimension sometimes including microphones above the heads of performers or other detail not intended to be included on screen.[30]

Loss of picture in the transition from big to small screen is not limited to films made in widescreen formats. Films made in the 1.33:1 format are also cropped, losing up to 30 per cent of the original picture by the time they reach the domestic television screen. Part of the original image (about 9 per cent) can be lost in the process of cinema projection, to ensure that frame lines and the boundaries of the image do not appear on screen and to take into account any misalignment between camera and projector. Another loss (some 6 per cent) occurs when the film image is scanned onto video, again to compensate for potential problems caused by misalignment.[31] Further cropping is imposed by the television set itself, in most cases, through a process known as over-scanning. As Anton Wilson puts it: 'The manufacturer does this to insure that the home viewer will never have to encounter those sinister black blanking areas that surround the transmitted picture. This black area that surrounds the picture is deemed so repulsive that manufacturers add from 9% to 15% of horizontal overscan to make absolutely certain that the viewer never need be subjected to the horrible sight of blanking area even under the most adverse conditions such as "brown-outs" or low voltage mains.'[32]

Between 24 and 30 per cent of the image originally captured by the camera can be lost, according to Wilson's figures, 15 to 21 per cent of this accounted for by the transition to the small screen. This can then be added to the losses involved with wider screen formats. The basic format today is 1.85:1. Transferred to television, the viewer gets 41 to 53 per cent of the picture projected in the cinema. For films shot in anamorphic widescreen processes such as Panavision and CinemaScope, usually a ratio of about 2.35:1, the television viewer receives 32 to 41 per cent. In the extreme case of Ultra-Panavision 70, the proportion reduced to a mere 28 to 35 per cent of the theatrical image, 'missing a good two-thirds of the film as it was projected in theatres.'[33]

Films shown on broadcast television are also subject to other potential indignities. They may be shown incomplete. Cuts are made to fit films into broadcast slots or to accommodate commercial breaks. Films can also be slowed down or speeded up to fit television schedules during the telecine transfer process. Censorship is common, including cuts or redubbing, on the basis of language, violence or sexual material. Quality of colour and textural detail is also lost. The contrast ratio of conventional video is approximately 10 times less than that of 35mm film. Video also uses a different colour process (additive rather than subtractive) which reduces the range of the colour spectrum that can be reproduced.[34]

Panning and scanning technologies have improved since the early 1960s, permitting more subtle treatment of widescreen films. The practice has remained a source of outrage (and ridicule) among some film-makers, critics and enthusiasts. How far this, or other losses in quality of image, affect the experience of more than a relatively small and unrepresentative number of viewers is uncertain. There is nothing to suggest that substantial numbers of viewers expressed objections to even the worst of pan/scan horrors, either in 1961 or in subsequent years. Cuts and interruptions by advert breaks have had identifiable commercial consequences, however; they helped to create the initial opening for the success of cable, showing films uninterrupted and uncut. Hollywood itself responded to the potential compositional strains between sources of income on big and small screen, in recognition of the need for its products to go at least some way towards meeting the requirements of both formats.

As early as 1962, the Research and Education Committee of the American Society of Cinematographers came up with a solution that appears to remain widely in operation today. It defined what it termed a 'safe action area' in the cinematic image: 'that portion of the picture area inside the camera aperture borders within which all significant action should take place for "safe" or full reproduction on the majority of black-and-white and color home receivers.'[35] The sanctity of this 'safe' area was underlined when it became marked with a dotted line on the viewfinders of many cameras, enabling filmmakers to keep in mind during the shooting process the implications of eventual transfer to small screen media.

The full scope of the widescreen image has been reigned in. Most filmmakers constrain themselves. They choose the confines of the 'safe action area', or the more moderate 1.85:1 widescreen format, rather than suffer the horrors of pan/scan. Extreme edge framing is generally avoided; or, at least, use of both lateral extremes. This is not an absolute requirement, but it is a strong tendency. Exactly how it might be traced historically remains open to some debate. The more striking examples of framing across the expanse of the wide screen did not disappear immediately, as is suggested by its use in *The Graduate*, released in 1967. Steve Neale argues that compositional practices began to change during the 1970s rather than the 1960s.[36] Examples of widescreen composition chosen by Neale are *Pat Garrett and Billy the Kid* (1973) and *Chinatown* (1974). For Neale, these are films that look both ways. They extend images and motifs of thematic relevance into the peripheries of the frame while keeping the principal characters and narrative actions within the proportions of 'safe action'. A similar pattern is identified in *Blade Runner* (1982).

Another compositional device identified in these films is what Neale calls 'the over-the-disposable-shoulder shot':

> All three of these films involve two-way conversation scenes which are composed in alternating two-shots. Each shot is in each case framed so as to show the face of one of the characters in medium close-up on one side of the frame and the shoulder of his or her interlocutor on the other. When subject to panning and scanning, the patterns of alternation are preserved – there is no need for subsequent 'editing' – and all that disappears are the shoulders.[37]

Two additional strategies are identified. In one, characters are grouped together in one particular sector of the frame 'whose dimensions correspond precisely to those of the television screen.'[38] The other – described by Neale as 'more distinctive, a real compositional hallmark of post-1960s widescreen films' – involves cross-cutting between set ups of two characters, each located in the frame at opposite extremes of the screen: 'The result is the generation of a symmetrical pattern or rhythm across a set of markedly asymmetrical components, and when viewed in the cinema is a bit like watching a tennis match. On television, however, the asymmetry is lost, and shots appear to be framed more conventionally.'[39]

What these strategies have in common is a form of composition that is able to pay heed to the requirements of the 'safe action area' without entirely abandoning any significant use of the margins of the screen. These films offer a different compositional experience on big screen and small, but only within limitations. Key aspects of Hollywood films such as character and significant narrative action are usually subject to the protective custody of the television-sized frame, even if a few extras or some different effects are allowed around the edges. The central point is that the strategies identified by Neale permit transfer to television easily and at relatively low cost.

It would make sense to expect the limitations of the television frame to have become more pressing in the decades since the 1960s, in keeping with the growing importance of delivery channels such as cable and video. Other factors also intrude. Neale's first two examples, along with *The Graduate*, are films associated with the Hollywood Renaissance. They might, as a result, be expected to make more creative use of devices such as marginal framing in the widescreen image. This could be explained in terms of both the degree of 'arty' or innovative effects found in films of the Renaissance and in their thematic concerns, which sometimes involve a marginalization and/or questioning of the 'heroic' status of the central character. A movement towards a 'recentering' of heroic character, in both senses, is often found in the more mainstream blockbuster productions from the second half of the 1970s and the 1980s. This soon merges into the period in which televisual media began to account for a substantial share of Hollywood revenues. As is often the case, the characteristics of Hollywood films can be explained in more than one manner. A movement towards a more television-friendly aesthetic can also be understood in more general terms of less innovative cinematic style.

Not all home viewing occurs in the usual television format of 1.33:1. Many films are also released on video in their original widescreen format, or something close to it. Some broadcasters also show films in the form known as 'letterboxing', in which the full width (or something approximating it) spreads across the centre of the screen, leaving black borders at the top and bottom of the frame. None of this is likely to have had much impact on the question of cinema/television composition, because these practices tend to be found in the commercial margins. The number of copies of films sold in widescreen format is a small percentage of the total. Widescreen copies are rarely found in rental outlets, while broadcasts in widescreen are usually reserved for minority channels (almost exclusively limited to BBC2 and Channel Four in British terrestrial television, for example) or niche markets on cable or satellite.

Is this about to change with the advent of widescreen television and DVD? Widescreen televisions have become more affordable in recent years, their uptake encouraged by the broadcast of some mainstream programming in wider screen formats. The prevalence of widescreen televisions is likely to spread, reducing the problems associated with the transfer of widescreen cinematic formats (although the currently dominant 16x9 format still requires an element of letterboxing with films shot in the 2.35:1 format used by many features).

The advent of DVD, a format gaining rapidly increased penetration in the early 2000s, introduced a new complication. The default format on DVD is often the original widescreen (some discs offer the viewer of choice of either widescreen or pan-scanned formats). Whether this will continue to be the case remains to be seen. DVD began as a niche market for the enthusiast, sold on the basis of greater image quality and fidelity, a market that could be expected to embrace widescreen letterboxing. This might change when DVD begins to take over the much larger market previously occupied by videotape (a development to be expected soon, particularly with the launch of recordable DVD[40]). As a mass market product, DVD might move away from widescreen formats towards which most viewers are assumed to be hostile. A significantly increased take-up of widescreen television might counter any such tendency, however. New DVD or DVD–ROM type formats might also increase the capacity of discs, encouraging more producers to offer both wide and pan-scanned versions. Where the balance of all these developments might lie in the near future remains open to question, and with it the precise implications for the use of, and composition within, wider formats in the cinema.

New technologies such as widescreen television, DVD, digital transmission, future high-definition, plasma-screen or wall-mounted television and other new formats offer the prospect of a reduction in the loss of sound and image quality found in the move from big screen to small. A sizeable difference will remain, however. Sophisticated and high fidelity 'home cinema' systems remain well short of theatrical capacities and are unlikely to be embraced in the near future by anything other than a specialist audience. Most viewers in search of impressive sound and visuals are more likely to continue to seek these from the cinema than to invest large sums of money in domestic screen entertainment.[41]

The differences between the experience of films in the cinema and on the small screen are not merely issues of size, quality, editing or technical fidelity. Each usually occurs in a very different social environment: that of the theatre or the home. Each tends, as a result, to be watched rather differently. Films watched in the cinema are usually given closer attention. The audience sits in the dark, in rows, facing the screen and has usually paid and made an outing to the cinema for the privilege. Those viewed in the home are often watched more casually and amid a multitude of potential distractions, ranging from interruptions by other people to indignities such as channel-hopping, video rewind and fast-forward and the tendency to combine viewing with other activities.

The regime that governs the viewing of films in the cinema is characterized by John Ellis as that of the 'gaze', an intensity of rapt attention.[42] Watching television is characterized by the 'glance', a far less sustained mode of attention. This, for Ellis, has consequences for the kinds of programming that are encouraged. An assumption of a high degree of audience attention encourages the production of tightly organized narratives for consumption in the cinema (it also encourages analysts such as Ellis and many others to interpret the viewing experience in terms of processes such as voyeurism and fetishism drawn from psychoanalytic theory). Television programming, aimed at a less attentive audience, tends towards the use of open-ended and ongoing formats divided into relatively short segments that are only loosely connected.

Distinctions such as those made by Ellis are based on a combination of the formal and social characteristics of big and small screen media. The impact of the sheer size of the cinema screen is magnified by the social convention of viewing it in a special place in the dark in which talking or other activities are discouraged. The reduced audio-visual impact of the small screen is exacerbated by the fact that it is watched usually in normal lighting conditions amid a world of domestic distractions. It is possible to over-state these distinctions. The cinema screen is not always the subject of uninterrupted rapt attention. Far from it. One of the failings of some film theory, especially a tradition developed from psychoanalytic approaches, is an undue assumption that the viewer is entirely captivated by the big-screen image. Plenty of distractions remain available, from other cinemagoers and from the variety of levels of attention or inattention given by the individual viewer.

Television can be watched more attentively than is usually assumed to be the case. It may sometimes form the kind of undifferentiated background identified by Raymond Williams in his classic conception of television in terms of a 'flow' of sound and image.[43] Many programme formats are designed to permit casual or interrupted viewing. But individual programmes are also separated out quite distinctly and liable to be treated differently from one viewer to another. Some are designed and promoted as special 'events', encouraging more sustained and exclusive viewing, including 'prestige' productions such as the TV movie, series and mini-series and, of course, premiere screenings of Hollywood films.[44]

The distinctions drawn by Ellis are best seen, as he suggests, as relative tendencies rather than absolutes. Big and small screen lend themselves to different uses, as a result of both their audio-visual qualities and the particular social and economic contexts in which each has been developed. What, then, are the dominant characteristics of the small screen aesthetic? And how might these have been accommodated by Hollywood in recent decades? One way to approach this question is to start with a comparison between two films from the genre in which a number of the widescreen films of the 1950s and 1960s were located: the Roman (or Biblico-Roman) epic. What differences might be found between the formal characteristics of a film such as *Spartacus* (1960) and the revisitation of the genre in *Gladiator* (2000)?

## *Spartacus* vs. *Gladiator*

Extreme long-shot from above. Massed ranks of Roman soldiers manoeuvre slowly into position for battle; tiny figures reduced to mere components in an abstract chessboard design. Cut briefly to extreme long shot from the side, as the troops advance towards the rebel slave enemy, shields whipping into position. Cut back to the distant overhead perspective. Cut to a less extreme long shot, overhead, from behind the line of Roman advance, troops marching upwards into the frame. A brief long shot of the rebel leaders, signalling their attack. Cut back to the previous set-up, as flaming obstacles are lit. Cut to a higher and more distant perspective. Several more shots follow, including a mid-shot of the rebel leader Spartacus (Kirk Douglas), before the flaming devices are sent rolling into the Roman ranks. The first line of Romans is sent into retreat, followed by a great horde of rebels that fills the expanse of the screen as battle commences.

The remainder of the climactic battle of *Spartacus* is shot mostly in long and mid-shots, the camera panning and tilting to follow elements of the action, although generally relatively static. Most of the fighting is shot from slightly above, except for one sequence in which we are given a ground-level perspective on Spartacus wielding his sword from horseback. Blurry figures pass closer to the camera, out of focus, during this sequence, creating an occasional impression of greater proximity to the action. This latter tendency is greatly extended in *Gladiator*, which adopts very different formal strategies overall. The major battle sequence is placed at the opening of the film rather than at the climax. A few

12. Spectacle designed for the big screen: massed ranks fill the width of the frame, shot from distance and high above in *Spartacus*, © Universal Pictures Company, 1959. British Film Institute

long-shots are provided, capturing the broad sweep of Roman soldiers and the fire rained down upon their Barbarian enemy. But these are held only momentarily. The dominant formal strategy involves rapid cutting and rapid and unstable camera movement (hand-held), creating a disorienting impression of immersion in the chaos.

Similar contrasts are found in many other sequences of action and spectacle in the two films. *Spartacus* makes frequent use of the extreme long shot, especially in the depiction of large masses of people moving across the widescreen landscape. A key scene of gladiatorial combat between Spartacus and another slave, Draba (Woody Strode), is shot in more or less conventional 'classical' style, although with some composition taking advantage of the wider screen frame. The emphasis is on 'objective' mid and long shots mixed with the occasional more 'subjective' camera position (such as a shot taken through the mesh of a net wielded by Draba): a mix characteristic of the classical style. The 180 degree line is 'crossed' once or twice. Spartacus is pulled from his feet to screen left in one shot, only to be seen on the ground on screen right in the next; he then fights back onto his feet from screen left again in the next. A reversal occurs twice, in the relative placement of the two figures on the screen. This is a departure from dominant Hollywood convention, the effect of which is to heighten the graphic and dynamic impact of the incident.

Strategies such as this, used occasionally in *Spartacus*, become part of the dominant aesthetic of *Gladiator*. Varied combinations of rapid editing and dizzying camera movement are utilized in its set-pieces sequences of gladiatorial combat. A clear sense of the relative position of figures – or even of what exactly happens in some cases – is sacrificed in favour of an impressionistic creation of a sense of violent speed and impact. How might we explain these differences?

A number of factors come into play. We might attribute the extreme detachment found at times in *Spartacus* to the influence of the director, Stanley Kubrick. It is a characteristic of the visual style found in many of his films. *Spartacus* was not a production over which he had the level of authorial control found in his later work, however, and the film's visual strategies do not depart significantly from the norm for Biblico-Roman epics of the period. The blurry/grainy/crazily-disoriented cinematography used to heighten some of the action scenes of *Gladiator* is lifted from the combat sequences in *Saving Private Ryan* (1998).[45] The latter established a new convention for the creation of an impression of 'authentic' impact in the depiction of harrowing combat action, dependent partly on the use of camera-shutter effects that make the highly mobile image strobe, as if immersed in and barely able to keep up with the action. It is not hard to see the appeal of this style to the makers of *Gladiator*. It offers the injection of a fresh and contemporary-seeming dynamic into a form of action-spectacular noted in the past for a tendency towards lumbering sword-and-shield play, especially when compared with the high-octane action-adventure diet with which many of its potential viewers were likely to be familiar.

The different formal approaches used by *Spartacus* and *Gladiator* can also be understood in terms of aesthetics best suited to the big and small screen experiences. *Spartacus* is quite clearly designed to play on the big screen. Does this make *Gladiator* a film consciously designed for the small screen? It is not so easy to say with any certainty. But, by design or otherwise, *Gladiator* offers a form of spectacular Roman epic that is likely to lose a good deal less than *Spartacus* and its contemporaries

13. Up close and painful: camera close to the action in *Gladiator*, ©
DreamWorks LLC and Universal Studios, 2000. Ronald Grant archive

in translation to the small screen. *Spartacus* depends on scale for much
of its spectacular impact. Sheer massed numbers are mobilized and
choreographed to achieve this effect. Many of the 'big' spectacular
shots are held for relatively long periods, inviting the viewer to examine
at leisure the detail within the frame, a typical characteristic of 1950s
and 1960s widescreen cinema. *Gladiator* depends to a far larger extent
on the effects of montage–editing and rapid and unstable camera
movement: effects that translate more effectively to the small screen.

   *Spartacus* loses much in transition to the television screen, in which
two main options are available. The first is to reframe the film into the
1.33:1 format, which involves cutting off the edges of the frame and
panning/scanning: destroying, in the process, much of the impact
created by its spectacular scale and composition. The second is to show

it in letterbox format, which maintains something close to the original composition but at the expense of an even greater shinkage of detail within the image. *Gladiator* also loses a good deal of its impact in the move to small screen, as must even the most intimate and small scale production. It does so, however, to significantly lesser extent.

*Gladiator* makes much less use of the extremes of the widescreen image, and so is less prone to its effects being undermined by pan/scan or a demand for complete or partial letterboxing. The dialogue scenes are shot primarily in one-shots, cutting from one character to another. These are framed off-centre but not with the degree of asymmetry found in the examples examined by Neale. A shift into shot/reverse-shot regimes is found at the point where key dialogues become more intimate and intense, but these are also framed in such as way as to loose little in transition to small screen. In the early scene in which the ageing emperor Marcus Aurelius (Richard Harris) asks the hero Maximus (Russell Crowe ) to take over the reigns of power after his death, we move from separate shots of the two into Neale's over-the-disposable-shoulder style of shot/reverse shot. A similar move occurs in the sequence in which Maximus and Lucilla (Connie Nielsen) declare their love, although in this case the result is a non-disposable-over-the-shoulder, the two being framed closely enough for the presence of both to be maintained in shot on the small screen. Most striking about *Gladiator*, however, is the extent to which its action sequences obey a logic closer to the dominant aesthetic used in television itself.

The conventional television screen is limited in size and resolution, and thus in the amount of visual information that can be supplied at any particular moment. This is why the detailed vista of the big screen image does not work well on the small screen. The single television image is limited in what it can carry. One way around this problem is to use more rapid editing or camera movement to maintain visual interest. As Ellis puts it: 'Variation is provided by changing the image shown rather than by introducing a complexity of elements into a single image.'[46] Television tends to reduce background detail in favour of an emphasis on close-ups, especially head or head-and-shoulders shots of people.

*Gladiator* provides some sweeping vistas, in which fine detail is important, including its digitally augmented recreation of the Coliseum. These are liable to lose their impact on the small screen, but their use is minimal compared with the epic productions of the 1950s and 1960s. The spectacular impact of the film is constructed to large extent through the fast editing and camera movement used in the combat sequences. This also loses some of its effect when reduced to television scale, but to a lesser extent. The image in these sequences undergoes constant and rapid change of the kind likely to maintain dynamic interest within the limited confines of the small screen. No time is available for a leisurely exploration of the contents of a lavishly filled widescreen composition, so little is lost in that dimension. *Gladiator* is not alone in the use of such techniques. Explosive montage editing and rapid, unsteady camera movement have become two of the signatures of the major set-piece sequences of the contemporary Hollywood action cinema, as I have suggested elsewhere.[47] 'It is notable that the *Saving Private Ryan/Gladiator*' aesthetic was translated intact to the small screen in the Spielberg executive – produced series *Bond of Brothers* (2001).'

*Gladiator* and *Spartacus* offer examples of two different ways of constructing spectacular impact. One seeks to emphasize the real scale of the pro-filmic event, the large-scale or dramatic action staged before the camera. The other uses montage techniques more impressionistically, spectacular impact being heightened – or often created – by an intensity of editing or a combination of editing and camera movement. The use of the latter strategy in *Gladiator* can be explained in part as a simple act of product differentiation. A successful return to a genre remembered with a mixture of fond nostalgia and ridicule needed to find a way to breathe new life into earlier conventions, especially in the high-profile combat sequences. *Gladiator* offers a blend of the old and the new: a familiar but recently neglected genre combined with state-of-the-art digital special effects and the latest in contemporary action montage and strobed-image shutter-speed techniques.

The difference between *Spartacus* and *Gladiator* can be measured quantitatively in terms of average shot-length (ASL), calculated by dividing the running time by the number of shots. *Spartacus* has an ASL of 7.89 seconds, according to my calculation, while the figure for *Gladiator* is strikingly lower, at 3.36 seconds, a figure that drops to between 2.08 and 0.59 seconds for sequences of battle or gladiatorial combat (*The Fall of the*

*Roman Empire*, 1964, the epic on which *Gladiator* is partly based, has an ASL of 8.72 seconds). Some historical-technological developments in Hollywood can be charted through changing ASL figures. Shot lengths typically grew longer with the initial development of sound and, again, in the early widescreen era. They have subsequently undergone a process of gradual reduction. The pattern indicated by a comparison between the extremes represented by *Spartacus* and *Gladiator* is of more general historical validity, although a range of possibilities remain available within broad tendencies such as this.[48] Many action films of the 1990s have an ASL of between 3 and 4 seconds. Differences are found between different types of film as well as between those of one era and another. *Armageddon* has an extremely short ASL of 2.07, for example, while that for *Deep Impact*, reflecting its less bombastic style, is a more leisurely 5.165. Differences among earlier action-adventure examples such as *The Charge of the Light Brigade* (1936, 6.51 seconds) and *The Adventures of Robin Hood* (1938, 4.52) further complicate the picture.

The use in *Gladiator* of formal devices that translate better than most to the small screen cannot be explained *simply* as a response to the industrial centrality of small screen media outlets. Other factors intervene. The impact-aesthetic style derived from *Saving Private Ryan* was used originally to create an impression of 'authenticity' deemed necessary to the positioning of that production as a 'serious' and 'responsible' work.[49] The use of impact-montage editing in Hollywood action cinema more generally can be explained by the internal development of the format, seeking new ways to increase the level of sensational impact. Rapid editing and violently unsteady camerawork – combined with a jolting thrusting of objects apparently out from the screen – is a source of the particular pleasure taken by some devotees of the action film. Does the fact that these styles work relatively well on the small screen mean they were developed with that specifically in mind? This might be the case to some extent.

Charles Eidsvik suggests a connection between the economic importance of small screen media and the use of unfettered styles of camera movement permitted by the development of technologies such as the Steadicam and the Louma-type crane. New patterns of fluid camera movement, he suggests, 'are not so much the consequence of technologically created opportunity as of an economics- and video-driven loss of other esthetic options.'[50] Styles such as rapid editing and camera movement might also be explained as a result of other influences associated with the small screen, most notably the impact of aesthetics developed in advertising and music video.

## MTV and the ad aesthetic

Fast, flashing editing. Stark, sometimes startling, 'in-your-face' images. Bright back-lighting. Emphatic camera-movement, fluid or shakily hand-held. These are some of the characteristics of contemporary Hollywood, especially in action-oriented features. They are also formal devices often associated with advertising and music video. A turn towards these forms in Hollywood might be explained by the desire of the industry to appeal to generations familiar with the rhythms of television advertisements and MTV, particularly as an overlap is likely between these and core target audiences (relatively youthful and heavier than average media consumers).

The style of some Hollywood productions might thus have been influenced by aesthetics developed on the small screen, but indirectly: because these forms have a popular cultural currency rather as a result of their immediate suitability for broadcast or video screenings. Exactly how such influences occur, to what extent and where, is not easy to specify beyond the bald assertions found in some (usually critical) accounts. Other factors tend to complicate the picture, as we have seen. Some basis for an assumption of influence can be found in the movement of personnel between one medium and the other. Many directors working in Hollywood moved into feature films from advertising (including Ridley Scott, director of *Gladiator*) and music video. In the argument of Justin Wyatt encountered in the previous chapter, advertising and music video have affected the styles of films as a result of a blurring of distinctions between all three media in the heavily marketing oriented strategy of corporate Hollywood.[51]

The influence of advertising and music video is usually assumed to be a harmful one, like that of small screen media in general. A disapprovingly evaluative tone is often found in accounts of these phenomena, reflecting the lower cultural esteem with which television, music video and especially advertising are usually regarded.[52] Cinema tends to have a greater prestige, partly because it often has greater financial resources but also because it is consumed less habitually and is less readily available, at the push of a button, than television. It is for this reason that that some television programmes, advertisements and music videos have used marginally wider formats than 1.33:1, a tendency starting well before the advent of widescreen television. The presence of the characteristic black bands at the top and bottom of the screen is, in these cases, a signifier not of something missing but of an aspiration to the higher cultural status of the cinematic.

The quality or scope of Hollywood filmmaking is often assumed to have been reduced by its connections with the world of small screen media. This might be true in some respects. The available repertoire of compositional strategies has been reduced by the demand that films can play without too great a loss – or too great a cost of conversion – on the small screen. For critics such as Mark Crispin Miller, 'today's Hollywood movie works without, or against, the potential depth and latitude of cinema, in favour of that systematic overemphasis deployed in advertising (and all other propaganda).'[53] Many examples seem to bear this out. Take *Armageddon* (1998), a spectacular action-effects blockbuster shot to a large extent in close and mid shots.

The ease with which most of the images of *Armageddon* translate to small screen is figured several times within the film itself, through its deployment of images on monitor screens that appear within the frame. In one case the hero Harry Stamper (Bruce Willis) is saying farewell to his daughter Grace (Liv Tyler) before sacrificing himself to save the world. Stamper appears to us in big close-up, from chin to forehead, in the right half of the 2.35:1 widescreen picture. His image is relayed to Grace via ranks of television monitors in Mission Control, where it appears as the film itself might appear on the domestic small screen: his face fits into and fills the frame of the monitor with no loss of primary content. *Armageddon* is packed with the kind of over-emphatic rapid-impact editing described by Miller. Typical of its style are the scenes in which one space shuttle crashes and the other lands heavily on a rogue meteor they have been sent to intercept. Big close-ups dominate, along with fast cutting, shaky camerawork and flashing white light. The effect is a 'shallowness' and brightness of individual images, the impact of which comes almost entirely from the rapidity of editing, camera movement and strobing light; a style that might well be explained by the director Michael Bay's background in advertisements and music video.

Framing in great depth or width, without constant editing, is almost entirely absent from *Armageddon*, even in its most large-scale action set-pieces. Not that the more exaggerated compositional novelties of the earlier widescreen era should be unduly fetishized. They have their merits, like other formal devices, but they can be just as contrived as any framing designed to take account of the safe-action area in the age of television and video. Many of these films might appear static and pedestrian today, hamstrung by the compulsion to hold single shots long enough to show off accumulated detail within the frame. They are not part of what is usually taken to be the 'classical' Hollywood style, their prominence in the Hollywood mainstream being a product of the very specific context of the 1950s and 1960s. Classical composition, in David Bordwell's account, privileges a T-shaped zone comprised by 'the upper one-third and the central vertical third' of the screen, a zone unthreatened by translation to the small screen.[54]

The fact that some films are shown on television or video in formats more narrow than those in which they are released in the cinema does not necessarily involve an act of destructive intervention. Some films are still shot in the 1.33:1 ratio and then masked during projection, to create a wider shape on the cinema screen. In the past this was a way to create a widescreen impression on the cheap. Today it might be done with the shape of the television screen in mind from the start. The widescreen version is not, in this case, an 'original', the 'vision of the filmmakers' that has subsequently been damaged. A number of versions might exist, none of which has any essential privilege over the others.[55] This might have unfavourable implications for the use of the full expressive resources of the medium. Compromises might be involved in both directions: limitations on the use of width, when considering the move from cinema to television, but also limitations on the use of the full height of the 1.33:1 frame when it is to be cropped for theatrical exhibition. The latter impact is generally given less consideration, the relative status of the two media and the history of some pan/scan horrors ensuring that the 'cinematic' shape of the wider screen is seen by many commentators – if not by the majority of television viewers – as intrinsically 'superior'.

Another characteristic of television production identified by Ellis makes a connection between the debates encountered in this and the previous chapter. In the television action series, Ellis suggests, 'the narrative enigma (the aim of the heroes' quest), is relatively absent. It provides the ground for a series of relatively self-contained segments that deal with particular actions.'[56] This sounds very similar to the verdict of many commentators on the contemporary Hollywood action-spectacular. In the case of television, the argument is based on the assumption that the dominant conditions of reception work against any great or sustained investment in tightly constructed narrative. Could this be another potential explanation for a lack of narrative coherence in Hollywood, or the development of more segmented narrative forms such as those associated with the serial? Might this aspect of the small screen experience also be taken into account in the construction of Hollywood films?

It could be added to the list of possible factors detailed in chapter 6, although only with substantial qualification, not least because of the extent to which many of the most action-packed and spectacular films still continue to manifest substantial and over-arching narrative frame-works. It might be another way to try to account for the particular high-peaking narrative/spectacle-action profile found in the Hollywood action cinema of recent years. The gradual build-up of the 'rising action' curve might not function so well on the domestic small-screen, where harder work is generally required to maintain audience attention, and might be less well suited to the series format favoured by television. The roller-coaster aesthetic, offering a regular series of noisy attention-grabbers amid a looser narrative structure, might be expected to function more effectively in this environment. This is at least a more specific and materially rooted explanation for the shape of such films than more general – and widespread – diagnosis of what is taken to be a 'reduced attention span' among contemporary viewers.

The economic importance of domestic small screen media has been drawn in other ways into debates about the fate of narrative in contemporary Hollywood. Films shown on commercial television, videotape and disc are subject to levels of interruption additional to the fact of location amid the distractions of the home environment. Advertisements break into the narrative flow, as might use of the TV remote control and the video stop, pause, rewind or fast-forward. Have films been structured to take this into account? Commercial television programmes are designed with reference to the rhythms imposed by advertisement breaks. What about films destined eventually for television screenings? I am not aware of any argument or evidence to support such a conclusion in this case. Kristen Thompson suggests that Hollywood features tend to break down into segments averaging between 20 and 30 minutes – which does not seem to accord with the dominant rhythm of advertisement breaks in American television – a structure identified in films made both before and after the age in which television became an important element of the industrial calculation.[57] The appeal of screenings on satellite and cable networks is often based on the fact that they show films uninterrupted.

Films shown on television or video are potentially subject to a variety of interruptions and re-orderings by remote control. These have con-siderable implications for theories of the experience of viewing. How films themselves might conceivably be structured to take this into account is not clear, if only because of the sheer variety of viewing strategies available. The assumption that viewers might fast-forward from one spectacular action set-piece to another might be used to account for the existence of a stylistic feature such as the roller-coaster format. But the ease with which such manipulations can be achieved might obviate any argument about the need to offer a particular kind of structured relationship in the first place. A demand for greater narrative redundancy might be attributed to uncertainty about the mode in which films are received on broadcast television, video or DVD. But a strong measure of redundancy is already a standard feature of Hollywood narrative style, rooted in existing allowances for the vagaries of potentially different levels of attention or understanding among diverse cinema audiences at home and abroad. Mainstream Hollywood films

14. Superficial glitz, or Hollywood avant-garde? Multi-layered rear projections in *Natural Born Killers*, © Warner Bros., 1994. Ronald Grant archive

are designed to achieve the maximum level of legibility for the maximum number of viewers. A basic threshold of attention is presupposed however, which is unlikely to include allowances for the most active users of the remote control.

Formal devices drawn from media such as advertising and music video have encouraged the adoption of some more radical, experimental or almost avant-garde strategies in Hollywood, in addition to the more negative influences highlighted by many commentators. *Natural Born Killers* (1994), for example, unleashes a panoply of effects of the kind that might usually be found in music video or advertising: extensive use of back-projected images, the precise motivations of which are not always immediately clear; rapid shifts between different formats (including moves between colour and monochrome and from 35mm to 16mm and Super-8), canted framing, fast and slow motion, animation sequences and a spoof sitcom. *Romeo + Juliet* (1996) is distinctly William Shakespeare for the MTV generation, director Baz Luhrmann drawing on a background in music video in a hyperkinetic style including devices such as hyperbolic whip-pans and zooms. *Three Kings* (1999) also displays a mixture of visual styles, audacious in what appears to be a mainstream action-adventure. It uses different film stocks and methods of processing in different parts of the film, to create stylized colour effects, along with unusually grainy, wide-angled and sometimes rapidly cut and panned sequences, the latter modelled in part on the style of television news coverage.

From a social-cultural perspective, styles such as these have often been interpreted as symptoms of a 'postmodern' tendency in recent or contemporary cultural production. MTV, and music video in general, has been seen by several commentators as the acme of the postmodern, in its violations of traditional cause–effect narrative structures, its mixture of elements drawn from 'high' and 'low' culture, its manipulations of the image, and so on.[58] The relative departures from classical Hollywood style found in some films of the Hollywood Renaissance might be understood as a variant of modernism (albeit limited), defined sometimes as a 'thickening' of the means of representation to the point at which its formal strategies are thrust into the foreground. This has often been seen as a type of formal experimentation that has radical political potential, laying bare the constructed nature of representations. Films that draw on the styles of music video and advertising might, in these terms, be defined as postmodern. The postmodern is seen by many commentators as reactionary or apolitical in nature, refusing the stability of any reference point and highly implicated in the realm of capitalist consumerism.

How far these oppositions hold up, and how far the characteristics of Hollywood films can be explained this way, remains very much open to question.[59] Interpretations in terms of sweeping epochal changes are tempting but open to dangers of oversimplification, as we have seen in previous chapters. It might be possible to make connections between the use of particular stylistic devices and assertions of such large-scale cultural change, but the picture tends to be more complex. Many of the less conventional formal strategies inspired by advertising or music video, for example, had themselves been raided from the work of 'modernist' avant-garde filmmakers. An industrial perspective, based on the importance of small screen media, offers a simpler and more immediate explanation; one that might be easier to demonstrate because it depends on fewer other intervening factors. It need not be a question of one or the other. One of the aims of this book has been to show how particular New Hollywood phenomena might be explicable in more than one way. The use of innovative techniques drawn from media such as advertising and music video can also be explained as a way individual directors seek to leave a stylistic imprint, to increase their market value, a process that can lead to the wider adoption and absorption of such devices within the available Hollywood repertoire. [60]

Films such as *Natural Born Killers*, *Romeo + Juliet* and *Three Kings* appear to have adopted elements of the frenetic aesthetic of advertising or MTV, postmodern or otherwise. This does not mean that they have abandoned the potential scope and breadth of the wider image, however. The multi-layered texture of *Natural Born Killers* loses much on the small screen. *Romeo + Juliet* and *Three Kings* make pointed use sometimes of frame-edge compositions in the 2.35:1 format (the heads of the rival Montague and Capulet families are framed at one point at extremes of the image, figuring their separation very much like the image of Benjamin and Mrs Robinson in *The Graduate*; one of the opening images of *Three Kings* gives us an American soldier's helmeted face in extreme and lower right while the figure of an Iraqi who is about to be shot is in the extreme top-left). *Three Kings* also uses composition in depth, performers often being framed close to the camera while action continues in the background. Widescreen and deep focus effects have not been abandoned in Hollywood, even if they are used less extensively than on particular occasions in the past and perhaps most often in films that depart from the conventional mainstream. As these examples show, they can be combined very effectively with the strategies most associated with the creation of impact in the limited frame of the small screen.

If close and mid shots dominate many features, fitting comfortably into the small screen, we should not forget that they have always formed an essential part of the Hollywood style, along with its more epic sweep. [61] A blend of scale/impact and intimacy has been a more or less constant feature of Hollywood production – along with a mixture of spectacle and narrative. The balance does appear to have changed somewhat in recent decades, however, a factor that might be attributed at least in part to the economic centrality of small-screen media. The facial close up has always been an important source of emotional impact but it was used more sparingly in the past.[62] A comparison between *Spartacus* and *Gladiator* reveals notable differences. Close and medium shots account for some 78 per cent of *Gladiator*, compared with 64 per cent of *Spartacus*. The real contrast lies in the proportions of close and close-medium shots (42 per cent in *Gladiator*, 14 per cent in *Spartacus*) and extra-long and extreme-long shots (9 per cent and 19 per cent, respectively).[63] *The Fall of the Roman Empire* produces figures similar to those of *Spartacus* (a slightly higher proportion of longer shots, in fact), confirming that the shot-scale approach of *Spartacus* should not be attributed primarily to the distinctive imprint of Kubrick. *Armageddon* and *Deep Impact* are both dominated by close and medium shots (78 per cent and 82 per cent), despite their contrasting average shot lengths. Longer shots are deployed more extensively in the 'classical' examples I have used, *The Charge of the Light Brigade* and *The Adventures of Robin Hood*, each of which has proportions of long and extra/extreme-shots close to 50 per cent and low proportions of close shots (9 per cent and 4 per cent). Significant changes are revealed by comparisons such as these, although larger samples would be required for more definitive conclusions to be suggested. Hollywood is far from having been converted to a cinema of televisual 'talking heads', however, despite the impression given by some of these examples. And for good reason.

The larger scale and impact of the theatrical experience remains central to the Hollywood economy, even for films that go on to make more money on the small screen. The aura of the cinema screening, as special event, has if anything been increased by the number of viewings that take place in the domesticated settings of the television set. Success in the cinema remains the key indicator of likely revenues elsewhere. The profitability of Hollywood films on broadcast television, video and future delivery channels is established largely by their association with the prestige of cinema, which often carries a more 'glamorous' or higher cultural status even when reduced to the confines of the small screen. Hollywood features need to work effectively in both dimensions.

Spectacular impact created through explosive montage and/or hyperbolic camera movement is one form that translates particularly well. But broader expanses and vistas are still to be found on the big screen, even if few mainstream features rely entirely on these qualities for their spectacular impact. The climactic battle scenes of the historical epic *The Patriot* (2000) offer numerous large sweeping images of the massed ranks of English and rebel American forces, spread out across the width of the screen. These are combined with faster-cut sequences of close-up battle that in some fleeting instances approach the strobing/chaotic aesthetic of *Gladiator*. The distinction might partly be driven by the imperatives of big and small screen media. But it can also be understood as a classically Hollywood tendency to shift between the bigger and smaller picture, the epic sweep of historical events and the close-up focus on the travails of the heroes and their close associates.

# Notes

## Introduction

1 'Theses on the philosophy of Hollywood history', 6

2 For an outline, and critique, of this argument, see Asu Aksoy and Kevin Robins, 'Hollywood for the 21st century: global competition for critical mass in image markets', *Cambridge Journal of Economics*, 16, 1992

3 Thomas Doherty, *Pre-code Hollywood*

4 See, for example, Michael Ryan and Douglas Kellner, *Camera Politica: The Politics and Ideology of Contemporary Hollywood Film*

## Chapter One

1 *Easy Riders, Raging Bulls: How the Sex 'N' Drugs 'N' Rock 'N' Roll Generation Saved Hollywood*, 17

2 Damon Wise, 'Hollywood plays the smart card', *Screen*, 8, 16 January 2000

3 Michael Pye and Lynda Myles, *The Movie Brats: How the Film Generation Took Over Hollywood*

4 For an overview see William Chafe, *The Unfinished Journey: America Since World War II*

5 See, for example, Robin Wood, *Hollywood from Vietnam to Reagan*, chapters 5 and 6, and Sumiko Higashi, '*Night of the Living Dead*: A Horror Film about the Horrors of the Vietnam Era'

6 As is the demon in *The Exorcist* (1973), which might not by mere coincidence have been set in the Washington of the early 1970s

7 Peter Cowie, *Coppola*, 81

8 The first of these statistics are from Jim Hillier, *The New Hollywood*, 13; the figures for 1980 and 2000 are based on my calculations taken from annual admissions statistics in the Motion Picture Association of America *2000 US Economic Review*

9  Kristin Thompson, *Exporting Entertainment*

10  Gomery, *The Hollywood Studio System*, 8–14

11  'A Mature Oligopoly', 255

12  The detail below comes mostly from Balio, 'A Mature Oligopoly'

13  Jon Lewis, *Hollywood v. Hard Core: How the Struggle over Censorship Saved the Modern Film Industry*, 57

14  Biskind, *Easy Riders*, 18, 20

15  Richard Maltby, 'Sticks, Hicks and Flaps'

16  Maltby, 'Sticks, Hicks and Flaps', 25

17  Lewis, *Hollywood v. Hard Core*, 101

18  For the list of banned subjects see Frank Miller, *Censored Hollywood: Sex, Sin and Violence on Screen*

19  Miller, *Censored Hollywood*, 162

20  Miller, *Censored Hollywood*, 168

21  Jon Lewis, 'Money Matters: Hollywood in the Corporate Era', 91–2

22  'Money Matters', 93

23  Lewis, *Hollywood v. Hard Core*, 150

24  Richard Maltby, '"Nobody knows everything": Post-classical historiographies and consolidated entertainment', 31

25  *Doctor Dolittle* budget $18 million, gross $9.05 million; *Star!* budget $14 million, gross $4 million; *Hello, Dolly!* budget $26.4 million, gross $9 million (Internet Movie Database)

26  John Izod, *Hollywood and the Box Office*, 173; Maltby, '"Nobody knows everything"', 32

27  Summaries of some of these borrowings are given in Robert Ray, *A Certain Tendency of the Hollywood Cinema, 1930–1980*, 269–95, and David Bordwell and Janet Staiger, 'Historical implications of the classical Hollywood cinema', in Bordwell, Staiger and Kristin Thompson, *The Classical Hollywood Cinema: Film Style and Mode of Production to 1960*

28  Close inspection suggests that strictly speaking there is no departure from the 180 degree rule, although as Ray suggests the cutting does create a sense of unease

29  Michael Pye and Lynda Myles, *The Movie Brats: How the Film Generation Took Over Hollywood*, 210

30  Pye and Myles, *The Movie Brats*, 192

31  *A Certain Tendency*, 288

32 'The classical Hollywood style, 1917–60', in Bordwell, Staiger and Kristin Thompson, *The Classical Hollywood Cinema*

33 Amy Taubin, *Taxi Driver*, 46

34 A contrast made by Bordwell and Staiger, 'Historical implications of the classical Hollywood cinema', in Bordwell, Staiger and Thompson, *The Classical Hollywood Cinema*, 375–7, although they err in suggesting that the protagonist of *Blow Up* has no access to other than the photograph of the murder: he does actually see the body at one point

35 See Bordwell, 'The classical Hollywood style, 1917–60', in Bordwell, Staiger and Thompson, *The Classical Hollywood Cinema*, 72–4

36 Kristin Thompson, *Storytelling in the New Hollywood: Understanding Classical Narrative Technique*, 5, citing figures from Eddie Dorman Kay, *Box-Office Champs: The Most Popular Movies of the Last 50 Years*

## Chapter 2

1 'Theses on the philosophy of Hollywood history', 11

2 Brian Fuson, '"Scream 3" kills theaters record', *The Hollywood Reporter*, 4–6 February 2000

3 Figures from the Motion Picture Association of America (MPAA), as reported in 'Movie Box-Office Gross and Attendance', Grolier, Inc. web site, March 2000, and in the MPPA's *2000 US Economic Review*, slide 5

4 'Top 20 Films of All-Time (adjusted for inflation)', Grolier Inc., March 2000

5 MPPA, *2000 US Economic Review*, and Nicholas Garnham, *Capitalism and Communication*, 181

6 Different figures are cited by different commentators, the differences depending probably on exactly how the output of the majors and other companies with links to the majors are defined. Richard Maltby puts the total in 1975 at 120 ('Nobody knows everything', 32), while David Cook suggests an average as low as 100 a year by the end of the decade (*Lost Illusions: America in the Shadow of Watergate and Vietnam, 1970–1979*, 349)

7 Peter Bart, *The Gross*, 31

8 See Tino Balio, *Grand Design: Hollywood as a Modern Business Enterprise*, 179–211

9 Previous exceptions to the rule were *Gone with the Wind* (1939) and *Duel*

*in the Sun* (1946), which were widely released amid extensive publicity, but untypical of their time

10  Figures from Thomas Schatz, 'The New Hollywood', 27, and Eileen Meehan, '"Holy Commodity Fetish, Batman!"': The Political Economy of a Commercial Intertext, 60

11  Figures from the Internet Movie Database

12  Bart, *The Gross*, 176

13  Schatz, 'The New Hollywood', 18

14  These and the following figures are from the Motion Picture Association of America, *2000 US Economic Review*

15  Kirk Honeycutt, 'Wide tracks of "Godzilla" lead to a holiday record', *The Hollywood Reporter*, 15 April 1998

16  Bart, *The Gross*, 200; Mike Goodridge, 'Aiming for the heart', *Screen International*, 12 June 1998, 16

17  Honeycutt, 'Wide tracks of "Godzilla"'

18  Garnham, *Capitalism and Communication*, 191

19  John Izod, *Hollywood and the Box Office*, 178

20  Tino Balio, '"A major presence in all the world's important markets": the globalization of Hollywood in the 1990s', 60

21  *Screen Digest*, 'Worldwide cinema: Weaknesses hidden by record growth', September 1998, 202–203

22  Don Groves, 'Boffo B.O. bucks foreign coin ills', *Variety*, 18–31 December 2000, 9, 74

23  *Screen Digest*, 'Top 10 films take huge chunk of global revenues', January 2000, 29. The extent to which earnings are concentrated on a small proportion of titles is further increased when sources such as video are taken into account

24  The following is based partly on Garnham

25  Tino Balio, 'Adjusting to the new global economy: Hollywood in the 1990s', 30–1; Jim Hillier, *The New Hollywood*, 19–20

26  Balio, 'Adjusting', 30

27  Balio, 'Adjusting', 35

28  *Screen Digest*, February 1998, 'From Studio to Screen: The majors' integrated strategy', 33

29  David Cook, *Lost Illusions*, 19

30  See A.D. Murphy, 'Distribution and Exhibition: An Overview'. Two main

practices are used. In one, the distributor takes 90 per cent of the gross after the deduction of the 'house nut' – the operating expenses of the exhibitor. In cases when the gross is relatively low, and this calculation is less beneficial to the distributor, a simple percentage of the gross is demanded

31 David Kaplan, 'How George Lucas orchestrated the biggest movie-marketing campaign of all time and made *Phantom* a must-see, no matter what critics say', *Newsweek*, 17 May 1999, 64–8

32 Izod, *Hollywood and the Box Office*, 192

33 Bart, *The Gross*, 199; 'Economies of Scale', opinion/editorial, *Screen International*, 5 June 1998, 11

34 Bart, *The Gross*, 175

35 Statistics: Internet Movie Database

36 Cook, *Lost Illusions*, 353

37 Izod, *Hollywood and the Box Office*, 176

38 Izod, *Hollywood and the Box Office*, 176–7

39 See Stephen Prince, *A New Pot of Gold: Hollywood Under the Electronic Rainbow, 1980–1989*, 22

40 Bart, *The Gross*, 101

41 Bart, *The Gross*, 202

42 Veronis Suhler merchant bank, 14th annual *Communications Industry Forecast*, August 2000

43 Janet Wasko, *Hollywood in the Information Age*, 62

44 *The Movie Game*, 25

45 'Corporate history' from Loews Cineplex Entertainment website, http://www.loewscineplex.com; Tino Balio, '"A major presence in all of the world's markets"', 61

46 Jeffrey Daniels, 'Global economics slam Sony', *The Hollywood Reporter*, 29 October 1998

47 Correspondence to the author from Al Ovadia, executive vice-president, consumer products, February 2001

48 Interview with John Calley, *The Hollywood Reporter*, 28 September 1999

49 Sony Corporation, *Annual Report*, 1999, 36, 39

50 Sony Corporation, *Annual Report*, 2000, 29

51 Balio, 'A major presence', 69

52 Balio, 'A major presence', 69

53 Figure supplied to the author

54  Dale, *The Movie Game*, 27

55  *The Gross*, 205

56  Nik Jamgocyan, 'Godzilla TV rights go cheap', *Screen International*, 5 June 1998, 5

57  See Eileen Meehan, '"Holy Commodity Fetish, Batman!": The Political Economy of a Commercial Intertext'

58  '"Holy Commodity Fetish, Batman!"', 53

59  This and the following detail is taken from Jon Lewis, 'Money Matters: Hollywood in the Corporate Era', 103

60  The commission imposed some conditions on the deal, including the requirement that the company open up to competitors its next generation of instant-messaging services

61  Paul Sweeting, 'Vid chains vie for early edge in digital domain', *Variety*, 6–12 March, 2000

62  Lewis, 'Money Matters: Hollywood in the Corporate Era', 97

63  *Screen Digest* press release, 'Electronic cinema set to transform the movie business', September 2000

64  Wasko, *Hollywood in the Information Age*

65  Douglas Gomery, 'The Coming of the Sound: Technological Change in the American Film Industry'

66  'The New Hollywood', 19

67  *Time Warner 1999 Fact Book*, 13

68  Goodridge, 'Aiming for the heart'

69  Dade Hayes, 'Sequels try for triples', *Variety*, 24–30 July 2000, 1, 70

70  Cathy Dunkley, 'Baker [sic] paints a Dis franchise', *The Hollywood Reporter*, 17 April 2000

71  Claude Brodesser, 'Sony's twice-told tales', *Variety*, 27 November–3 December 2000, 1, 74

72  Justin Wyatt, 'The formation of the major independent: Miramax, New Line and the New Hollywood'

## Chapter 3

1  Quoted in Michael Pye and Linda Myles, *The Movie Brats: How the film generation took over Hollywood*, 194

2  'A close encounter with *Raiders of the Lost Ark*: notes on narrative aspects of the New Hollywood Blockbuster', 168

3 'A Certain Tendency of the French Cinema', *Cahiers du Cinéma*, January 1954

4 See Robert Philip Kolker, *A Cinema of Loneliness: Penn, Kubrick, Scorsese, Spielberg, Altman*, chapter 2

5 'Notes on the auteur theory in 1962', 64

6 'Notes', 64

7 'Towards a theory of film history', 65

8 Pye and Myles, *The Movie Brats*, 191

9 Pye and Myles, *The Movie Brats*, 10

10 David A. Cook, 'Auteur Cinema and the "Film Generation" in 1970s Hollywood', 18

11 *Whom God Wishes to Destroy...: Francis Coppola and the New Hollywood*, 47

12 See Mark Litwak, *Reel Power: The Struggle for Influence and Success in the New Hollywood*, 66, 147

13 Lewis, *Whom God Wishes to Destroy*, 2

14 Kolker, *A Cinema of Loneliness*, 304

15 See David Thompson and Ian Christie (eds), *Scorsese on Scorsese*, 116–45

16 Peter Biskind, *Easy Riders, Raging Bulls*, 126, 136–37

17 Quoted in Biskind, *Easy Riders*, 52

18 Biskind, *Easy Riders*, 76

19 Lewis, *Whom God Wishes to Destroy*, 13

20 Lewis, *Whom God Wishes to Destroy*, 16

21 Biskind, *Easy Riders*, 177, 184, 185–7

22 Lewis, *Whom God Wishes to Destroy*, 14

23 Lewis, *Whom God Wishes to Destroy*, 16–8

24 The following is based again on the detailed account in Lewis, *Whom God Wishes to Destroy*

25 Lewis, *Whom God Wishes to Destroy*, 10

26 Lewis, *Whom God Wishes to Destroy*, 55

27 Lewis, *Whom God Wishes to Destroy*, chapter 2

28 For more background see John Baxter, *George Lucas: A Biography*

29 Cook, 'Auteur Cinema and the "Film Generation" in 1970s Hollywood', 21–2

30 Joseph McBride, *Steven Spielberg: A Biography*, 363

31 McBride, *Steven Spielberg*, 380

32  McBride, 445; Jon Hazelton, 'Delayed Impact', *Screen International*, 29 August 1997, 12

33  Hazelton, 'Delayed Impact', 12–13

34  For an account of this theme in *Jurassic Park* see my *Spectacular Narratives: Hollywood in the Age of the Blockbuster*, chapter 2

35  Quoted in McBride, *Steven Spielberg*, 327

36  For one example explored in more detail, see Buckland, 'A close encounter with *Raiders of the Lost Ark*', on Spielberg's deployment of the 'off-screen presence', a device not exclusive to Spielberg but which, Buckland suggests, is used in a manner that contributes to the distinctive impression created by the film

37  *A Cinema of Loneliness: Penn, Kubrick, Scorsese, Spielberg, Altman*, 239

38  See Janet Wolff, *The Social Production of Art*

39  'The Classical Hollywood Style, 1917–60', in Bordwell, Janet Staiger and Kristin Thompson, *The Classical Hollywood Cinema: Film Style and Mode of Production to 1960*, 80–1

40  'The death of the author', 211

41  McBride, *Steven Spielberg*, 290

42  Paul Sammon, *Future Noir: The Making of Blade Runner*, 368

43  Eileen Meehan, '"Holy Commodity Fetish, Batman!": The Political Economy of a Commercial Intertext', 53

44  'Auteurs and the New Hollywood', 42

45  Peter Bart, 'Coppola: technophile Renaissance man', *Daily Variety*, 24 March 2000

## Chapter 4

1  *Gunfighter Nation: The Myth of the Frontier in Twentieth-Century America*, 8

2  *Film/Genre*, 64

3  Exactly to what extent audiences 'identify' with characters has been the subject of much debate in film theory. For a useful contribution which suggests a range of possibilities see Murray Smith, *Engaging Characters: Fiction, Emotion, and the Cinema*

4  'A Semantic/Syntactic Approach to Film Genre'

5  The classic structural account of the western is found in Jim Kitses, *Horizons West*. See also Thomas Schatz, *Hollywood Genres*. For an outline of this kind of approach to science fiction see Geoff King and Tanya Krzywinska,

*Science Fiction Cinema: From Outerspace to Cyberspace*. The definitive version of this way of reading the Hollywood musical is Rick Altman, *The American Film Musical*. For a reading of comedy in terms of the opposition between normality and comic disruption see Frank Krutnik, 'The Clown-Prints of Comedy'

6  The concept of regeneration through violence is a central feature of American frontier mythology according to Richard Slotkin, *Regeneration Through Violence: The Mythology of the American Frontier 1600–1860*

7  Especially 'The Structural Study of Myth'

8  'Criticism and the Western', 10

9  See Douglas Pye's useful overview, 'Criticism and the Western', 15–18

10  For examples and further references, see Steve Neale, *Genre and Hollywood*, 136

11  'Genericity in the Nineties: Eclectic Irony and the New Sincerity'

12  See Schatz, *Hollywood Genres*, 37

13  'Shoot-Out at the Genre Corral: Problems in the "Evolution" of the Western'

14  Gallagher, 'Shoot-Out', 252

15  Gallagher, 'Shoot-Out', 253–4

16  Rick Altman, *Film/Genre*, 112

17  The connection has been much discussed by critics and the filmmakers themselves

18  Slotkin, *Regeneration Through Violence*, 94–111

19  Peter Kramer, 'A Powerful Cinema-going Force? Hollywood and the Female Audience since the 1960s', 96

20  Kramer, 'A Powerful Cinema-going Force?', 95

21  For an overview see John Hill, 'Film and postmodernism'

22  For an example of the latter see Brian Henderson, 'Romantic Comedy Today: Semi-Tough or Impossible?', *Film Quarterly*, vol. 31, no. 4, Summer 1978

23  See my *Film Comedy*

24  *Film/Genre*, 149

25  *Genre and Hollywood*, 244–51

26  Marc Vernet, 'Film noir on the edge of doom'; Steve Neale, *Genre and Hollywood*, chapter 4

27  *Film/Genre*, 127

28  For a detailed study of how this process worked in the early stages of development of the musical, the western and the biopic, see Altman, *Film/Genre*, chapter 3

29  *Film/Genre*, 162

30  See my *Spectacular Narratives: Hollywood in the Age of the Blockbuster*, chapter 6

31  *Film/Genre*, 115

32  *Film/Genre*, 115

33  *Genre and Hollywood*, 211

34  See also Christine Gledhill, 'Rethinking genre'

35  See Robin Wood, 'Ideology, Genre, Auteur'

36  Neale, *Genre and Hollywood*, 225–29

## Chapter 5

1  *Reel Power: The Struggle for Influence and Success in the New Hollywood*, 211

2  'Reconceptualising Stardom', 180

3  The character left the series in 1999

4  'Articulating Stardom'

5  'Re-examining stardom: questions of texts, bodies and performance'

6  Barry King, 'Articulating Stardom', 178

7  Tessa Perkins, 'The Politics of "Jane Fonda"', 247

8  'The Politics of "Jane Fonda"', 247

9  For an examination of what we can learn about the distinctive contributions of particular performers by imagining their replacement by others, see John O. Thompson, 'Screen acting and the commutation test'

10  See Richard DeCordova, 'The emergence of the star system in America'

11  *The Hollywood Reporter*, 'Star Power' survey, 1999

12  See Paul McDonald, *The Star System: Hollywood's Production of Popular Identities*, 88–93

13  For the comments of numerous studio executives on this, see the 1999 'Star Power' survey by *The Hollywood Reporter*

14  Diane Taylor and Jane Cassidy, 'Trust me, I'm a doctor', *Guardian*, section 2, 27 June 1997, 4–5

15  Barry King, 'Stardom as an occupation', 166

16  'Stardom as an occupation', 166

17  'Stardom as an occupation', 166

18   *A New Pot of Gold: Hollywood Under the Electronic Rainbow, 1980–1989*, 160–1

19   Dyer puts such variations in terms of the extent to which star image 'fits' with the character played. He suggests three main categories: 'selective use' of certain aspects of star image only; 'perfect fit' between star image and character; and 'problematic fit', in which various contradictions might occur between the two. (*Stars*, 142–49)

20   William Leith, 'Big Ears flies again', *Observer*, 'Life' magazine, 20 December 1998, 7

21   Joe Rhodes, 'Iron Will', *Premiere*, November 1998, 91–3

22   For more on the significance of biracial 'buddy' relationships in Hollywood, see Donald Bogle, *Toms, Coons, Mulattoes, Mammies, and Bucks: An Interpretive History of Blacks in American Films*, 271–76

23   Lyons, Charles, 'Passion for Slashin'', *Variety*, 26 June–9 July 2000

24   See, for example, Ned Zeman, 'Will Smith Rides High', *Vanity Fair*, July 1999

25   An issue I explore in relation to contemporary Hollywood 'action' films in *Spectacular Narratives*, chapter 4

26   *Stars*, 30

27   *Stars*, 22

28   See, for example, Yvonne Tasker, *Spectacular Bodies: Gender, genre and the action cinema* and a brief summary of such approaches in Paul McDonald, 'Star Studies', 89

29   On *Play Misty for Me*, see Adam Knee, 'The Dialectic of Female Power and Male Hysteria in *Play Misty for Me*'; on *Tightrope*, see Paul Smith, *Clint Eastwood: A Cultural Production*, 134–5

30   See, for example, Michael Ryan and Douglas Kellner, *Camera Politica: The Politics and Ideology of Contemporary Hollywood Film*, 42–6

31   See, for examples, Zeman, 'Will Smith Rides High' and William Leith, 'Big Ears flies again'

32   For a study of various dimensions of DiCaprio fandom in relation to *Titanic* (1997), see Melanie Nash and Martti Lahti, '"Almost Ashamed to Say I Am One of Those Girls": *Titanic*, Leonardo DiCaprio, and the Paradoxes of Girls' Fandom'

33   For outline summaries see, for example, McDonald, 'Star Studies', 86–90, and Jackie Stacey, *Star Gazing: Hollywood cinema and female spectatorship*, chapters 2 and 5

34   A complex issue that cannot be discussed here in full. Some of the debates
     around this ideological reading of star images is found in Dyer, *Stars*, 'Part
     Three: Stars as Signs'
35   *Engaging Characters: Fiction, Emotion, and the Cinema*
36   *Star Gazing*, chapter 5
37   See, for example, Edward Branigan, *Narrative Comprehension and Film*,
     13–17

## Chapter 6

 1   'Dickens, Griffith, and Film Theory Today', 26
 2   *The Classical Hollywood Cinema: Film Style and Mode of Production to 1960*,
     'Part One, The classical Hollywood style, 1917–60', 12–3
 3   *Hollywood Cinema: An Introduction*, 7
 4   For a useful summary, see Elizabeth Cowie, 'Storytelling: classical
     Hollywood cinema and classical narrative'
 5   'Storytelling', 178
 6   Cowie, 'Storytelling' and Altman, 'Dickens, Griffith, and Film Theory
     Today'
 7   Cowie, 'Storytelling', 185
 8   *The Classical Hollywood Cinema*, 20
 9   *The Classical Hollywood Cinema*, 21
10   Steve Neale, *Genre and Hollywood*, 180–81
11   *Genre and Hollywood*, 202
12   Fred Pfeil, 'From Pillar to Postmodernism: Race, Class, and Gender in
     the Male Rampage Film', 180
13   'From Pillar to Postmodernism', 181
14   For more on *Armageddon* see *Spectacular Narratives*, chapter 6
15   See, for example, Martin Rubin, *Showstoppers: Busby Berkeley and the
     Tradition of Spectacle*
16   'From Pillar to Postmodernism', 180
17   William Paul, 'The K-mart audience at the mall movies', 488
18   For more on this see *Spectacular Narratives*, chapter 7 and/or my 'Ride-
     Films and Films as Rides in the Contemporary Hollywood Cinema of
     Attractions'
19   'Zooming Out: The End of Offscreen Space', 266
20   For more on this see *Spectacular Narratives*, 187–8, and Geoff King and

Tanya Krzywinska, *Science Fiction Cinema: From Outerspace to Cyberspace*, 99–102

21  Motion Picture Association, *1999 Motion Picture Attendance*

22  *Distinction: A social critique of the judgement of taste*

23  See, for example, Mike Goodridge, 'Aiming for the heart', *Screen International*, 12 June 1998, 16

24  See Matthew Bernstein, '"Floating Triumphantly": The American Critics on *Titanic*', 23–4

25  Studio surveys showed that older moviegoers narrowly outnumbered the young at the opening of *Deep Impact*: Peter Bart, *The Gross*, 174

26  Richard Maltby and Ian Craven, *Hollywood Cinema*, 11

27  Motion Picture Association, *1999 Motion Picture Attendance*

28  Denis Seguin, 'Middle-aged spread brings BO dividends', *Screen International*, no. 1267, 14–20 July 2000

29  Andrew Brown, vice-president, international advertising media for United International Pictures, the international distributors of the film, in correspondence with the author

30  Dade Hayes, 'Women Taking Action at B.O.', *Variety*, 31 July–6 August 2000, 7–8

31  *Knowing Audiences:* Judge Dredd*, Its Friends, Fans and Foes*, 150

32  Warren Buckland, 'A close encounter with *Raiders of the Lost Ark*: notes on narrative aspects of the New Hollywood blockbuster', 172

33  For examples cited by Cowie, see 'Storytelling', 185

34  See Brian Taves, 'The B Film: Hollywood's Other Half'

35  'The New Hollywood', 23

36  'The New Hollywood', 24

37  *Hollywood Cinema: An Introduction*, 35–6

38  For numerous examples see *Spectacular Narratives*

39  Wasko, *Hollywood in the Information Age*, 205

40  Sony Corporation, 'Annual Report 2000', 'Composition of Sales and Operating Revenue by Business and Geographic Segment'

41  For a flavour of this see Mark Litvak, *Reel Power: The Struggle for Influence and Success in the New Hollywood*

42  See, for example, Robert Allen, 'Home Alone Together: Hollywood and the "family film"', 110

43  'To the rear of the back end: The economics of independent cinema', 94

44  'Advertising: End of Story', 193

45  'Advertising', 197

46  'Advertising', 191

47  *Spectacular Narratives*, 24

48  *High Concept: Movies and Marketing in Hollywood*, 40

49  *High Concept*, 41

50  *High Concept*, 46

51  *High Concept*, 60

52  *A Cinema Without Walls: Movies and Culture after Vietnam*, 161

53  *A Cinema Without Walls*, 166

54  'Conglomerates and Content: Remakes, Sequels and Series in the New Hollywood'

55  *A Cinema Without Walls*, 170

56  Wasko, *Hollywood in the Information Age*, 206. As Wasko points out, movie tie-ins are not embraced with open arms by all toy manufacturers, some of whom see them as a risky proposition

57  'The New Hollywood', 34

58  See Charles Eckert, 'The Carole Lombard in Macey's Window'

59  Kristen Thompson, *Storytelling in the New Hollywood*, 338, 347

## Chapter 7

1  Quoted in John Belton, *Widescreen Cinema*, 198

2  'Glorious Technicolor, Breathtaking CinemaScope, and Stereophonic Sound', 207

3  Estimates based on studies of data from various sources, including the MPAA, supplied by *Screen Digest* to the author

4  Average screen size before the adoption of widescreen processes in the 1950s was 20 x 16ft, which increased to 65ft or more in some cases with formats such as Cinerama and CinemaScope (Belton, *Widescreen Cinema*, 159); conventional television sets were limited at the time of writing to a maximum of some 36ins, or 46ins using rear-projection

5  Tino Balio, Introduction to Part I of Balio (ed.) *Hollywood in the Age of Television*, 21

6  Balio, 'Introduction', 21

7  Peter Kramer, 'The Lure of the Big Picture: Film, Television and Hollywood'

8   Balio, 'Introduction', 21–23

9   Balio, 'Introduction', 36. For more detail see Christopher Anderson,
    *Hollywood TV: The Studio System in the Fifties*

10  Balio, 'Introduction', 17; Richard Maltby, '"Nobody knows everything":
    post-classical historiographies and consolidated entertainment'

11  Christopher Anderson, *Hollywood TV*, 159

12  William Lafferty, 'Feature Films on Prime-Time Television', 242

13  Balio, 'Introduction', 31; initially, the studios mostly only sold or leased
    features made before 1948, unions representing actors, writers and directors
    having secured rights to residual compensation for films made after that
    year

14  Balio, 'Introduction', 39

15  This detail, and most of the above, is from Janet Wasko, *Hollywood in the
    Information Age*

16  Wasko, *Hollywood in the Information Age*, 126–29

17  See Wasko for more detail

18  *2000 Economic Review*, slide 28

19  Tino Balio, 'Introduction' to Part II of Balio (ed.), *Hollywood in the Age of
    Television*, 268

20  'Home Alone Together', 112

21  Scott Hettrick, 'Tarzan puts Grinch in vidlock', 1

22  Wasko, *Hollywood in the Information Age*, 91–2

23  MPPA, *1999 Economic Review*, slide 38; pay cable subscription figures are
    listed only from 1982 while the figure for 1999 shows a drop to 33.2 million
    attributed 'in part to redefinition of some pay channels to basic cable'

24  See Wasko, *Hollywood in the Information Age*

25  Widescreen process had been available decades earlier but did not come
    into widespread use for various reasons discussed by Belton, *Widescreen
    Cinema*

26  Belton, *Widescreen Cinema*, 198

27  *Widescreen Cinema*, 216; Balio, 'Introduction', 37

28  Belton, *Widescreen Cinema*, 217

29  Belton, *Widescreen Cinema*, 281

30  Belton, *Widescreen Cinema*, 218; in the case of *Bonnie and Clyde*, Belton
    notes, the 'full-frame' version reveals more of Faye Dunaway's body than
    had been intended in the opening sequence examined in chapter 1

31   Anton Wilson, *Anton Wilson's Cinema Workshop*, 61, 81

32   *Cinema Workshop*, 81

33   *Cinema Workshop*, 82

34   John Belton, 'Looking through Video: The Psychology of Video and Film', 71

35   Quoted in Belton, *Widescreen Cinema*, 225

36   'Widescreen composition', 134–35

37   'Widescreen composition', 135

38   'Widescreen composition', 135

39   'Widescreen composition', 136

40   The lack of ability to record appears to have been the principal reason for the past failure of the laserdisk to challenge videotape, despite its greater quality of reproduction

41   Dan Fleming, 'Dial "M" for Movies: New Technologies, New Relations', 252

42   *Visible Fictions: Cinema, Television, Video*

43   *Television: Technology and Cultural Form*, 86–118

44   Martin McLoone, 'Boxed In?: The Aesthetics of Film and Television', 92–3; Ellis, *Visible Fictions*, 116. As Sean Cubitt suggests, differences in the mode of reception are also found from one culture or country to another: *Timeshift: On Video Culture*, 27

45   For more on *Saving Private Ryan* see my *Spectacular Narratives*, chapter 5; on the technique as used in *Gladiator* see Douglas Bankston, 'Death or Glory' and 'Veni, Vidi, Vici', an interview with Ridley Scott, in *American Cinematographer*, vol. 81, no. 5, May 2000, 38, 52

46   *Visible Fictions*, 132

47   *Spectacular Narratives*, chapter 4

48   I am grateful to Barry Salt for making available unpublished ASL and other statistics on a sample of thousands of films from the silent era to the late 1990s. See also David Bordwell, 'The classical Hollywood Style', in Bordwell, Janet Staiger and Kristin Thompson, *The Classical Hollywood Cinema*, 61

49   For more on this, see *Spectacular Narratives*, chapter 5

50   'Machines of the Invisible: Changes in Film Technology in the Age of Video', *Film Quarterly*, vol. 42, no. 2, winter 1988–89, 21

51   *High Concept: Movies and Marketing in Hollywood*, chapter 2

52  See, for example, Mark Crispin Miller, 'Advertising: End of Story'

53  'Advertising', 205

54  'The classical Hollywood style, 1917–60', in Bordwell, Janet Staiger and Kristen Thompson, *The Classical Hollywood Cinema: Film Style and Mode of Production to 1960*, 51

55  For examples, see David Bordwell and Kristin Thompson, *Film Art: An Introduction*, 5th edition, 233

56  *Visible Fictions*, 152

57  *Storytelling in the New Hollywood: Understanding Classical Narrative Technique*, 36

58  See in particular E. Ann Kaplan, *Rocking Around the Clock: Music Television, Postmodernism and Consumer Culture*; for a critique of such accounts see Will Straw, 'Popular Music and Postmodernism in the 1980s' and Andrew Goodwin, 'Fatal Distractions: MTV meets Postmodern Theory'

59  See, for example, Anne Friedberg, *Window Shopping: Cinema and the Postmodern*, chapter 4

60  Henry Jenkins, 'Historical Poetics', 115

61  For a similar argument see Martin McLoone, 'Boxed In?', 81

62  Pierre Sorlin, 'Television and the Close-up: Interference or Correspondence?', 119

63  According to my own calculations. Such findings are approximate. The exact boundaries between one type of shot and another are not always clear and can be complicated by the use of techniques such as mobile camerawork that shifts scale during the shot

# Bibliography

Aksoy, Asu, and Kevin Robins, 'Hollywood for the 21st century: global competition for critical mass in image markets', *Cambridge Journal of Economics*, 16, 1992

Allen, Robert, 'Home Alone Together: Hollywood and the "family film"', in Melvyn Stokes and Maltby (eds), *Identifying Hollywood's Audiences*, London: BFI, 1999

Altman, Rick, 'A Semantic/Syntactic Approach to Film Genre', in Barry Keith Grant (ed.), *Film Genre Reader*, Austin: University of Texas Press, 1986

— *The American Film Musical*, Bloomington: Indiana University Press, 1987

— 'Dickens, Griffith, and Film Theory Today', in Jane Gaines (ed.), *Classical Hollywood Narrative: The Paradigm Wars*, Durham: Duke University Press, 1992

— *Film/Genre*, London: BFI, 1999

Anderson, Christopher, *Hollywood TV: The Studio System in the Fifties*, Austin: University of Texas Press, 1994

Balio, Tino, 'A Mature Oligopoly, 1930–1948', in Balio (ed.), *The American Film Industry*, Madison: University of Wisconsin Press, 1985

— Introduction' to Part I and Part II of Balio (ed.) *Hollywood in the Age of Television*, Boston: Unwin Hyman, 1990

— *Grand Design: Hollywood as a Modern Business Enterprise, 1930–1939*, Berkeley: University of California Press, 1993

— '"A major presence in all the world's important markets": the globalization of Hollywood in the 1990s', in Steve Neale and Murray Smith (eds), *Contemporary Hollywood Cinema*, London: Routledge, 1998

— 'Adjusting to the new global economy: Hollywood in the 1990s', in Albert Moran (ed.), *Film Policy: International, national and regional perspectives*, London: Routledge, 1996

Bankston, Douglas, 'Death or Glory' and 'Veni, Vidi, Vici', *American Cinematographer*, vol. 81, no. 5, May 2000, 38, 52

Barker, Martin, and Kate Brooks, *Knowing Audiences:* Judge Dredd, *Its Friends, Fans and Foes*, Luton: University of Luton Press, 1998

Bart, Peter, *The Gross*, New York: St Martin's Press, 1999

— 'Coppola: technophile Renaissance man', *Daily Variety*, 24 March 2000

Barthes, Roland, 'The death of the author', extract in John Caughie (ed.), *Theories of Authorship*, London: Routledge, 1981

Baxter, John, *George Lucas: A Biography*, London: HarperCollins, 1999

Belton, John, 'Glorious Technicolor, Breathtaking CinemaScope, and Stereophonic Sound', in Tino Balio (ed.), *Hollywood in the Age of Television*, Boston: Unwin Hyman, 1990

— *Widescreen Cinema*, Cambridge, Mass.: Harvard University Press, 1992

— 'Looking through Video: The Psychology of Video and Film', in Michael Renov and Erika Suderburg (eds), *Resolutions: Contemporary Video Practices*, Minneapolis: University of Minnesota Press, 1996

Bernstein, Matthew, '"Floating Triumphantly": The American Critics on *Titanic*', in Kevin Sandler and Gaylyn Studlar, *Titanic: Anatomy of a Blockbuster*, New Brunswick: Rutgers University Press, 1999

Biskind, Peter, *Easy Riders, Raging Bulls: How the Sex 'N' Drugs 'N' Rock 'N' Roll Generation Saved Hollywood*, London: Bloomsbury, 1998

Bogle, Donald, *Toms, Coons, Mulattoes, Mammies, and Bucks: An Interpretive History of Blacks in American Films*, New York: Continuum, 1993

Bordwell, David, 'The classical Hollywood style, 1917–60', in Bordwell, Janet Staiger and Kristin Thompson, *The Classical Hollywood Cinema: Film Style and Mode of Production to 1960*, London: Routledge, 1985

Bordwell, David, and Janet Staiger, 'Historical implications of the classical Hollywood cinema', in Bordwell, Staiger and Kristin Thompson, *The Classical Hollywood Cinema: Film Style and Mode of Production to 1960*, London: Routledge, 1985

Bordwell, David, and Kristin Thompson, *Film Art: An Introduction*, 5th edition, New York: McGraw Hill, 1997

Bourdieu, Pierre, *Distinction: A social critique of the judgement of taste*, trans. London: Routledge, 1984

Brodesser, Claude, 'Sony's twice-told tales', *Variety*, November 27–December 3, 2000, 1, 74

Buckland, Warren, 'A close encounter with *Raiders of the Lost Ark*: notes on narrative aspects of the New Hollywood blockbuster', in Steve Neale and Murray Smith (eds), *Contemporary Hollywood Cinema*, London: Routledge, 1998

Bukatman, Scott, 'Zooming Out: The End of Offscreen Space', in Jon Lewis (ed.), *The New American Cinema*, Durham: Duke University Press, 1998

Caughie, John, (ed.), *Theories of Authorship*, London: Routledge, 1981

Chafe, William, *The Unfinished Journey: America Since World War II*, Oxford: Oxford University Press, 1991

Collins, Jim, 'Genericity in the Nineties: Eclectic Irony and the New Sincerity', in Collins, Hilary Radner and Ava Preacher Collins, *Film Theory Goes to the Movies*, New York: Routledge, 1993

Cook, David A., 'Auteur Cinema and the "Film Generation" in 1970s Hollywood', in Jon Lewis (ed.), *The New American Cinema*, Durham: Duke University Press, 1998

— *Lost Illusions: America in the Shadow of Watergate and Vietnam, 1970–1979*, New York: Charles Scribner's Sons, 2000

Corrigan, Timothy, *A Cinema Without Walls: Movies and Culture after Vietnam*, London: Routledge, 1991

Cowie, Elizabeth, 'Storytelling: classical Hollywood cinema and classical narrative', in Steve Neale and Murray Smith (eds), *Contemporary Hollywood Cinema*, London: BFi, 1998

Cowie, Peter, *Coppola*, London: Faber, 1989

Cubitt, Sean, *Timeshift: On Video Culture*, London: Routledge, 1991

Dale, Martin, *The Movie Game: The Film Business in Britain, Europe and America*, London: Cassell, 1997

Daniels, Jeffrey, 'Global economics slam Sony', *The Hollywood Reporter*, October 29, 1998, http:/www.hollywoodreporter/archive/hollywood/archive/1998/thr1029/sonyearn.as

DeCordova, Richard, 'The emergence of the star system in America', in Christine Gledhill (ed.), *Stardom: Industry of Desire*, London: Routledge, 1991

Doherty, Thomas, *Pre-code Hollywood*, New York: Columbia University Press, 1999

Dunkley, Cathy, 'Baker [sic] paints a Dis franchise', *The Hollywood Reporter*, April 17, 2000, http:/www.hollywoodreporter.com/archive/hollywood/archive/2000/thr0417/bakerpai.as

Dyer, Richard, *Stars*, London: BFI, 1979

Eckert, Charles, 'The Carole Lombard in Macey's Window', *Quarterly Review of Film Studies*, vol. 3, winter 1978

Eidsvik, Charles, 'Machines of the Invisible: Changes in Film Technology in the Age of Video', *Film Quarterly*, vol. 42, no. 2, winter 1988–89

Ellis, John, *Visible Fictions: Cinema, Television, Video*, revised edition, London: Routledge, 1989

Fleming, Dan, 'Dial "M" for Movies: New Technologies, New Relations', in John Hill and Martin McLoone (eds), *Big Picture, Small Screen: The Relations between Film and Television*, Luton: John Libbey, 1997

Friedberg, Anne, *Window Shopping: Cinema and the Postmodern*, Berkeley: University of California Press, 1993

Fuson, Brian, '"Scream 3" kills theaters record', *The Hollywood Reporter*, February 4–6 2000, http://www.hollywoodreporter.com/archive/hollywood/archive/2000/thr0204/t0254bc-.as

Gallagher, Tag, 'Shoot-Out at the Genre Corral: Problems in the "Evolution" of the Western', in Barry Keith Grant (ed.), *Film Genre Reader*, Austin: University of Texas Press, 1986

Garnham, Nicholas, *Capitalism and Communication*, London: Sage, 1990

Geraghty, Christine, 'Re-examining stardom: questions of texts, bodies and performance', in Christine Gledhill and Linda Williams (eds), *Reinventing Film Studies*, London: Arnold, 2000

Gledhill, Christine, 'Rethinking genre', in Gledhill and Linda Williams (eds), *Reinventing Film Studies*, London: Arnold, 2000

Gomery, Douglas, 'The Coming of the Sound: Technological Change in the American Film Industry, in Tino Balio (ed.), *The American Film Industry*, Madison: University of Wisconsin Press, 1985

— *The Hollywood Studio System*, Basingstoke: Macmillan, 1986

— 'Hollywood corporate business practice and periodizing contemporary film history', in Neale and Smith (eds), *Contemporary Hollywood Cinema*, London: Routledge, 1998

Goodridge, Mike, 'Aiming for the heart', *Screen International*, 12 June 1998, 16

Andrew Goodwin, 'Fatal Distractions: MTV meets Postmodern Theory', in Simon Frith, Goodwin and Lawrence Grossberg (eds), *Sound and Vision: The Music Video Reader*, London: Routledge, 1993

Grolier Inc., 'Movie Box-Office Gross and Attendance', March 2000, http://ea.grolier.com/ea-online/wsja/text/ch09/tables/me004.htm

Groves, Don, 'Boffo B.O. bucks foreign coin ills', *Variety*, December 18–31, 2000, 9, 74

Hayes, Dade, 'Sequels try for triples', *Variety*, July 24–30, 2000, 1, 70

— 'Women Taking Action at B.O.', *Variety*, July 31–August 6, 2000

Hazelton, Jon, 'Delayed Impact', *Screen International*, 29 August 1997, 12

Henderson, Brian, 'Romantic Comedy Today: Semi-Tough or Impossible?', *Film Quarterly*, vol. 31, no. 4, Summer 1978; also in Barry Keith Grant, (ed.) *Film Genre Reader*, Austin: University of Texas Press, 1986

Hettrick, Scott, 'Tarzan puts Grinch in vidlock', *Variety*, 8–14 January, 2000

Higashi, Sumiko, '*Night of the Living Dead*: A Horror Film about the Horrors of the Vietnam Era', in Linda Dittmar and Gene Michaud (eds), *From Hanoi to Hollywood: The Vietnam War in American Film*, New Brunswick: Rutgers University Press, 1990

Hill, John, 'Film and postmodernism', in Hill and Pamela Church Gibson (eds), *The Oxford Guide to Film Studies*, Oxford: Oxford University Press, 1998

Hillier, Jim, *The New Hollywood*, London: Studio Vista, 1992

*Hollywood Reporter, The*, interview with John Calley, September 28, 1999, http://www.hollywoodreporter.com/archive/hollywood/archive/1999/thr1008/col2.as

*Hollywood Reporter, The,* 'Star Power' survey, 1999

Honeycutt, Kirk, 'Wide tracks of "Godzilla" lead to a holiday record', *The Hollywood Reporter*, April 15, 1998, http://www.hollywoodreporter/archive/hollywood/archive/1998/thr0415/godzil2.as

Internet Movie Database, 'Toy Outlets Complain About Godzilla Secrecy', Studio Business, 30 March 1998

Izod, John, *Hollywood and the Box Office*

Jamgocyan, Nik, 'Godzilla TV rights go cheap', *Screen International*, 5 June 1998, 5

Jenkins, Henry, 'Historical poetics', in Joanne Hollows and Mark Jancovich (eds), *Approaches to Popular Film*, Manchester: Manchester University Press, 1995

Kaplan, David, 'How George Lucas orchestrated the biggest movie-marketing campaign of all time and made *Phantom* a must-see, no matter what critics say', *Newsweek*, May 17, 1999, 64–8

Kaplan, E. Ann, *Rocking Around the Clock: Music Television, Postmodernism and Consumer Culture*, New York: Methuen, 1987

King, Barry, 'Stardom as an occupation', in Paul Kerr (ed.), *The Hollywood Film Industry: A Reader*, London: Routledge, 1986

— 'Articulating Stardom', in Christine Gledhill (ed.), *Stardom: Industry of Desire*, London: Routledge, 1991

King, Geoff, 'Ride-Films and Films as Rides in the Contemporary Hollywood Cinema of Attractions', *Cineaction* 51, February 2000

— *Spectacular Narratives: Hollywood in the Age of the Blockbuster*, London: I.B.Tauris, 2000

— *Film Comedy*, London: Wallflower Press, 2002

King, Geoff, and Tanya Krzywinska, *Science Fiction Cinema: From Outerspace to Cyberspace*, London: Wallflower Press, 2000

Kitses, Jim, *Horizons West*, London: Thames and Hudson, 1969

Kolker, Robert, *A Cinema of Loneliness: Penn, Kubrick, Scorsese, Spielberg, Altman*, 2nd edition, Oxford: Oxford University Press, 1988

Knee, Adam, 'The Dialectic of Female Power and Male Hysteria in *Play Misty for Me*', in Steven Cohan and Ina Rae Hark (eds), *Screening the Male: Exploring Masculinities in Hollywood Cinema*, London: Routledge, 1993

Kramer, Peter, 'The Lure of the Big Picture: Film, Television and Hollywood', in John Hill and Martin McLoone (eds), *Big Picture, Small Screen: The Relations between Film and Television*, Luton: John Libbey, 1997

— 'A Powerful Cinema-going Force? Hollywood and the Female Audience since the 1960s', in Melvyn Stokes and Maltby (eds), *Identifying Hollywood's Audiences*, London: BFI, 1999

Krutnik, 'The Clown-Prints of Comedy', *Screen*, 25, 1984

Lafferty, William, 'Feature Films on Prime-Time Television', in Balio (ed.), *Hollywood in the Age of Television*, Boston: Unwin Hyman, 1990

Leith, William, 'Big Ears flies again', *The Observer*, 'Life' magazine, 20 December, 1998, 7

Lewis, Jon, *Whom God Wishes to Destroy... Francis Coppola and the New Hollywood*, Durham: Duke University Press, 1995

— 'Money Matters: Hollywood in the Corporate Era', in Lewis (ed.), *The New American Cinema*, Durham: Duke University Press, 1998

— *Hollywood v. Hard Core: How the Struggle over Censorship Saved the Modern Film Industry*, New York: New York University Press, 2000

Levi-Strauss, Claude, 'The Structural Study of Myth', in *Structural Anthropology*, trans. Harmondsworth: Penguin, 1972

Litwak, Mark, *Reel Power: The Struggle for Influence and Success in the New Hollywood*, Los Angeles: Silman-James, 1986

Loews Cineplex Entertainment, 'Corporate History' entry on website at http://www.loewscineplex.com

Lyons, Charles, 'Passion for Slashin'', *Variety*, June 26–July 9, 2000

Maltby, Richard, '"Nobody knows everything": Post-classical historiographies and consolidated entertainment', in Steve Neale and Murray Smith (eds), *Contemporary Hollywood Cinema*, London: BFI, 1998

— 'Sticks, Hicks and Flaps', in Melvyn Stokes and Maltby (eds), *Identifying Hollywood's Audiences*, London: BFI, 1999

Maltby, Richard, and Ian Craven, *Hollywood Cinema: An Introduction*, Oxford: Blackwell, 1995

McBride, Joseph, *Steven Spielberg: A Biography*, London: Faber, 1997

McDonald, Paul, 'Star Studies', in Joanne Hollows and Mark Jancovich (eds), *Approaches to Popular Film*, Manchester: Manchester University Press, 1995

— 'Reconceptualising Stardom', in Richard Dyer, *Stars*, revised edition, London: British Film Institute, 1998

— *The Star System: Hollywood's Production of Popular Identities*, London: Wallflower Press, 2000

McLoone, Martin, 'Boxed In?: The Aesthetics of Film and Television', in John Hill and McLoone (eds), *Big Picture, Small Screen*, Luton: John Libbey, 1997

Meehan, Eileen, '"Holy Commodity Fetish, Batman!": The Political Economy of a Commercial Intertext', in Roberta Pearson and William Uricchio (eds), *The Many Lives of the Batman: Critical Approaches to a Superhero and His Media*, London: BFI, 1991

Miller, Frank, *Censored Hollywood: Sex, Sin and Violence on Screen*, Atlanta: Turner Publishing, 1994

Miller, Mark Crispin, 'Advertising: End of Story', in Miller (ed.), *Seeing Through Movies*, New York: Pantheon, 1990

Motion Picture Association of America, *1999 US Economic Review*, available at http://www.mpaa.org

— *1999 Motion Picture Attendance*, available at http://www.mpaa.org

— *2000 US Economic Review*, available at http://www.mpaa.org

Murphy, A.D., 'Distribution and Exhibition: An Overview', in Jason Squire, (ed.), *The Movie Business Book*, New York: Simon and Schuster, 1992

Nash, Melanie, and Martti Lahti, '"Almost Ashamed to Say I Am One of Those Girls": *Titanic*, Leonardo DiCaprio, and the Paradoxes of Girls' Fandom', in Kevin Sandler and Gaylyn Studlar (eds), *Titanic: Anatomy of a Blockbuster*, New Brunswick: Rutgers University Press, 1999

Neale, Steve, 'Widescreen composition in the age of television', in Neale and Smith (eds), *Contemporary Hollywood Cinema*, London: Routledge, 1998

— *Genre and Hollywood*, London: Routledge, 2000

Paul, William, 'The K-mart audience at the mall movies, *Film History*, vol. 6, 1994

Perkins, Tessa, 'The Politics of "Jane Fonda"', in Christine Gledhill (ed.), *Stardom: Industry of Desire*, London: Routledge, 1991

Pfeil, Fred, 'From Pillar to Postmodernism: Race, Class, and Gender in the Male Rampage Film', in Jon Lewis (ed.), *The New American Cinema*, Durham: Duke University Press, 1998

Prince, Stephen, *A New Pot of Gold: Hollywood Under the Electronic Rainbow, 1980–1989*, New York: Charles Scribner's Sons, 2000

Pye, Douglas, 'Criticism and the Western', in Ian Cameron and Pye (eds), *The Movie Book of the Western*, London: Studio Vista, 1996

Pye, Michael, and Lynda Myles, *The Movie Brats: How the Film Generation Took Over Hollywood*, New York: Holt, Rinehart and Winston, 1979

Ray, Robert, *A Certain Tendency of the Hollywood Cinema, 1930–1980*, Princeton: Princeton University Press, 1985

Rhodes, Joe, 'Iron Will', *Premiere*, November 1998, 91–3

Rubin, Martin, *Showstoppers: Busby Berkeley and the Tradition of Spectacle*, New York: Columbia University Press, 1993

Ryan, Michael, and Douglas Kellner, *Camera Politica: The Politics and Ideology of Contemporary Hollywood Film*, Bloomington: Indiana University Press, 1988

Sammon, Paul, *Future Noir: The Making of Blade Runner*, London: Orion, 1996

Sarris, Andrew, 'Notes on the auteur theory in 1962', extract in John Caughie, (ed.), *Theories of Authorship*, London: Routledge, 1981

— 'Towards a theory of film history', extract in Caughie

Schamus, James, 'To the rear of the back end: The economics of independent cinema', in Steve Neale and Murray Smith (eds), *Contemporary Hollywood Cinema*, London: BFI, 1998

Schatz, Thomas, *Hollywood Genres*, Austin: University of Texas Press, 1981

— 'The New Hollywood', in Jim Collins, Hilary Radner and Ava

Preacher Collins, *Film Theory Goes to the Movies*, New York: Routledge, 1993

*Screen Digest*, 'From Studio to Screen: The majors' integrated strategy', February 1998, 33

— 'Worldwide cinema: Weaknesses hidden by record growth', September 1998, 202–203

— 'Top 10 films take huge chunk of global revenues', January 2000, 29

— 'Electronic cinema set to transform the movie business', press release, September 2000, http://www.screendigest.com/press_ecine.htm

*Screen International*, editorial, 'Economies of Scale', June 5, 1998

Seguin, Denis, 'Middle-aged spread brings BO dividends', *Screen International*, July 14–20, 2000

Simonet, Thomas, 'Conglomerates and Content: Remakes, Sequels and Series in the New Hollywood', in Bruce Austin (ed.), *Current Research in Film: Audiences, Economics, and Law*, vol. 3, Norwood, NJ: Ablex Publishing Corporation, 1987

Slotkin, Richard, *Regeneration Through Violence: The Mythology of the American Frontier 1600–1860*, Middletown: Wesleyan University Press, 1973

— *Gunfighter Nation: The Myth of the Frontier in Twentieth-Century America*, New York: Atheneum, 1992

Smith, Murray, *Engaging Characters: Fiction, Emotion and the Cinema*, Oxford: Clarendon Press, 1995

— 'Theses on the philosophy of Hollywood history', in Steve Neale and Murray Smith (eds), *Contemporary Hollywood Cinema*, London: BFI, 1998

Smith, Paul, *Clint Eastwood: A Cultural Production*, Minneapolis: University of Minnesota Press, 1993

Sony Corporation, *Annual Report*, 1999

— *Annual Report*, 2000

Sorlin, Pierre, 'Television and the Close-up: Interference or Correspondence?', in Thomas Elsaesser and Kay Hoffman (eds), *Cinema Futures: Cain, Abel or Cable? The Screen Arts in the Digital Age*, Amsterdam: Amsterdam University Press, 1998

Stacey, Jackie, *Star Gazing: Hollywood cinema and female spectatorship*, London: Routledge, 1994

Straw, Will, 'Popular Music and Postmodernism in the 1980s', in Simon Frith, Andrew Goodwin and Lawrence Grossberg (eds), *Sound and Vision: The Music Video Reader*, London: Routledge, 1993

Sweeting, Paul, 'Vid chains vie for early edge in digital domain', *Variety*, 6–12 March, 2000

Tasker, Yvonne, *Spectacular Bodies: Gender, genre and the action cinema*, London: Routledge, 1993

Taubin, Amy, *Taxi Driver*, London: BFI, 2000

Taves, Brian, 'The B Film: Hollywood's Other Half', in Tino Balio, *Grand Design: Hollywood as a Modern Business Enterprise, 1930–1939*, Berkeley: University of California Press, 1993

Taylor, Diane, and Jane Cassidy, 'Trust me, I'm a doctor', *The Guardian*, section 2, 27 June 1997, 4–5

Thompson, David, and Ian Christie (eds), *Scorsese on Scorsese*, London: Faber, 1989

Thompson, John O., 'Screen acting and the commutation test', in Christine Gledhill (ed.), *Stardom: Industry of Desire*, London: Routledge, 1991

Thompson, Kristin, *Exporting Entertainment: America in the World Film Market 1907–1934*, London: BFI, 1985

— *Storytelling in the New Hollywood: Understanding Classical Narrative Technique*, Cambridge, Mass.: Harvard University Press, 1999

Time Warner, *1999 Fact Book*

Truffaut, Francois, 'A Certain Tendency of the French Cinema', *Cahiers du Cinéma*, January 1954; reprinted in Bill Nichols (ed.), *Movies and Methods*, Volume I, Berkeley: University of California Press, 1976

Vernet, Mark, 'Film noir on the edge of doom', in Joan Copjec (ed.), *Shades of Noir: a reader*, London: Verso, 1993

Veronis Suhler, 14th annual *Communications Industry Forecast*, August 2000, at http://www.veronissuhler.com/articles/article_202.htm

Wasko, Janet, *Hollywood in the Information Age*, Cambridge: Polity, 1994

Williams, Raymond, *Television: Technology and Cultural Form*, London: Routledge, 1990

Wilson, Anton, *Anton Wilson's Cinema Workshop*, Hollywood: A.S.C Holding Corp., 1983

Wise, Damon, 'Hollywood plays the smart card', *Observer*, 'Screen', 8, 16 January 2000

Wolff, Janet, *The Social Production of Art*, Basingstoke: Macmillan, 1981

Wood, Robin, *Hollywood from Vietnam to Reagan*, New York: Columbia University Press, 1986

Wyatt, Justin, *High Concept: Movies and Marketing in Hollywood*, Austin: University of Texas Press, 1994

— 'The formation of the major independent: Miramax, New Line and the New Hollywood', in Steve Neale and Murray Smith (eds), *Contemporary Hollywood Cinema*, London: BFI, 1998

Zeman, Ned, 'Will Smith Rides High', *Vanity Fair*, July 1999

# Index